The Vampire State
in Africa

This book is to be returned on
or before the date stamped below

2 2 MAR 2001

The Vampire State in Africa

in Africa
The Political Economy
of Decline in Ghana

JONATHAN H. FRIMPONG-ANSAH

Executive Secretary, African Capacity Building Foundation
Senior Consultant, Standard Chartered Bank
Formerly Governor of the Bank of Ghana

JAMES CURREY • London
AFRICA WORLD PRESS • Trenton

James Currey Ltd
54b Thornhill Square, Islington
London N1 1BE

Africa World Press
PO Box 1892
Trenton, New Jersey 08608

British Library Cataloguing in Publication Data

Frimpong-Ansah, Jonathan, H.
    The vampire state in Africa : the political economy
    of decline in Ghana.
    I. Title
    330.966705

    ISBN 0-85255-124-X (cloth)
    ISBN 0-85255-123-1 (paper)

Library of Congress Catalog Card Number: 91-76223

    ISBN 0-86543-278-3   (cloth)
    ISBN 0-86543-279-1   (paper)

Typeset in 10/11 pt Garamond with Optima display
by Opus 43, Cumbria, England
Printed in the United States of America

To the memory of
my grandfather Yaw Frimpong Mensah
& of my father Kwadwo Owusu Ansah,
the two men who shaped my life

Contents

Tables and Figures

Figures

Tables in the Annex

Figures in Annex

Acknowledgements

This book would not have been completed without advice, encouragement and sacrifice from many sources. I owe a particular debt of gratitude to Dr Barbara M. Ingham who was my supervisor in the doctoral research from which this book has been developed. I cannot thank Sir Sydney Caine enough for travelling specially from the country to London to give me insights into the environment in the Colonial Office and some aspects of colonial economic policy. Institutions that facilitated my research include the Ghana Academy of Arts and Sciences, Accra, the Public Record Office in London and the British Library of Political and Economic Science (London School of Economics). The Development Economics Research Centre, University of Warwick, assisted me by organizing seminars and a one-day workshop at which my ideas were discussed. My gratitude goes to all my colleagues there, particularly to Professor Ravi Kanbur.

Ghanaians and authorities on the Ghanaian economy, who have been more than generous with their time, are too many to list. Their help is greatly appreciated. I mention here particularly Dr O.A. Akoto, International Coffee Organization, Dr Oware Gyekye, University of Ghana, Dr Michael Roemer and Dr Joseph Stern, Harvard Institute for International Development, Professor Tony Killick, Overseas Development Institute, Mr J. Odling-Smee, UK Treasury and former Economic Adviser to Prime Minister Busia, Mr M. Boye-Anawomah, former Principal Assistant to Prime Minister Busia, Mr Kofi Adjepong-Boateng, St. John's College, Oxford, Professor Kweku Andah, former Master of Mensah Sarbah Hall, Legon and Minister of Agriculture, and Reverend Col. K.A. Quashie, former Commissioner (Minister) for Trade, Ghana. My thanks also go to Miss Margaret Cornell for her work in editing and preparing the text for publication and to an anonymous reader for valuable comments on an earlier draft.

Finally, to my wife and family, who have endured much neglect and nevertheless have been the source of encouragement that made this work possible, my deepest gratitude.

Jonathan H. Frimpong-Ansah
Asante Mampong

Abbreviations

ADB	African Development Bank
ADC	Agricultural Development Corporation
AFRC	Armed Forces Revolutionary Council
ARPB	Association of Recognized Professional Bodies
C	cedi
CBS	Central Bureau of Statistics
CEAC	Colonial Economic Advisory Committee
CMB	Cocoa Marketing Board
CO	Colonial Office (Prefix to Colonial Office Files)
COCOBOD	Ghana Cocoa Board
CPC	Cocoa Purchasing Company
CPP	Convention People's Party
ECA	Economic Commission for Africa
ECOWAS	Economic Community of West African States
ERP	Economic Recovery Programme
FPD	Front for the Prevention of Dictatorship
GDC	Gonja Development Corporation
GDP	Gross Domestic Product
GDFCF	Gross Domestic Fixed Capital Formulation
GIS	Ghana Information Service
IDC	Industrial Development Corporation
IMF	International Monetary Fund
ISSER	Institute of Statistical, Social & Economic Research
m	million
MIT	Massachusetts Institute of Technology
NAL	National Alliance of Liberals
NEP	New Economic Policy
NDM	New Democratic Movement
NLC	National Liberation Movement
NRC	National Redemption Council
ODI	Overseas Development Institute
OFY	Operation Feed Yourself
OGS	Office of the Government Statistician
PMFJ	People's Movement for Freedom and Justice
PNDC	Provisional National Defence Council
PP	Progress Party
PPP	Purchasing Power Parity
SMC	Supreme Military Council
TYIP	Three Year Investment Programme
UAC	United Africa Company
UGFCC	United Ghana Farmers' Council Cooperatives
UGCC	United Gold Coast Convention
VRA	Volta River Authority
WACRI	West Africa Cocoa Research Institute
WAWC	West African War Council

Notes

Asante has the same interpretation as Ashanti. The former is the more correct word.

Gold Coast was the former name of Ghana. In the colonial period Gold Coast referred to what is now southern Ghana. Asante and the Northern Territories were administered with the Gold Coast as Protectorates.

Ghana has a **total area** of 238.5 thousand square kilometers, approximately the size of the United Kingdom.

Population in 1987 was estimated at 14.5 million, growing at 2.9 per cent per annum. Population in agriculture is 62 per cent; the urban population is 38 per cent.

Cedi is the national currency of Ghana, usually denoted by 'C'. Previous currencies were the West African pound and the Ghana pound, both with equivalent value to the pound sterling and convertible until June 1961.

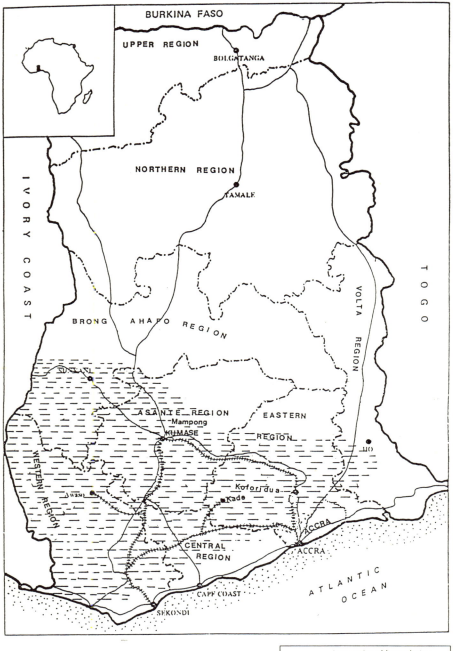

International boundaries
Regional boundaries
Trunk roads
Railways
Cocoa land

Ghana: The Regions and Cocoa Areas

Introduction
Background and Objectives

> To fail to speak to a man who is capable of benefiting is to let man go to
> waste. To speak to a man who is not capable of benefiting is to let one's
> words go to waste. A wise man lets neither man nor words go to waste.
> Confucius (*Analects*, XV. 8)

This study investigates the nature of Ghana's efforts at economic development during most
of this century, particularly in the period after independence, and how and why they failed.
This is not the first time that such a study has been attempted, but on most previous
occasions the discussion has related to shorter historical periods.[1] The whole story has not
been told, and therefore the whole explanation has not been given. A long-term inter-
disciplinary project may be required for the full story. This study is intended as a
contribution to such a project from the standpoint of political economy, placing the Ghana
case in a long-run historical framework.

The hundred years just ended have witnessed a political and socio-economic transformation
in Africa that has had no parallel in the continent's long history.[2] Small ethnic groups
became united and formed themselves into new states under European rule, developed new
forms of economic activity and became involved in large-scale international trade. These
new states then revolted against foreign rule, or negotiated with foreign rulers to gain
political and economic independence, and undertook far-reaching development
programmes in the attempt to improve their welfare, with widely differing results.[3]

During this period, development economics has evolved considerably. Until about the
early 1950s, the organized study of economics, as it related to the problems of the
underdeveloped regions of the world, hardly existed. The earliest ideas on the planned
development of Africa were formulated as part of the colonial economic development
debate (Lewis, 1944a, b, c).[4] The published works around this time were concerned with
the development problems of Southern Europe (Rosenstein-Rodan, 1943, Mandelbaum,
1945). The first debates on economic development of the underdeveloped areas centred on
aggregates of output and the mobilization of savings (Lewis, 1955). Thereafter a wider
definition was sought in modernization, seen as an all-embracing process of social change;
most post-independence African political leaders and academics adopted this view.
Modernization was usually based on industrialization programmes, such as those for import
substitution (Lewis, 1954), and strategies of unbalanced economic development
(Hirschman, 1958). Some of these theories of development led to development
programmes which failed to achieve the desired results;[5] in certain situations, they resulted
in injuriously rapid rural–urban population shifts (Stoces, 1966). The debate has therefore
moved, in recent times, to a distributive or social justice definition of development,
particularly in the late 1960s to 1970s (Seers, 1970), which was much promoted by the
World Bank in the McNamara era and by radical economists and politicians alike for its
emphasis on the reduction of poverty and on the equitable redistribution of the burden of
development between the various classes of the population.

The debate continues, enriched by the empirical analyses of actual experiences,[6] and has been joined by a large number of scholars including many from the developing countries. The more recent emphasis has been on self-reliance and economic independence.[7] But fundamental questions remain to be tackled from the African perspective, questions debated by economists of pre-industrial Britain in much the same way as they engage the attention of economists who are studying Africa today. What limits the pace of modernization and industrialization from the primary state? What environment, in terms of political economy, is most conducive to economic development?

In the early days of economic thought in Britain, the first question was answered in a preliminary way by Sir James Steuart (Steuart, 1767), who gave it as the rate of productivity increase, induced by appropriately high prices, of farmers remaining on the land and whose marketable surpluses would subsequently be exchanged for the new manufactured goods.[8] Adam Smith, nine years later, extended this answer to take account of the export of manufactures, thus including the external sector in the model (Smith, 1776). In more recent times, Arthur Lewis, himself from a developing country, acknowledged the pioneering works of Steuart and Smith[9] when he re-interpreted the classical contributions in a development policy framework for the Colonial Office (Lewis, 1944a, b, c), for the West Indies (Lewis, 1950) and for Ghana (Lewis, 1953). For the Colonial Office his emphasis was on agricultural and industrial revolutions, for the West Indies he put greater weight on agriculture, and in the case of Ghana, equal emphasis was placed on agriculture and import-substitution industrialization. These differences in emphasis were fair. The Colonial Office was distant from the people it governed and lethargic about direct involvement in development (see Chapter 4); in Lewis's view radical intervention by the government was needed.[10] In Ghana in 1953, the cocoa sector was at its peak of price incentive and production was rising in relation to the population (see Chapter 7). In the West Indian islands, commercial agriculture could not assure the levels of rural income that would justify a market for a wide range of import-substituting manufacturing.

What has been assumed in the theoretical development models is that political leaders and economic managers in Africa, in both the colonial and post-independence periods, would take rational decisions and ensure that their public policies preserved and consolidated the role of primary agriculture for domestic and external markets. It has also been assumed that agricultural output for both sectors would be pushed to its respective margins of advantage through price and other incentives during the period of initial development. In practice, the new programmes of modernization, particularly in the post-independence period, have tended to generate their own momentum, chiefly for ideological reasons. This momentum has appeared to dominate decision-making, to the detriment of primary production.

The empirical evidence shows many failures of development programmes, carried out ostensibly within the framework of development theories. The often disastrous effects on the populations of the countries concerned have prompted debates on the dangers inherent in too simplistic an application of the doctrines of development economics. With the resurgence of neo-classical economics, some researchers and writers have warned against the neglect of the market and price discipline in the theory and practice of development economics (Lal, 1983), in the hope of improving the quality of development management. Most World Bank- and IMF-initiated economic restructuring and stabilization in Africa has also, in recent times, taken a similar market-oriented approach.

Against the background of intellectual debate and economic reconstruction on the ground in Africa, significant advances are being made in technology and management in the advanced countries of the world, facilitated by major strides in information technology. This structural transformation has yet to evolve fully, but the indications are of a sharp contrast between the fast rate of technological advancement in the past two decades in the advanced countries and the stagnation and decline in most parts of Africa, particularly in those countries where attempts at post-independence economic development have failed.

The Nature of the Problem

Ghana is a classic case of economic stagnation and decline in the contemporary period in Africa. Its experience since the turn of the century may well define the limits of success and failure of the African development effort. After well-organized military resistance to British colonization by the armies of the inland kingdoms, lasting close on eighty years (1825–1903),[11] Ghana (then the Gold Coast) settled down very quickly to become one of the fastest-growing new states of Africa (Szereszewski, 1965:74). Twenty-five years later, it was exporting large quantities of agricultural produce and minerals and was described as one of the most advanced colonial territories south of the Sahara (Ormsby-Gore, 1926).

Endowed with considerable financial, human and natural resources for the kind of development then possible, and under two charismatic leaders, Guggisberg (1919–27)[12] and Nkrumah (1950–66), it was one of the first countries in Africa to make a bold attempt at planned economic development. Sadly, Ghanaians were also the first on the African continent to suffer real failure in economic development, and to resign themselves to the humiliating disintegration of a post-independence political economy. Ghana therefore offers a prime example of the economic and political processes limiting the pace of development in Africa.

As in most pre-industrial states in Africa, agriculture and the services related to it have been the pivot of Ghana's economic activities. Minerals, particularly gold (from which the country gained its earlier name), bauxite, diamonds and manganese, have also played a significant role. Commercial agriculture began at the close of the last century with the advent of cocoa. Before that period most agricultural exports, particularly palm oil and natural rubber, came from sylviculture. The acceptance of cocoa, in a period when peasants had little capital, was facilitated by the ease of its initial cultivation among food crops, a peasant innovation adopted from sylviculture. The new cocoa industry developed so rapidly that within two decades Ghana had become the world's leading producer and exporter (using peasant methods only), and accounted for 40% of world output. Dominated by cocoa (see Chapter 7), agriculture remained the predominant activity throughout the first half of this century.

On the eve of decolonization, however, there were identifiable weaknesses in the Ghanaian economy which would limit the pace of economic development. By imposing an excessive tax burden on the cocoa industry to finance an attempt to accelerate initial development, public policy failed to recognize that industry as the most important contributor to the country's economic progress. Public policy also ignored the common-sense view that a successful programme of economic growth will take into account the impediments to development and nourish the foundations on which economic development may be erected. If this principle had been adhered to, Ghana's massive economic decline could have been avoided. Instead, the attempt at development failed and the cocoa industry was destroyed. Economic recovery and resumption of development would be a slow process.

The Proper Approach

This study is inspired by what the writer perceives to be an inadequate comprehension, in policy circles, of the proper approach to development from the pre-industrial state. There is need for a long-run analysis which seeks to discover the salient weaknesses of Ghana's political economy since its early years of nationhood, and the kind of knowledge that can provide better management of economic development. From the evidence of the current efforts at economic and monetary stabilization,[13] there appears to be the desire in Ghana and in a number of other African countries[14] to re-examine economic management strategies and to reconstruct their damaged economies after nearly three decades of euphoric adventures in development. If these efforts are genuine, then they deserve to be placed in a wider theoretical framework.

This study is also motivated by the plight of the many people in the declining states of Africa whose welfare continues to be eroded by inappropriate economic management. Many have become the innocent victims of various forms of economic and political instability.[15] There are older people who are experiencing the frustration and indignity of their life's savings being eroded by inflation and who have been reduced to begging for their daily sustenance.[16] There are also the younger people whose future recedes steadily into a bleak unknown.

Lastly, this study has been inspired by the need to widen the perspective of African intellectual opinion. African academics and intellectuals have a responsibility for the continent's post-independence economic reconstruction and development.

Of the contemporary writers on the Ghanaian political economy and development, the most prominent have been Killick, Roemer and Chazan. Others who have referred to Ghana in their major works include Bates, and Dunn and Robertson. A substantial African contribution is still awaited The more significant works relating to the colonial political economy of the Gold Coast are by Guggisberg, McPhee, Cardinall, Seers and Ross, and Arthur Lewis. Though Killick (1978: 3) concentrates on the early post-independence period, he does refer to some of the 'obvious characteristics of the colonial past' and suggests that at the beginning of the 1960s the economy still largely retained the structural framework which emerged at the beginning of the century. His primary objective did not include an attempt to define this structure but it is clear from his results that a fuller understanding of the characteristics of the inherited colonial economic strategies would contribute to a greater understanding of the subsequent events.

Similarly, Roemer (1983:1), whose work covers the period 1950–1980, notes that Ghana was thought to be a country with substantial growth potential which successive governments had failed to realize. This view raises the question of investigating the characteristics of this 'potential' and how it should have been managed in order to preserve and increase it. In a similar vein, Chazan (1983:154–78) states that the story of Ghana's economy since independence has been one of stagnation and decay and that, having failed to live up to its declared potential, Ghana during the 1970–80 period underwent a process of accelerated decay. Again characteristics of the 'declared potential' remain vague, yet they would seem to be taken for granted as the yardstick for measuring subsequent performance. All these arguments point to the danger of drawing a distinct historical line between the colonial and post-independence periods in assessing the performance of economic management in Ghana.

Political economists who have focused on the rural economy, however, have a different perception. Bates (1983), for example, takes a long-term view and draws attention to weaknesses in indigenous production and marketing fostered by the colonial coalition of bureaucrats, miners and traders and compares the effect (Bates, 1981) with the indigenous coalition of the post-independence period. Dunn and Robertson (1973) note weaknesses in the development of the cocoa industry in Ahafo introduced by conflicts in the political economy during the periods of decolonization and transition to independence.

The opinions of writers who observed economic conditions in the colonial period and at the eve of decolonization, some of whose ideas and theories have since become well known, also throw a somewhat different light on the long-term development and management problems of the economy. After praising the colonial governments of the West African states for achieving what he described as an economic revolution, McPhee (1926: 309) went on to question whether the 'mandatory system of native development of economic resources under a rule which may be described as "autocratic paternalism" did not pose serious dangers' of exposing producers to adverse international competition and of inducing internal revolt. This was an issue that had much to do with the political economy of primary production and economic stability, which has persisted under a different manifestation in the post-independence period.

Cardinall (1931: 99) also drew attention to the emerging excessive concentration on the single crop of cocoa. He observed that 'the Gold Coast peasant farmer, if he is to survive, must remember ... that the crops which produce small but certain profits are those on which his existence depends'. The problems of monoculture were to surface more seriously in the post-independence development phase. Even more potent were the warnings from the academic economists who studied the Ghana economy on the eve of decolonization, a period assumed by more recent writers to have held great promise.

In 1951 Dudley Seers and C.R. Ross were commissioned by the Colonial Office in London to 'enquire into building costs in the Gold Coast and into the organization and utilization of building resources in relation to the economy of the territory and to make recommendations'.[17] Their Report (1952) reveals that on their arrival in the Gold Coast they were confronted with issues more serious than building costs, and quite fundamental to the future of the economy if an attempt was to be made to accelerate the pace of development. They described the economy as 'fragile' because it did not have the mechanisms to moderate over-response to monetary acceleration. When, in the following year, Professor W. Arthur Lewis was invited by the Gold Coast transitional government, headed by Nkrumah, to study the strategies of industrialization, he was also in no doubt that the priority was 'a concentrated attack on the system of growing food ... so as to set in motion an ever increasing productivity'. (Lewis, 1953: para 253).

Objectives

This study therefore addresses a long-term theme of public policy relating to the promotion of the primary sectors of production. It adds a dimension to previous attempts in that it seeks to link the common characteristics of the post-independence period with those of the colonial period in determining the long-term reasons for some of the difficulties of the Ghana economy.

Some specific questions come under scrutiny:
1. What were the principal characteristics of the pre-industrial state which some have described as offering potential for growth, but which earlier scholars described as fragile? What aspects can be identified from the standpoint of political economy?
2. Can it be established through long-term historical analysis that a significant decline has taken place in Ghana, and how is such a decline to be explained?
3. What evidence is there, in both colonial and initial post-independence political philosophies and economic strategies, of clear ideas on economic development? Is there evidence of concern on the part of governments, or of an understanding of appropriate management methods?
4. How good was the professional economic advice that became available to the country towards the end of the decolonization era and in the early period of independence? Of what relevance was that advice to contemporary economic management and to subsequent development policy?
5. What evidence is there of recognition, in public and official opinion, of the importance of the primary producing sectors of the Ghana economy, especially cocoa, to long-term economic development?

6. What has been the nature of public policy towards farmers, particularly cocoa farmers, in both the colonial and post-independence periods? What has been the nature and the effect on economic development of farmers' responses to public policy?
7. The period since 1975 has been recognized in the literature as a period of uninterrupted economic decline. How can this decline be explained? To what extent was the adverse trend recognized by policy-makers and what were the characteristics of their response?
8. What are the policy implications of these analyses for Ghana's economic recovery programme and for development theory?

The study is organized in three Parts and eight chapters. Part I presents a conceptual and interpretative framework for studying economic development. Chapter 1 surveys the standard development theories and their relevance to post-independence African economic development. Chapter 2 traces the evolution of economic development thinking in the Gold Coast up to the eve of independence. Chapter 3 introduces a theoretical and conceptual model of decline. Since this is a study of the economic management of development, an analysis of the economic approach to the political process is a central theme. This leads to the choice of a model in the political economy of decline, particularly regarding conflicts in the taxation of the primary sectors to finance economic development. Useful models for this purpose emerge from the new literature on taxation, such as that of the 'Revenue-maximizing Leviathan' in the context of a fiscal constitution (Brennan and Buchanan, 1980), the 'Deleterious Coalition Theory' (Bates, 1981), which describes the predatory tendencies of the ruling coalition in the process of industrialization and of the 'Predatory State' (Lal, 1981, 1984, 1988), which explores the net revenue maximizing behaviour of an inefficient charismatic autocracy. The contribution of these models to the interpretative model of the study is discussed.

Part II then reviews the long-term performance of the economy in the colonial period (Chapter 4), the immediate post-independence period (Chapter 5), and the period of decline since 1961 (Chapter 6), using the interpretative model.

Part III provides a case study of the cocoa industry and draws conclusions from the study as a whole. Chapter 7 is a quantitative and historical analysis of the cocoa industry, illustrating public policy towards a principal economic sector in the initial process of economic development. It discusses the long-term production base of the industry, and the direct and indirect distortions arising out of taxation and exchange-rate over-valuation. It estimates short-run and long-run supply elasticities with respect to producer price and the industry's capacity base, and then traces producer responses. The analysis covers the period from the turn of the century, when the industry was introduced, to 1985 in most cases, and to 1988 where data permit.

The concluding chapter summarizes the principal findings of the study and discusses them in the context of the current Economic Recovery Programme in Ghana, and the political economy of development. The findings identify the weakness of the Ghana economy on the eve of independence, and show that post-independence regimes, in their attempts to develop, did not always recognize the structural and financial limitations inherent in this weakness. The interrelationships between economic decline and conflicts in the political economy are stressed. The neglect of the important role of the cocoa industry in economic decline is a principal feature. The performance of the Economic Recovery Programme is reviewed against this background and questions are raised as to whether the recovery programme, as at present designed, recognizes the primary problems and is sustainable in the long term.

Notes

1. Examples of the major works include Birmingham *et al.* (1960), Killick (1978), Roemer (1983a), Chazan (1983; 1988).
2. Since the Berlin Conference of 1885 which initiated the colonial partition of Africa.
3. See particularly the Statistical Appendix to Morawetz, D. *Twenty-five Years of Economic Development, 1950–1975*, Johns Hopkins University Press, 1977, pp. 77–101. Also illustrative of this point are the statistical annexes of the various issues of the World Development Report (World Bank).
4. These documents emerged in the course of research for this study, in the Colonial Office Records. Arthur Lewis then served as Secretary of the Colonial Advisory Committee. The contents are discussed in detail in Chapter 2.
5. For example the Ghana 7-Year Development Plan (1963–70) based on the Harrod-Domar model failed partly because the concept and estimation of capital stock and incremental capital-output ratios had both estimation and theoretical defects. There were also other problems of implementation such as the wrong estimation of export earnings (see Bissue, 1965).
6. See Chenery, H. and Syrquin, M. *Patterns of Development, 1950–1970*, Oxford University Press, 1975. Also the World Bank internal memoranda on the subject, especially those of the Development Research Department.
7. The ideas of collective self-reliance have been best articulated by the Group of 77 Developing Countries in their various decisions since the mid-1970s. They include the Mexico Decision, 13–22 September 1976, the Arusha Decision, (UNCTAD TD/236, 28 February 1979), and the Caracas Programme of Action, 13–19 May 1981. In Africa, the mechanism for collective self-reliance has been regional economic integration promoted by the Economic Commission for Africa since 1975.
8. Hart (1982) articulates Steuart's theory and how it would apply to West Africa.
9. Meier and Seers (1985) p. 121.
10. Lord Bauer would argue, however, that 'development' in the colonies was better encouraged by the minimum of government interference (see Bauer, 1984 Chap. 6). Bauer defends the policy of 'limited government, including limited intervention in economic life; reliance on local institutions as far as possible; acceptance of traditional leaders and local councils as representatives of African opinion and interests; and gradual evolution of reforms of traditional authorities in preparation for independence.' p. 91.
11. The reference here is to the Asante Wars.
12. Niculescu (1965: 63) has suggested that the Guggisberg 10-Year Development Programme, 1920–30, could be one of the very first development plans ever drawn up and implemented. See further Chapter 4 for some assessments of the Guggisberg Programme.
13. The huge adjustment of the nominal exchange rate since April 1983 (from 2.75 cedis = 1 US$ to 261.91 cedis = 1 US$ in April 1989, parallel rate at 350 cedis = 1 US$) and the consequent contraction of fiscal and monetary policies, is sufficient evidence of the will to stabilize the Ghana economy.
14. Nigeria, which has voluntarily undertaken rigorous monetary stabilization since 1985, is one of several African countries submitting to radical economic and monetary reforms.
15. The reference here is to the excessive Ghanaian refugee problem in Africa (an estimated 1.5 million Ghanaians were driven out of Nigeria in 1983), the high increase in the levels of Ghanaian female prostitution in neighbouring countries, (from discussions with Mrs Campbell, of the Attorney General's Office, Accra, a member of a women's delegation to neighbouring states to study the subject) and the massive Ghanaian brain drain.
16. I have often been asked by our elderly people when 'independence would be ended so that prosperity can return'.
17. The Colonial Office was disappointed with the modifications in the study. Comments on the Report are to be found on File CO554/747 in the Public Record Office, London.

Part I
Theories of Development and Decline

The three chapters contained in this Part follow a methodology which first reviews the orthodox development theories as they relate to the African condition. Next comes a study of the evolution of development theories and strategies adopted by the principal writers and policy-makers who have addressed the development problems of Ghana in the course of this century, comparing such theories and strategies with the orthodox literature. An attempt is made to illustrate in particular the primary weaknesses in the structure of the Ghanaian economy and to discuss how far these have been recognized in the theory and strategies of development. Part I concludes by introducing, on the basis of this analysis, a theoretical interpretative model for the study of economic decline in Ghana.

1 Development Theory and the African Experience

> In unenlightened circles agriculture and industry are often considered as alternatives to each other. The truth is that industrialization for a home market can make little progress unless agriculture is progressing vigorously at the same time. If agriculture is stagnant, industry cannot grow.
>
> W. Arthur Lewis (1953: 2)

Progress has been the consistent endeavour of mankind, whether individually or in groups, at all levels of development and in all historical periods. The central purpose of economics has been the development of a body of knowledge to aid analysis of the conditions under which this effort can be enhanced and monitored. From the classical economists like Steuart, Adam Smith, Ricardo and Karl Marx, to the host of neo-classical economists and those of more modern times,[1] the contribution of economists has been to set down, in an organized manner, the analysis of human progress by different methods which seek to interpret or describe the processes of economic growth.

The idea of distinguishing between the problems of growth of the advanced and the less advanced societies began only in the late 1940s. The literature of that time, which emphasized economic growth in terms of incomes as well as transformations in social and economic structures,[2] has tended to shape the course of economic thought and knowledge of modern economic development in less developed societies. A large volume of literature has been produced since the 1950s, when the subject of economic development became formalized both in the advanced teaching of economics and in the practical application of development economics by policy-makers in developing countries. Nevertheless, no single development theory has yet emerged, indicating that the rate, content and direction of the structural changes needed for economic development vary too greatly to permit theoretical generalizations. The pioneers of development thought have therefore introduced different ideas based on their experiences in the different regions of the world,[3] their engagement in particular roles[4] or their analysis of empirical evidence on the historical evolution of development in advanced societies. [5]

It is difficult, even to this day, to agree on what is mainstream development economics. There are structural dimensions, variously illustrating trade pessimism, emphasis on physical capital, the use of surplus labour, the use of state planning, reliance on import substitution, or on foreign capital flows. But issues of approach have been equally important, such as balanced versus unbalanced growth, agriculture versus industrialization, import substitution versus export promotion, and planning versus market forces.

African Development in the Context of the Evolved Development Theories

Development theories, as they have been absorbed into policy-making, have posed a few problems for economic growth in Africa. These have derived principally from a bias towards the structural approach to development, in particular, the emphasis on the capital constraints approach and on the idea of centralized planning and the consequent excessive state initiatives that underlie the principal theories. As a corollary, there has been less effort to solve the more relevant, and more controversial, development issues that arise in Africa's specific circumstances. Such issues are the appropriate strategies in the progression from agriculture to industrialization and from import substitution to export substitution (Ranis and Okhawa, 1985), questions of state promotion of development under freer market conditions (Pacific Basin model) versus central planning involving state participation, and the whole controversy between balanced and unbalanced strategies.

Evidence from Africa indicates that the idea that development may be achieved by overcoming the capital constraint problem has adversely influenced macroeconomic management of the external sectors in most countries. In the design of development plans it has induced indiscriminate external and internal mobilization of capital for use mostly by the state and in some instances by favoured private entrepreneurs. The 1986 Africa Memorandum to the United Nations General Assembly[6] on external resource assistance for development has offered a classic opportunity to test the appropriateness and value of such assistance in the present context. Responding to this initiative, the African Development Bank (ADB) and the UN Economic Commission for Africa (ECA) mounted a joint study on the ability of African countries to mobilize two-thirds of the amount promised in the Memorandum.[7] Its results clearly indicated that the African counterpart of $82.5 billion could not be mobilized in the 1986–90 period. The ability and the institutional capability to mobilize savings in Africa was found to have been significantly eroded since the mid-1970s.

Further studies have also shown the tendency towards the misuse of publicly mobilized savings (ADB Annual Symposium, 1988),[8] excessive reliance on external borrowing for social infrastructure and inappropriate industrial investment. It would appear that the assumption underlying the two-gap model (Chenery and Eckstein, 1970)[9] has worked in reverse in most of Africa. It is rational to assume that external capital is essential for development because extra domestic savings cannot always be converted into capital goods and are therefore frustrated. However, the evidence gathered in the ADB/ECA (1987) Study indicated that the rate of domestic savings was in reverse order to that of external capital inflow in the large majority of countries, as was also the relationship with economic growth except in situations of major economic recovery (Ghana since 1984) and of established external private sector investment collaboration (Côte d'Ivoire). The ADB/ECA study indicated that until domestic capital was mobilized to the maximum, external capital could not be advantageous to development. These findings supported the views of Haavelmo (1965)[10] and showed that the value of capital in economic development in Africa was not in the capital *per se* but in the conditions enabling the sustained growth of savings in the productive sectors at their maximum levels of both mobilization and management.

Further relevant results are the following. First, exports and taxation emerge as the most important determinants of savings in Africa. These determinants have not been reliable in recent years, however. The export sector, largely of traditional primary commodities, has shown consistent decline in most of the post-independence period. Recent studies have shown that, for the majority of African countries, barter terms of trade have been adverse in the whole of the post-war period (Svedberg, 1991). Also, export volumes have collapsed since the mid-1970s, largely due to direct and indirect internal policy factors (Balassa, 1977; Krueger, Schiff & Valdes, 1987; Svedberg, 1991). Taxation, though significant in the results, is mixed in its benefits to capital mobilization; only in a minority of countries does it correlate positively with savings. It is clear that the large transfers of private financial savings to governments have been at the expense of investments in vital productive sectors of the African economy.

Economic conditions provide the second important influence on domestic and external capital mobilization. Major changes in economic conditions have altered the principal determinants of capital mobilization significantly, whether they are the results of political changes, as in Ethiopia in 1974 and Ghana in 1972, or oil price changes, as in Nigeria in 1973 and 1979, or the collapse of commodity prices, as in Côte d'Ivoire since the late 1970s. Thirdly, institutional capability for capital mobilization has declined significantly as economies in Africa have stagnated or declined (ADB, 1987; ACMS, 1985), and formal economic sectors have been stifled by restrictions and exchange-rate over-valuation (Leith, 1974).

Though all these results confirm the severe capital constraint on development in Africa, they do not suggest that development can be more easily achieved if that constraint is overcome. Rather, they indicate the futility of any massive external mobilization of capital to fill the gap assumed by the Chenery–Eckstein hypothesis. The results suggest a more deep-seated weakness of the African economy that development theory has to address more seriously. This has to do with the management of the limits to which the underdeveloped economy can accept capital, the types of capital and their productivity. These factors relate closely to the strategies for the steady transition from an agriculture-dominated economy to industrialization through modernization rather than destruction of the agricultural base. (This subject is taken up, in the Ghanaian context, in some detail in Chapter 2.) If this condition is not met, the availability of excess capital, from whatever source, has the tendency to retard rather than promote development. It is reasonable to hypothesize, from the African experience, that the countries that were better endowed with capital at independence (Ghana, Zambia, Zaire) or gained windfall capital (from oil in Nigeria, for example), have been more prone to failure in development than those that were less endowed (Kenya, Côte d'Ivoire). This reasoning points to a much more fundamental problem.

The examples of Kenya and Côte d'Ivoire indicate an emphasis on agriculture and moderation in macroeconomic management in the transition from colonialism, while the relative successes of Botswana and Cameroon point to moderately conservative financial management as an important condition for development from the pre-industrial state.

The second major difficulty with the development theories has been the implied reliance on taxation for capital mobilization. Apart from the general limitations discussed above, empirical evidence indicates that the primary export sectors of the African economy have been the conventional source of the bulk of taxation and have borne a more than justifiable burden of capital mobilization, except in countries where the primary agricultural sector has developed into a politically sensitive interest group, as in Kenya (Bates, 1983).[11] Table 1.1 shows the average effective taxation on primary exports in a selection of African countries. Table 1.2 on Ghana compares the taxes on cocoa and those on some primary non-agricultural exports and shows the high discriminatory taxation against cocoa. Table 1.3 shows, for a number of developing countries, including four from Africa, the effective direct and indirect rates of taxation against the principal export commodities. These results reveal very high levies on primary production generally in the developing world and illustrate the discriminatory treatment of the relatively more advanced economic sector in the immediate post-independence period when the need for capital mobilization for development was greatest.

A number of problems also arise from the application of the theory of unbalanced development (Hirschman, 1958) by those countries that opted for the more aggressive disequilibrium strategies in their development programmes. First, the role of the private sector has been limited because of the indivisibility of the capital outlays required in situations where a wide gap exists between social and private profitability. This problem is bigger where the economic environment is less developed. Second, as resources have

Table 1.1   Producer Price Ratios to Border Prices at Official Exchange Rates in Selected African Countries and Selected Commodities, 1979–80

Country	Currency over-valuation average 1978–80 1970 = 1.00	Groundnuts	Coffee	Cocoa	Cotton seed
1	2	3	4	5	6
Ghana	3.96	6.09	0.45	0.34	0.73
Zaire	0.84	2.22	0.06	0.34	1.28
Nigeria	2.43	1.70	0.69	0.88	0.85
Cote d'Ivoire	1.87	0.33	0.44	0.43	0.53
Niger	1.82	0.65	0.80		
Cameroon	1.75	1.40	0.46	0.43	0.35
Senegal	1.68	0.59	0.35		
Somalia	1.67	0.57		0.58	
Central African Rep.	1.66	0.41	0.23		0.35
Tanzania	1.42	1.40	0.47	0.32	0.50
Kenya	1.42	0.59	1.01		0.63
Burkina Faso	1.40	0.41		0.38	
Madagascar	1.40	0.66	0.31	0.07	0.58
Zambia	1.24	1.40		0.83	
Malawi	1.15	0.60	0.27		0.38
Zimbabwe	1.11	1.01	0.38	0.75	
Sierra Leone	1.05	0.59	0.59	0.66	

Source: ECA (1986), p. 25.

Table 1.2 Tax Distortions Within the Ghana Export Sector, 1955–66

Year	Cocoa tax rate(%)	Wood tax rate(%)	Diamond tax rate(%)	Average non-cocoa export tax rate (%)
1955	44.74	1.67	4.89	1.40
1956	13.22	1.99	4.93	1.74
1957	33.79	1.72	5.20	1.58
1958	49.55	1.93	5.20	1.65
1959	37.07	2.26	5.04	1.76
1960	19.68	2.94	3.87	1.90
1961	39.70	2.88	4.34	1.85
1962	4.04	2.95	2.69	1.45
1963	22.73	2.98	2.98	1.52
1964	−3.02	2.42	1.83	1.14
1965	54.25	3.10	0.14	1.13
1966	40.59	3.39	0.02	1.08

Source: Leith (1974), p. 13

Table 1.3. Direct, Indirect and Total Nominal Protection Rates for Exported Products (%)

Country	Product	1975–79			1980–84		
		Direct	Indirect	Total	Direct	Indirect	Total
Argentina	Wheat	−25.1	−16.4	−41.4	−12.7	−36.7	−49.4
Brazil	Cotton	13.4	−31.9	−18.5	2.6	−13.7	−11.1
Chile	Grapes	1.0	22.4	23.4	0.0	−7.3	−7.3
Colombia	Coffee	−7.0	−24.5	−31.5	−4.9	−34.2	−39.1
Dominican Republic	Coffee	−14.9	−17.5	−32.4	−32.3	−19.3	−51.6
Egypt	Cotton	−36.3	−18.2	−54.4	−21.8	−13.9	−35.7
Ghana	Cocoa	25.6	−66.0	−40.4	34.0	−89.0	−55.0
Côte d'Ivoire	Coffee	−31.5	−32.6	−64.1	−25.2	−25.6	−50.8
Malaysia	Rubber	−25.2	−4.3	−29.5	−18.3	−9.5	−27.8
Pakistan	Cotton	−12.3	−48.4	−60.6	−7.3	−34.6	−41.8
Phil'pines	Copra	−10.7	−27.2	−37.9	−26.0	−26.0	−54.3
Portugal	Tomatoes	17.1	−5.3	11.8	17.1	−12.9	4.2
Sri Lanka	Rubber	−28.5	−34.6	−63.1	−31.3	−31.4	−62.7
Thailand	Rice	−27.7	−15.4	−43.1	−14.9	−19.1	−34.0
Turkey	Tobacco	1.8	−40.2	−38.4	−27.6	−35.3	−62.9
Zambia	Cotton	−13.4	−41.5	−55.0	−4.6	−57.1	−61.7

Source: Krueger, Schiff and Valdes (1987), p. 14

dwindled in more recent times, as in the case of Ghana, competing demands have imposed severe constraints on the maintenance of installed capacity and have led to the decay of some investments, particularly in the public sector, a prediction made by Lewis in 1959. [12]

Third, problems of excess capacity and of linkages between productive sectors have grown rather than shrunk as predicted in the disequilibrium models. This has been due to shortcomings in project design and to import compression (see further Chapter 6 and Annex 1) when the primary export sectors failed as a result of exogenous and domestic policy factors before the potentially favourable results of development could come to the fore. Fourth, the implied fiscal excesses in the unbalanced strategies, especially those arising from subsidies and other restrictive measures induced by permissive strategies, have had major adverse effects, direct and indirect, in the majority of African states (Krueger, Schiff & Valdes, 1987 and Stryker *et al.*, 1988).

Some difficulties have also been observed with the Lewis (1954) model, which is based not only on the assumption of infinite elasticity of labour supply at the subsistence wage but also on the ease of absorption of such labour. Though its validity, as a theory, remains unchallengeable, a state of inhibited labour absorption can reduce its usefulness to development. Notwithstanding the generally low population densities in Africa compared with some regions of the developing world, there are valid arguments based on the empirical evidence since the 1950s to justify the assumption of infinite labour supply. There has been phenomenal urbanization and the formation of large informal sectors in most African countries, particularly around the urban centres. There has also been some degree of technological unemployment following the importation of factories and agricultural machinery. The growth of women in employment outside the household has also been significant. But perhaps the most important evidence has been the unexpected rise in the rate of population increase; for most countries the rate is now closer to 3% compared with the 2% assumed in the 1950s.

Labour absorption, despite the above factors, has been hindered in two important ways. First, in many countries, the combination of minimum wage legislation and trade union action for higher wages, price controls, the low profitability of state commercial enterprises and excessive company taxation has had the effect of curtailing the rate of growth of profits and therefore of profit shares in the national income anticipated by Lewis in his model. Furthermore, the prevalence of exchange rate overvaluation has had the effect of reducing productive efficiency and profitability in the primary mining and agricultural export sectors, hampering their ability to maintain investment and labour absorption. Second, labour absorption has been impeded by urban demand for food rising faster than agricultural productivity (Akoto, 1985). These indicators would suggest a slowing down, if not a reversal, of the process of capital accumulation in the non-farm sectors of the economy and of the growth of non-farm employment, both of which are important results in the model. Far from reducing the theoretical validity of the model, these observations point to the importance of an appropriate organizational environment in the process of technological change and labour absorption. This important factor has been assumed in the model but not well articulated or emphasized as a condition. With hindsight, it is a very difficult problem of development, of at least the same significance as the core concepts of labour surplus and capital constraint.

To take the argument further, the Lewis (1955) model assumes success in introducing technological improvements into the traditional agricultural sector, which would have the effect of shifting the production function outward. Observations from Africa indicate that success depends on the following factors:

1.. *The strategies for the adoption of appropriate technology* (Dadson, 1970). The Japanese unimodal and the Mexican dualist approaches have been the standard ones in the literature. On the other hand, the evolution of new primary crops in West Africa demonstrates the case for indigenous adaptation. In the Gold Coast, the adaptation of sylviculture in cocoa was frowned upon by the authorities but the method turned out to be the most appropriate for farmers in terms of investment costs (Guggisberg, 1924).[13]
2.. *The ability to retain maximum incentives for agriculture.* This has not been emphasized adequately. On the contrary, the erosion of incentives through direct and indirect taxation would appear to be assumed as part of the solution to the capital constraint problem.
3.. *Resource allocation to agriculture* may be sub-optimal in the environment of price distortions created by factors such as price controls and subsidies, and therefore may not provide the maximum incentive for the adoption of technology (Akoto, 1985).
4.. *Subsidies can be ineffectual* in the environment of price distortions (Stryker *et al.*, 1988) as subsidized items find their way to the informal markets or are smuggled abroad.
5. *Bateman's limited incentive curve* (discussed in more detail in Chapter 7) demonstrates how farmer incentives come up against a ceiling effect. Factors observed to impose the ceiling include limited rural living comforts and lack of farmers' basic needs, leading to the habit of capital accumulation in urban centres that have better amenities.
6.. *The disparity between urban and rural prices* created by distorted transportation facilities and costs keeps peasant production permanently sub-optimal and unresponsive to incentives and technological ideas (see further Chapter 2). This last factor is perhaps the most telling of all.

Conclusion

One conclusion to be drawn from this analysis is that while freeing the mind from classical economic thinking enabled the academic pioneers to make new assumptions and produce development models that were thought to be relevant to economic growth in the underdeveloped societies, most of the new theories were not of general application. For the particular development problems of Africa, the Lewis models of 1954 and 1955 were the most relevant, but even these concentrated on the problem of capital constraint while neglecting problems of organization which were at least as important. The specific problem which the theory failed to tackle was that of the organization of development from the pre-industrial state. If the pre-industrial state is assumed to be one structured entirely as a peasant agricultural society and the objective of development is to change that structure by introducing industrialization to increase overall as well as per capita incomes, leading to increases in profit shares and hence in development capital, then the Lewisian tradition of labour absorption through productivity increases, not only in the new capitalist sector but more so in the agricultural sector, cannot easily be faulted. However, Lewis himself argues (1955: 279) that

> in practice, in most backward economies, the sector which usually responds least well to growth in other sectors, and which therefore acts as a brake to economic growth, is the agricultural sector, producing food for home consumption.

The theoretical framework has not adequately emphasized agricultural productivity, the proper design of the sequence of priorities, and the appropriate organization. One of the biggest gaps in development theory is work on public agricultural policy during the management of development from the nascent state.

Two important factors emerge from our analysis. First, the theories of development attach only marginal importance to the organization and management of development *ab initio* in the absence of natural factors acting rapidly to stimulate growth in agriculture and manufacturing. Second, the provision of appropriate incentives for production, in a situation in which little or no natural stimulus exists, has been neglected. These two factors are assumed for the advanced state of development and have been absent from the development literature. A real danger is posed when this vacuum is filled by strategies whose viability is incorrectly perceived or by an assumption of structural capability that is more apparent than real. Thus, in an attempt to escape from the capital constraint, many countries in Africa which, at independence or some time thereafter, possessed large external reserves, or had access to large amounts of international capital, embarked on aggressive development programmes in the Hirschmanian and Rosenstein-Rodan traditions or in Lewisian agricultural and industrial modernization, only to be thwarted by problems of organization, management, and low productive response capability. And others abandoned incentives to important established productive sectors in their search for capital for modernization, at immense cost to the development process itself.

Notes

1. A good listing of those economists and their works, that relate to this study, is contained in Meier and Seers, (1984) and Meier (1987).
2. See, for example, Schiavo-Campo, S. and Singer, H.W. *Perspectives of Economic Development*, Houghton Mifflin, Boston, 1970.
3. Lewis, for example, narrates the thought of 'unlimited supply of labour' coming to him in August 1952 in Bangkok. See Lewis 'Development Economics in the 1950s' in Meier and Seers (1984), p.132.
4. See also the influence on Hirschman of his exposure in Colombia. He states in half truth 'I went to Colombia in 1952 without any prior knowledge of, or reading about, economic development ... without theoretical preconceptions of any kind. Then when I returned to the United States after four and a half years' intensive experience as an official adviser and private consultant, I began to read up on the literature and discovered that I had acquired a point of view of my own that was considerably at odds with current doctrines.' Hirschman, however, was influenced by his observed process of industrialization in Colombia, in his opposition to the

'balanced' or 'big push' industrialization. (See Hirschman, A.O. 'A Dissenter's Confession' in Meier and Seers (1984), pp. 88, 96.

5. As for example Lewis did in arriving at his theory on the rate of investment required to be classified as advanced.

6. UN General Assembly Memorandum 'Ad Hoc Committee's Report on the Critical Economic Situation in Africa', May 27–31, 1986; 13th Special Session Agenda Item 6, Document No. A/S–13/AC.1/L.3, p. 16 Para. 12.

7. The study *Domestic Resource Mobilization in Africa* has been widely published in Africa and has largely debunked some false notions of the domestic capital mobilizing capability in Africa in the post-independence period, (ADB/ECA, 1987).

8. For proceedings of the symposium plus country case studies see Frimpong-Ansah, J.H. and Ingham, B.M. *Saving for Economic Recovery in Africa,* James Currey (forthcoming) 1992.

9. Chenery, H.B. (working with a number of authors, particularly Bruno, M., Adelman, I., Strout, A.M and Eckstein, P.) has argued that economic growth can be limited by the capacity for domestic savings and the capacity for importation (the two-gap model). Subsequent work (Chenery and MacEwan, 1966) has shown that human capacity is also an important determinant of growth.

10. T.Haavelmo's comment on W. Leontief's paper on 'The Rate of Long Run Economic Growth and Capital Transfer from Developed to Underdeveloped Areas' in *Study Week on the Economic Approach to Development Planning.* Pontificaiae Academia Scientiarum Scripta Varia No. 28, North-Holland, 1965. Haavelmo's hypothesis is that foreign aid induces a decline in domestic savings.

11. Bates R. (1983) provides an illuminating comparison between Kenya and Ghana in the relative authority of the farmer, illustrating the power of the colonial settler farmer and his successor, the politician, businessman or public servant farmer in Kenya.

12. Lewis, W.A. in his Valedictory Address to Fellows of the Ghana Economic Society: On Assessing a Development Plan (Lewis, 1959) had predicted that due to the rapid pace of investment in the 1950s and 1960s a time would come when the country would face maintenance problems.

13. The argument then was that farmers did not plant cocoa in rows as in modern agriculture, but irregularly with other crops.

2 The Evolution of Development Theory and Policy in Ghana

> It is better to be free to govern or misgovern yourself than to be governed by anybody else.
>
> Kwame Nkrumah (1957: vi)

Fortunately, the study of development phenomena in Ghana is helped by some important works on the philosophy of development by a number of authors, including some of the pioneers of the subject. These underpin the effort in the present study to reconstruct Ghana's attempt at development, to document the evolution of development thinking and policy, and to assess Ghana's development problems against the background both of the evolved orthodoxy and of the specific ideas indicated in specialist studies of the economy. To the authors noted in the Introduction (Cardinall, Seers and Ross, and Lewis for the period before independence, and Killick, Roemer and Chazan for the post-independence period) we can now add Guggisberg (1924)[1] for the colonial period and Nkrumah[2] for the post-independence period. Both developed specific ideas and also, in the policy sense, played perhaps the most important roles in shaping the path of development in Ghana.

The analysis in this chapter is undertaken within the framework of some of the questions posed in the Introduction. The particular issues addressed are: the evidence, in colonial economic development thinking, of clear ideas on the role of government and on development management methods; the quality and value of the professional economic advice available to the country towards the end of decolonization and in the early period of independence, and its impact on economic management and development policy; and the principal characteristics of the pre-industrial economy in Ghana which some recent writers have described as offering the potential for growth, but which earlier scholars described as fragile.

Gold Coast Strategies: Guggisberg and Cardinall

Of the early writers on Ghana's development theory and strategies, Sir Gordon Guggisberg, who was Governor of the Gold Coast from 1919 to 1927, was the most prominent.[3] The essence of the Guggisberg development philosophy is captured in the sentence: 'No country can develop trade to its full paying capacity without incurring a debt for the construction of the necessary infrastructure' (Guggisberg, 1924: 41). His objective bears the inevitable stamp of British imperial trade policy with which he conformed as a colonial governor. Yet the evidence of his work, as we shall observe later in this chapter, revealed the sincerity of his belief in broader development without too much colonial constraint. The value of this approach is recognized today, as it was during his time in office.

The Guggisberg development theory is described in his Development Programme of 1920–1930,[4] said to be the result of his own original thinking rather than the deliberations of the Colonial Office in London or the colonial government of the Gold Coast which he headed at the time (Kimble, 1963: 55). It has also been argued that this Development Programme was the first formally theorized development programme undertaken in the colonial empire and in Africa (Niculescu, 1957: 63). Guggisberg was a surveyor by training but his theory showed glimpses of the professional economist. Implicit in the Guggisberg Programme were the following assumptions: that land, though fixed, was not a constraint on development in the Gold Coast during the period with which he was concerned; that labour was abundant and therefore not a constraint, either; and that the shortage of capital *was* a constraint, particularly on the development of communications which he regarded as the bottleneck to development. Guggisberg also assumed a growing international market in the traditional sense of imperial trade, but that commodity prices were likely to fall in the plan period or after, due to general increases in primary production in the post-war period. A necessary condition for his programme was therefore a structure of production costs that would fall with improvements in transport and other communications. Thus Guggisberg's assumptions resembled those of the later neo-classical economists in terms of the non-fixity of labour, the acceptance of technological change, and the capital constraint.

Unlike them, however, Guggisberg studied the development problem within the rigid constraints of colonial economic management. This can be explained by use of the identity $(S - I) + (T - G) = X - M$,[5] where S is private sector saving, I is private sector investment, T is government tax revenue, G is government current and development spending, and X and M are exports and imports of goods and services.

Colonial management assumed a strict budgetary balance $(T - G = 0)$, with the implication that the private savings-investment gap $(S - I)$ must always be equal to the deficit in the balance of payments. Since it was also British Treasury policy to discourage external debt accumulation,[6] a condition for the accelerated development strategy implied in the Guggisberg theory was an acceleration in private saving and in taxation at the same rate as development spending. For the heavy investment spending envisaged in the Guggisberg plan, and for the current costs involved over the ten-year period, this condition demanded that taxation and external borrowing increase productivity and overall export performance in volume terms.[7] Therefore the core condition of Guggisberg's development theory, under the colonial constraint, was that there should be higher taxation that would nevertheless not be a disincentive to production. This meant that there must be room in the profits of businesses to absorb more export taxation.[8] It also meant that the higher levels of output and productivity, particularly in relation to local food, would absorb the higher income levels generated by the higher levels of domestic public sector spending.

Remarkably, these conditions were generally met in the Guggisberg Plan period up to 1928. Guggisberg had predicted correctly that in the case of cocoa the removal of the transportation bottleneck would expand supply from the existing tree stock, that the minerals sector which had shown high utilization of capacity in production would also respond to the removal of the transport bottleneck, and that the international market would remain buoyant in the years after the First World War (the last condition held until 1927, when the depression set in). In Table 4.6, the relationship of production in the cocoa and minerals sectors to the expansion of road and rail mileage is reported.

Labour absorption did take place, but in this case there appears to have been significant movement from the larger towns to the newly promoted cocoa and mining areas, in line with the emphasis on the development of primary export production (Table 2.1).[9] As may be observed from Table 2.1, Kumase, the capital city of Asante, and in particular Mampong the next largest town, were growing in population at rates significantly below average, whereas the new cocoa area of Asante Akyem and the mining area of Obuase-Bekwai were growing significantly above average. Polly Hill (1986: 127), describing migration from the Fante coastal towns, confirms similarly that 'a fair proportion of migrants sought work in gold mining communities up-country'. Labour movements in this growth period contrast with the patterns of economic growth based on industrialization where labour absorption is to the urban areas (Lewis, 1955).[10] The neo-classical economists' argument is that the process of migration from the countryside goes on until 'a position of equilibrium is reached, such that "both villager and townsman know that nothing is to be gained by moving" ' (Hill, 1986: 133). Lipton (1980: 6) has argued, however, that equilibrating movements of this nature would act slowly due to lack of information, and therefore rural–urban migration would tend to enhance urban bias.

Table 2.1 Population Distribution in the Eastern Province of Ashanti, 1921–31

	1921	1931	Annual increase %	Average increase %
Asante Akyem	29,757	55,235	85	6.38
Kumase	49,114	172,196	15	1.45
Mampong	47,491	50,295	5	0.06
Obuase-Bekwai	66,082	116,084	76	5.80
Total	292,444	393,810	34	3.02

Source: Cardinall (1931)

The value of the Guggisberg development theory and programme to this study is the insight it gives into probable productive responses to the removal of bottlenecks through appropriate capital costs, the provision of adequate incentives for farmers, not so much in terms of higher prices as in overall increases in incomes from higher output, and the strategies of public policy in mobilizing producers in support of development. The removal of the transportation bottleneck for the mining sector is illustrated by the result that for the period 1920–28 the rate of export expansion matched almost perfectly the rate of expansion of the road and rail network (significant linear correlation of .9711 from the data in Table 4.6). Guggisberg also successfully mobilized the farmers to construct, at their own expense, all the feeder roads from the principal roads to the farming villages (Slater, 1930: 88) – a recognition that the fragmentation in the peasant productive system caused by the inadequate feeder road network could be reduced (discussed later in this chapter).

The lesson of the Guggisberg theory of development, in the context of a rigidly constrained colonial management system, is that the proper diagnosis of development problems, together with the provision of maximum incentives to producers, the removal of identified bottlenecks to production potential, public capital mobilization, and the proper management of all these elements are essential ingredients for successful economic development. This distinguishes the Guggisberg theory from the later ideas of abstract theoreticians and ambitious politicians. In the history of Ghana, Guggisberg's was the best thought-out development programme and the only one which was successfully implemented; some of its significant results for the export sector are illustrated in Tables 4.3 and 4.4.

Cardinall was a Census officer in the 1921–31 period, whose work brought together detailed information on economic growth in the period covered by the Guggisberg Plan (Cardinall, 1931). It therefore provides a test of the Guggisberg strategy rather than contributing to development theory. Cardinall predicted the long-term impracticability of a development strategy which, even in colonial terms, lacked adequate diversification; drew attention to the existing hired labour structure in the cocoa sector and the tendency towards absenteeism and urban migration of the wealthier farmers; and made observations on the capacity for agricultural modernization (Cardinall, 1931: 85, 99). The following paragraphs analyse his observations, which help to explain the handicaps that existed even then in the agricultural structure and which, together with certain other factors, may have frustrated the fullest implementation of the Guggisberg strategies.[11]

Cardinall's call for diversification was directed towards the export sector and not towards a general diversification and improvement in agriculture. In particular, he questioned the long-term effects of the relatively easier method of growing cocoa on the commercial farming culture in the forest belts of the country. He also commented on the major problem of excessive concentration of resources on a single farming sector. It should be noted, however, that considerable evidence exists in the official records of many attempts in the period, in other areas of the country, to introduce or develop on a commercial scale crops such as cotton, sisal, tobacco, copra, sheanuts, kola, oil-palm, rice and coffee. Most of these efforts were reported to have failed because of the 'inherent mistrust of new things by the natives' (Guggisberg, 1924: 46). But that could be interpreted as a lack of will for experimentation with less profitable crops, since several of the well-cultivated food and commercial export crops, including cocoa itself, were of foreign origin.

Cardinall also drew attention to the emerging commercialization of the labour structure, from family labour to hired labour. This was observed as a rapid increase in the wealth of cocoa farmers and the associated repudiation of communal ownership of land in favour of individual ownership. In his view it amounted to a revolution. The sale of land, a previously unheard-of practice, had begun and the industrious farmer was being forced 'to hire labour in order to cope with fruits of industry'. The farmer was 'gradually ceasing to be a working farmer with the inevitable result that in the course of time he would be a non-working landlord' (Cardinall, 1931: 84). This was the beginning of the process later analysed by Bateman (1971) as a possible explanation for the existence of a ceiling on farmer incentives. Based on observations of cocoa farmers' investment patterns, Bateman concludes that, under normal conditions, a farmer's planting response to the real producer price follows a non-linear path to a ceiling after which he will not invest additional income in the industry (see Chapter 7).[12]

The observations of Cardinall and others[13] on the commercial successes of cocoa in the early phases of the industry tend to cast doubt on certain ideas, long held then and now, on the non-entrepreneurial character of the African. The development of the industry was largely on the initiative of the peasant farmer, and arguments about forces inhibiting agricultural modernization, such as land tenure systems, communal ownership, the lack of desire for wealth accumulation, and the creation of a landless class are difficult to sustain. The development of the cocoa industry suggests that the farmers would respond, given the inducement of financial reward to work harder, and that attachment to custom and tradition in land ownership and inheritance could be abandoned. The official statement that the 'Gold Coast native sees small attraction in wandering far afield and consequently there is little real emigration'[14] cannot be upheld. Hill (1956, 1963) has documented this quite well and states in a more recent work (1986: 117) that

> the astonishingly rapid growth of the Gold Coast cocoa industry in the twenty years (or so) after 1895, when exports were negligible, had always been regarded as a 'miracle' until it was belatedly realized that the *migrant* farmers who bought large areas of forest land were initially responsible [emphasis added].

Further evidence from that period is provided by Beckett (1944).[15] Hart (1982: 123) also argues that

> this mobility is neither novel nor dysfunctional, for migration and movements were intrinsic to the indigenous population's way of life even before the concentration of economic opportunities on the coast set up today's asymmetrical drift from savannah villages to forest plantations and city slums.

The growth of cocoa enables one to postulate as follows on development from the nascent state. First, an assured and sustained high reward for work can induce higher productivity, and also change custom and tradition for the benefit of development. Second, the Ghanaian has the ability to adapt rapidly to production methods that increase the rate of financial return, such as switching to hired labour from family labour, or adopting share cropping (*abusa*), or adopting an entirely new crop or occupation, such as cocoa itself. Third, the farmer has the initiative, if he has the means, to enlarge his wealth by acquiring larger plantations. Cardinall quotes a survey of cocoa farmers in the south-east of Asante in 1920 which reported that most farmers owned more than one plantation, with the largest being 27 acres. The survey also mentioned that the 'process of "westernizing" the peasantry who had just emerged from the era of nomadism' had been hastened by the introduction of land sales, land transfers and mortgages (Cardinall, 1931: 93).

Coming, however, to Cardinall's third observation, we realize that major constraints still hindered the process of full commercialization of the small peasant system in agriculture. The Guggisberg road and rail transport system had increased production by removing the transportation bottleneck in the cocoa industry, but thereafter labour productivity could not increase beyond the capacity of manual labour. Again it can be postulated that the cocoa agricultural system of the time lacked the ingredients for long-run development after the removal of fragmentation in that it did not have the ability to release its labour at an increasing rate to other sectors of the economy without reducing its total output. The ability to accumulate and release savings was only beginning with the absentee farmer or *abusa* system, but was being manifested in real estate construction (see above and note 12). The greater accumulation needed for development in other sectors of the economy was to be seen only in the long term in circumstances in which farmer interest was maintained at the maximum Bateman incentive level for an extended period. This would ensure optimum cocoa output as well as the release of capital. Therefore, from Cardinall's analysis, the scope for agricultural modernization, which had started, could begin to have benefits for other sectors only in the long term. Lewis's assessment two decades later, discussed below, was similar (Lewis, 1953, 1954, 1955).

The conclusion from Cardinall's work on Ghana in 1931 is that, though he did not attempt to advance a development theory or a strategy, he made observations on the trend in development which were as pertinent to development policy then as they are today. He drew attention to the genesis of agricultural modernization but pointed out that major constraints remained which could only be resolved in the long term, even given the producer incentives that followed from the Guggisberg Programme. Thus Cardinall focused on the need both for diversification and for the maintenance of producer incentives as conditions for material progress from the underdeveloped state.

Theory and Policy after Guggisberg

A brief analysis of inter-war colonial development thinking cannot be omitted from this analysis; it not only bridges the gap between the Guggisberg development initiatives and those of Nkrumah, but also fills a gap in knowledge which few have so far attempted to reconstruct.[16] The analysis is designed to capture the thinking in the Colonial Office which provided overall guidance, that of the colonial government of the Gold Coast, and the responses of influential Africans in the period. It also helps in identifying some of the misconceptions regarding the strength of the Ghana economy at the time of independence.

A study of the economic thinking in the Colonial Office cannot fail to emphasize a conservatively detached approach to the general economic welfare of the colonies, except where the objectives related to the development of production for imperial trade (Crook, 1986).[17] However, such a study also shows a major change in attitudes, particularly from the late 1930s when several official pronouncements were made on decolonization.[18] The Colonial Development and Welfare Act (1940) was enacted to replace the 1929 Act. There were also individual initiatives by Lord Hailey and Malcolm MacDonald, the Secretary of State for the Colonies. Before the 1929 Act there was no special thinking on colonial development, as the colonies were lumped together with the more advanced Dominions. Ideas on development related to the coordination of the resources of the British Empire (Dominions, India and the colonies) by an Imperial Development Board that played only an advisory role in determining 'the means for the direction of Empire capital towards the development of Empire resources'.[19] The flow of capital favoured the Dominions against the underdeveloped colonial areas because it was linked with migration or was mainly from the private sector which preferred the more advanced territories or those with suitable climates. The Colonial Development Act of 1929 provided £1m to assist development through grants and loans for various development schemes in the colonies. The small size of the endowment illustrates the limited direct role that the Colonial Office expected to play. In the case of the Gold Coast the total amount disbursed under the Fund in the decade 1930–40 was £142,002 for the water supply, urban electrification, and an agricultural scholarships scheme.

The development thinking associated with the 1940 Act was somewhat wider in scope, as was the fund created under the Act, disbursing £5m annually for ten years. New initiatives introduced included the idea of planned expenditure on development, help from a Colonial Development and Welfare Committee in examining development plans, and the publication of the *Economic Survey of the Colonial Empire* to disseminate information on the resources, trade and financial strengths of the different colonies. Other new ideas were the supply of information by the Colonial Office on the international markets available for colonial produce, the strengthening of the Economic Department of the Colonial Office in order 'to meet the needs for an expanded policy of development in the Act of 1940',[20] and the establishment of a new Social Services Department in the Colonial Office to ensure that social advancement was not left behind. The Gold Coast received a total of £858,778 between 1941 and 1948 under the 1940 Act, for agricultural research, construction of educational institutions, urban water supply and electrification.

Though the 1940 efforts were a significant advancement on those of 1929, they could not be regarded as sufficient for initiating and managing development in the colonies. As Sir Edward Grigg said during the debate in Parliament on 26 November 1942:[21]

> I do not wish to disparage the importance of Scotland. But think of the attention one gave to the 5,000,000 people in Scotland compared with 75,000,000 in the Colonial Empire.... We have seen seven Colonial Secretaries in seven years ... this office is treated as a counter in the ordinary process of Empire politics ... and not by the convenience and welfare of the many millions at stake.

The importance to the present study of the 1940 Act lies, however, not in the amount it provided but in the development ideas that came from it. Events surrounding the 1940 Act helped to liberate some minds to question colonial development policies. They also exposed the asymmetry between the political trends towards decolonization and the evolution of economic development. The debate had begun on whether the colonies were being adequately prepared for economic independence in tandem with political liberation. This debate enabled the emergence in the 1940s of what appeared to be two schools of thought on colonial economic development. One school considered independence and economic development in the long term. Malcolm MacDonald, to whom the records seem to accord a pioneering role in the process of decolonization, may be said to belong to this school.[22] In pioneering official concern on the need for decolonization he stated in 1938:

we in this country have a passion for liberty....The same spirit guides our administration of the colonial empire. Even among the most backward races in Africa our main effort is to teach those peoples to stand always a little more steadily on their feet. *But it would take generations, perhaps even centuries, before that aim is accomplished in some cases* [emphasis added].[23]

MacDonald's apparently long-term perspective on decolonization justified the ideas of adherents to the more conservative school of thought on colonial development, best personified by Clauson.[24] It may also have provided justification for the idea that the real process of decolonization, despite the official pronouncements, could not have been initiated from the detached attitude of the Colonial Office (Crook, 1985) compared to the opposite view taken by Flint (1983).[25] The conservative or Clauson school held to the principles that policies on agriculture were to be emphasized, particularly those that supported imperial trade; that secondary industries might be discreetly encouraged but with the sole objective of providing for the simpler needs of the population; overseas purchasing power was to be retained in the colonies for the import of goods of greater social value; that the colonies must not be allowed to become a capital burden on Britain; and that heavy infrastructural expenditures, such as those immediately after the First World War, were to be discouraged. These views were held rather widely in the colonial administration by persons in authority and 'it was a lucky accident if a colony had a Governor capable of conceiving and carrying out development' within these constraints.[26]

The Committee on Post-war Reconstruction of the Colonies, popularly known as the Hailey Committee, though admitting that few colonies had the machinery for dealing with economic questions, nevertheless went on record against the recruitment, in the colonies, of specialists in economics or industries. It ruled that economic planning should be 'part of the normal development and outlook of the administrative staff'.[27]

The development-minded ideas were rather new and their supporters, like Caine, Cohen and Lewis, could not be described as having a large following. They did not appear to have been influenced by any source other than their individually inspired feelings towards the advancement of the colonial peoples.[28] As the only professionally trained economists in the Colonial Office, the proponents possessed greater intellectual articulateness. They were able to address the colonial development problem in a logical fashion, and questioned whether the Colonial Office understood the basic development needs of the colonial countries: the 1940 Act was no real improvement over that of 1929 because it failed to change attitudes from passive to active ones. They advocated state initiatives based on development planning, and a development authority which would operate on commercial lines to manage colonial economic development either at national or integrated regional level. They argued that urbanization had arrived, was set to grow and required development measures that recognized it, particularly in programmes for industrialization. Agricultural modernization was further required to improve rural productivity and release labour. They requested a resurrection of Arthur Lewis's development ideas which had been rejected by the Colonial Economic Advisory Committee in 1944.[29]

Lewis's 1944 ideas[30] may have had their antecedents in the ideas of James Steuart[31] and may also have been the seeds of his balanced growth theory (Lewis, 1955). But in 1944 he wrote in more radical terms, referring to an agricultural revolution and a process in which agricultural and industrial development would proceed hand in hand. These ideas were ignored for a number of reasons. Inflexible attitudes persisted on the role of a colony in the imperial scheme of trade and development. It has been shown that colonial governments tended to distance themselves from economic activities which were not directly related to imperial trade. There were virtually no studies of economic development *ab initio* in conditions resembling those facing Africa. There was total pessimism in high policy circles about the capability of colonial peoples to accept the personal and public obligations involved in economic development.[32] Most importantly, there was no commitment on the part of the Colonial Office to promote economic development on any scale outside the provisions of the Colonial Development and Welfare Fund of the 1940 Act.

In this environment Arthur Lewis's contribution was necessarily more in the nature of theoretical knowledge about development rather than the shaping of colonial development policy. These rather early contributions are less well known and are somewhat different in emphasis from the popular Lewis models. But it could be argued that they are of much more value to African development in that they address the question of economic development *ab initio*, and in a fragile environment. Lewis dealt with both agricultural and industrial development; in this review they are treated separately.

Lewis emphasized the primacy of agriculture in development, stating that 'in any programme of colonial development, agriculture must come first'.[33] He assumed that primary export production already had all the encouragement it needed and he therefore emphasized food production for the domestic market instead. The prescriptions for increasing agricultural productivity in food are increased knowledge of the problems of production, modernization of the methods of production and better economic organization of agricultural management; the latter two policy prescriptions were retained in his subsequent work. By increased knowledge, Lewis meant scientific and technical knowledge as well as the penetration of such knowledge to the village level – an idea very appealing to African leaders of the Gold Coast in the inter-war period. By modernization he meant enlargement of the farm unit and provision by the government of infrastructural facilities to support larger units of production, including the harnessing of water resources for irrigation, energy and flood control. The economic organization of agriculture and its management through government promotion were regarded by Lewis as fundamental to greater knowledge and productivity. Conscious of the brake that agricultural productivity placed on industrialization and on the construction of the social and economic infrastructure, Lewis was insistent that 'changes in agricultural organization [were] urgent; they are not something about which we can shrug our shoulders'.[34] In his view, countries would be doomed to long-term underdevelopment if agricultural organization was not radically modernized. For Lewis these ideas constituted an 'agricultural revolution'.

Parallel to the agricultural revolution Lewis also suggested an 'industrial revolution', supporting his ideas by the argument:

> it is undesirable to be entirely dependent on agriculture because the incomes of agricultural countries fluctuate more widely than the incomes of industrial countries. A colony may be better at agriculture than at industry, but if it specialises exclusively in agriculture, it will find its economy subject to much wider fluctuations than would be the case if it secured a better balance between the two. [35]

Lewis was careful to draw a distinction between development from a more advanced state and development *ab initio*. At the pre-industrial state the argument was that there was very limited scope for industrialization. At other stages the argument related to the economics of further industrialization through specialization. It was argued that markets had to be large enough and facilities such as energy, transportation, banking, research and training must be economically viable, and operating in a complementary manner. Lewis argued that because a colony could not industrialize economically on a small scale, particularly from the pre-industrial state, it did not follow that 'if properly developed, it would not indeed be most successful on a large scale. The moral of this is that it would be foolish to rely exclusively on haphazard rise of factories.'[36]

The essence of the Lewis (1944) argument for industrialization was that it was wrong to subject development *ab initio* to false comparison with the advanced countries where development had evolved over several centuries of experience in commerce and entrepreneurship. Rather, it was necessary for the government to promote industrialization through more judicious planning to avoid haphazard import substitution. Lewis's ideas for development *ab initio* were therefore not of the indiscriminate variety with which his name erroneously later became associated.

In proposing that the economics of industrialization depended on large-scale organization, Lewis's ideas were based on the condition that the appropriate scale could be reached quickly: thus the 'agricultural and industrial revolutions'. Lewis thought that planned and balanced industrial centres, possibly involving regional integration, could be a useful approach. He later acknowledged (Lewis, 1984: 127) the debt he owed to the ideas of Rosenstein-Rodan (1943). Industrialization on this scale, however, involved responsibility for centralized economic management which the Colonial Office was unwilling to accept.

The second condition was that agricultural modernization and industrialization must go hand in hand: 'the agricultural revolution releases labour from the land ... the industrial revolution in turn provides the farmer with a remunerative market, and if on sufficiently large scale, with cheap commodities' (Lewis, 1944: para.18). However, throughout the 1944 memorandum, Lewis maintained, in his principal thesis, that progress in agriculture would be compromised if the attempt at industrial development was made ahead of agriculture. An important condition for development *ab initio* was, in his view, that agricultural development must grow at least at the same pace as industrialization.

Like other economists of the period, Lewis recognized the capital constraint. Thus a third condition in this early development model was that the British Government should undertake to mobilize development finance, if necessary through the promotion of an international development bank, for accelerated agricultural and industrial development. Official preference at the time was for capital to the colonies to be attracted from the private market on the merits of the projects concerned (Lewis, 1944b).[37] The government therefore turned down any idea of large international loans for colonial development.[38]

The Lewis pre-independence development model would therefore suggest a three-way balance between urbanization, agricultural productivity and manufacturing, each stimulating the other to induce long-term balanced economic growth. In this model the external sector acts as the safety valve, while the domestic balance is determined by the propensity towards urbanization, and the respective elasticities of manufactured goods and agricultural products. The system succeeds if agricultural productivity keeps ahead of manufacturing and urbanization at least until the stage where manufactured production for both domestic and international markets replaces agriculture as the principal source of savings and employment. Failure will result if an attempt is made to raise manufacturing and social infrastructural activities prematurely while agricultural productivity is in an underdeveloped and stagnant state. There will also be the danger of economic decline if the higher demand of the urban and manufacturing sectors drains domestic and external savings and steadily reduces the share of resources going to the agricultural sector. When production in the agricultural sector declines the economy moves on to a downward path which becomes exceedingly difficult to reverse.

These ideas were too revolutionary to make any headway in official thinking, and faded with Lewis's resignation from the Economic Advisory Committee and Caine's posting to the Far East. We are therefore left with a passive and indifferent approach to economic development as the heritage of the colonial system, outside the tradeable sectors. This had two principal effects on economic development in the immediate post-independence period. First, there was little in the way of a 'culture' of economic development; there was little experience and much to learn about appropriate development ideas after independence.

Secondly, the economy of Ghana remained rather fragile despite the accumulation of large foreign exchange reserves from a booming export sector and a policy of maintaining a balanced budget. The colonial government had abstained almost entirely from development spending. Foreign reserves and other aspects which apparently manifested the robustness of the economy, such as the country's human and natural resources, concealed the fragilities, particularly a weak food-production base, which were to be aggravated later by urbanization and accelerated development (see Chapter 5).

Could the ideas Lewis put forward in 1944 have enabled the pre-decolonization colonial government to establish the basis for economic development and thus give the successor indigenous state a culture of development management, and perhaps a more viable economic future? Can it be said that this was possible for the francophone West African countries because the French retained economic control after independence? The countries belonging to the franc monetary zone exercised caution in the use of external reserves for the development of the social infrastructure as compared with the needs of agricultural and industrial development. Policies aimed to maintain maximum incentives in the primary sectors and to curtail inflationary tendencies through gradualist macroeconomic management. Economic management aimed at a slower pace of development more suited to the fragile base of the economy. It will be argued in the present study, however, that in the euphoria of independence, it is doubtful whether any indigenous government in Ghana would have maintained such moderation (see Chapter 6).

Development thinking and management of the colonial government of the Gold Coast in the post-Guggisberg period was more or less a reflection of Colonial Office policies. It is best to examine these by looking briefly at why the Guggisberg development strategy did not lead to economic growth as predicted.[39]

Shortly after Guggisberg left Ghana in 1927, a new set of circumstantial factors affected development thinking, for better or for worse. First, export prices of cocoa were badly hit by the worldwide depression. The total value of exports fell from £11.7m in 1927 to £4m in 1934 despite an increase in annual production from 210 to 230 thousand metric tons. Secondly, rail transport, which had played a major role in the removal of the transport bottleneck, fell victim to competition from road transport. Small indigenous road transport operators with few overheads reduced the cost of transportation, making rail haulage and passenger transportation uncompetitive. This would have been advantageous for cocoa and for development if public policy had not restricted the use of the cheaper road network (Bates, 1983: 67; Church, 1936: 137). Thirdly, throughout the decade of the 1930s, the depressed cocoa prices led to acrimonious exchanges between the government and farmers, the latter supported by African politicians.[40] Because of these events, the government decided, in the period 1929–40, to curtail economic expansion and to call for a 'consolidation and stabilization of government services for the time being'.[41]

An enquiry into the ensuing cocoa farmers' boycott on crop sales in 1937, however, reported more substantive problems with agricultural (cocoa) development which indicated some neglect in the years after Guggisberg. On the favourable side, the enquiry found that the modernization of cocoa production had already begun and that the concept of the peasant contractor was 'no longer true of more than a minority of farmers'.[42] There were multiple absentee owners and modernized land ownership, and there had emerged a 'native small capitalist [who] became possessed, either directly by the purchase of land or indirectly through the widespread notion of pledging farms for monetary loans, of numerous farms, often widely scattered'.[43] On the negative side, the basic requirements of commercial production had not developed. Appropriate farming methods covering such practices as drainage, pruning, manuring and pest control were not known. Also, an appropriate financial organization for production was virtually non-existent with the result that rural indebtedness had become commonplace.[44] Notwithstanding, therefore, that after four decades of production Ghana had emerged as the world's largest producer of cocoa, and that the crop earned a large percentage of the country's foreign exchange, the organization of its production was still rudimentary.

In a model of export-led development, higher real income should have facilitated the introduction of new technology to improve productivity. The internationalization of production should also have attracted external ideas of modernization. This was not the case with cocoa, which remained wholly indigenous in production. The mining sectors, which were entirely foreign-owned, did not respond either. In terms of classical economic theory, neither land nor labour could be said to be a constraint. Capital appeared not to be a principal constraint either, given the way the industries of cocoa and mining grew rapidly without evidence of heavy internal or external borrowing. But stagnant agricultural productivity and poor organization of production in other directions had the capacity to hinder development.

Economic Development and the Second World War

The demands of the Second World War brought efforts to increase productivity, and to integrate economic management regionally. The war affected colonial management in the Gold Coast, and in West Africa, in two principal ways. First, Accra and Takoradi, two principal cities, were made staging posts for American and British troops on their way to the Far Eastern front from 1941 to 1946. This led to increased shipping traffic, demanding more ships' stores and food for the troops. An objective of new policy therefore was to promote food production, especially meat and vegetables of varieties hitherto not produced by the indigenous population.

The loss of the Far Eastern colonies to Japan, and consequently the shortage of such primary commodities as rubber, palm oil and copra, created the second set of circumstances to change attitudes towards the development of production in West Africa. Earlier, when wartime economic policy was debated in the House of Commons in 1940, the principal problem of the colonial economies was seen as the disposal of surplus production resulting from the loss of European markets due to German occupation. By 1942 the problem was reversed, and in the Gold Coast there was new demand for forgotten primary products such as rubber, palm oil and kernel oil.[45] The changing demands of war led to the creation of the West African War Council (WAWC) in 1943, headed by Viscount Swinton (formerly Secretary of State for the Colonies and Minister for the Air Force) as Resident Minister in Accra. The Council had Military and Civil Divisions; our interest here is in the work of the Civil Division in coordinating the new production drive.

The Council's mandate was to integrate the four West African colonies (Gambia, Gold Coast, Nigeria and Sierra Leone) commercially, to ensure optimum local production for export, and to feed the foreign and local troops. Lord Swinton acted in the dual capacity of a *de facto* Federal Governor-General for West Africa and a British Cabinet Minister. These wartime initiatives involved better organization which contributed, in some measure, to economic development. The objectives of the Council were to establish production targets in the various commodities and to ensure that they were attained; to increase food production both for the indigenous population directly involved in the war effort and for British and American troops; to provide on-the-spot advice and decision-making to the colonial governors in the general management of the colonies; and to supervise and coordinate general economic development, including the establishment of secondary industries.[46]

To achieve these objectives the Council adopted a number of management strategies. It did not attempt any radical changes in the methods of production; rather, it provided monetary incentives, guaranteed purchases and transportation in order to maximize production with the existing technology. For the first time a price support system was provided for genuine production surpluses of selected crops, whose supply was estimated, in the long term, to fall short of demand. These included millet, guinea corn, rice, groundnuts, dried shallots, dried beans and peas; major staples like yam, plantain and maize were excluded. This strategy enabled the Council to create a two-month strategic stock of listed food items 'to meet sudden demands from existing stock and to avoid the necessity of being forced to buy suddenly at panic prices'.[47] Production was by joint military, government and private efforts. The military and the government's Agricultural Department ran vegetable and livestock farms, and the private farmers were organized in individual and cooperative farms for European-type vegetables and staple crops.

Producer response to the price and other incentives was marked, and the stock planning worked so well that it never became necessary to resort to the price protection scheme. In the period 1942–6, while the programme lasted, the Department of Agriculture reported the following increases in output: 4.5 million tons of vegetables, 7,156 head of pigs, 4,465 tons of cereal, and 103 tons of meat sold to ships and aircraft. The Director of Agriculture also reported that the additional production was achieved without the customary labour migration from the neighbouring French territories. He commented that it was 'surprising and encouraging to note how well the reduced farming population has met greatly increased demands, and marketed in the face of considerable difficulty.'[48] These results demonstrate how better organization and management, together with the appropriate incentives, could increase productivity, even without improvements initially in technology.

The closer involvement of Lord Swinton in the economic management of the Gold Coast and the positive results of his work also excited interest in development efforts which had been placed on the back burner since the departure of Guggisberg. In a memorandum entitled 'Economic Policy in West African Colonies' which he placed before the War Cabinet in London in February 1943, Swinton raised twenty-one neglected development issues,[49] covering the interests of the primary producers, emerging tension among Africans, Europeans and Lebanese (Syrians), ideas on how to promote and regulate local industries, finance, housing, education, communications, land tenure and modern plantation agriculture, all of which were highly important. They were not, however, pursued seriously by the Colonial Office or the colonial governments in West Africa, except where they promoted the specific war effort which was the mandate of the War Council.

The work of the Council is a wholly unresearched area and will remain so until a large number of closed files are made available. The following paragraphs summarize the conclusions to be drawn from the limited evidence available on the relevance of the War Council's efforts to the evolution of development thinking in the colonial period.

The coordinated and on-the-spot management by the WAWC provided the kind of concerned administration required for economic development. No such leadership could be provided by a colonial government directed generally from London by personnel largely ignorant of, or out of touch with, local conditions. This vindicated Caine's hypothesis that less passivity and more activity were needed to promote economic development from the colonial underdeveloped state.

The Council's rapid successes in increasing food production by price incentives and better organization was enough to demolish the entrenched misconception that Africans lacked a desire to increase their material wealth. It became clear that the capacity existed to increase productivity by current methods of production, even if it was limited.

The Council's experience also demonstrated a method of coping with the unstoppable process of urbanization. In Caine's words 'many social evils of urbanization are developing in Africa because of an unwillingness to admit that the urbanized, detribalized native has come to stay and must be properly provided for.'[50]

The activities of the WAWC were part of a programme of war emergency. In 1945 the Council was dissolved and was not replaced by any organ of government, either in the individual West African colonies or by one common to the four countries, which could pursue the objectives of increased agricultural productivity.[51] The Americans were the first to pull out at the end of the war in Europe. This led to the rapid decline and ultimate closure of the largest vegetable farm near Accra (Medea). A cocoa butter export scheme was wound up at approximately the same time. By 1946 most of the vegetable gardens had been closed down. Finally, with the recapture of the Far Eastern colonies late in 1945, the drive for the production of rubber, copra, palm oil and palm-kernel also came to an end, and the Gold Coast reverted to the pre-war levels of export and domestic food production. These events show, however, that ideas of development were not absent from the colonial mind during the Second World War; on the contrary, development ideas seem to have been given more prominence at this time than ever before, making the era something of a watershed in official thinking.

African Opinions

The opinions of African leaders also shed valuable light on development thinking at the time, particularly on the above observations concerning colonial development. The evidence points to African leaders as consisting of a few traditional leaders (chiefs) and legal and medical practitioners who had been nominated to the Legislative Council by the government. The views expressed are derived from their contributions to Legislative Council debates, and from memoranda dispatched by the chiefs to the colonial government or to the British government in London. Of greatest influence in formulating African ideas were Nana Ofori-Atta I, the Paramount Chief of Akyem Abuakwa, a leading traditional leader; Dr J.B. Danquah,[52] a lawyer and the leading nationalist politician at the time; and Dr Nanka-Bruce, a medical practitioner.

The ideas considered here, deriving from the study of African philosophy, politics and development thinking at the time,[53] include greater stress on the importance of economic development from the grass roots, and a perceived capital constraint on development. Also included is the relevance of the participatory role of the state in promoting indigenous development by protecting initiatives from the predatory tendencies of foreign enterprises.

Traditional philosophy at the time required African leadership 'to conceive and carry out development schemes for improving general social conditions and industry in the state'.[54] African leaders naturally viewed this responsibility in a much wider sense than the concentration on production for empire trade in primary commodities. They listed a number of areas where greater emphasis should be placed. These included agricultural education for the youth and for farmers, a more responsible attitude on the part of the government in the persistent dispute between the cocoa farmers and the produce buyers,[55] the development of indigenous expertise and the greater involvement of such expertise in agricultural extension.

In the 1934 Memorandum to the British government the African leaders indicated that the provision of agricultural training should go in tandem with the technical training in artisan trades that had been instituted in technical trade schools. They predicted the lagging behind of agricultural modernization and the dangers of urban unemployment:[56]

The prosperity of the Gold Coast, to a large extent, depends upon agriculture, yet in some general way, instruction in agriculture is not given a place in the school timetables. The result cannot but be that the pupils leave school with no bent for agriculture or farming, a situation which helps to increase unhappiness because of want of employment.

Also recognized was the need for modernization of farming methods through better communication in local languages. The African members of the Legislative Council stated in 1939 their unanimous desire:

> to stress the importance of sending agricultural officers into the country and ensuring that they give instructions to the farmers and make closer contact with them. [57]

These development ideas correspond with some of the later ideas of Arthur Lewis on the modernization of peasant agriculture, and on the proper balance between agricultural productivity and economic modernization in a modern economy.

Like the classical development theorists, the African leaders of the inter-war period recognized the importance of capital accumulation to development. The most important ideas related to the use of taxation in the mobilization of resources for development, and the role of traditional and rural administrators in the use of such resources. In the inter-war period taxes were levied principally on international trade. Following the Guggisberg principle, additional taxation was justified for the development of infrastructure related to the production of tradables.

African opinion in the inter-war years was that the use of tax revenues by the central government for grass-roots development was also justified. African development opinion, however, did not advocate direct government involvement in the financing of rural development. It expected the government to allocate funds for this purpose to the traditional authorities. Nor did African opinion agree with the colonial government that the local authorities should not only mobilize development funds from local taxation but also 'contribute a portion of tax towards the heavy cost of central administration in the colony'.[58] African opinion was that, from a long-term development perspective, it was wrong for the government to concentrate wealth in the urban areas where it operated, exclusively fostering foreign trade in which the imperial power had an interest. In this sense African opinion in this period regarded the Guggisberg strategy as a necessary but not a sufficient strategy for long-run development.

However, by the latter half of the inter-war period, the role of the traditional authorities was rapidly declining, and they therefore could not be the focus of development strategies. This situation was not well recognized at the time, either by the traditional leaders themselves or by the African political leaders in the Legislative Council. The real problem, it would appear, was that the institutional mechanisms did not exist for the administration of development from the grass roots. In this sense, lack of capital, though recognized as a problem, was only one, and probably not the major, factor in a general management problem.

African opinion on the role of capital centred on the issue of the distribution of available capital between urban (colonial) and rural (traditional) employment, and between current and capital expenditure. African opinion was that 'a small axe put on public sector emoluments: just 10%, will satisfy everybody ... what the government has failed to see is, there is a point beyond which expenditure cannot go.'[59] The biggest industry involving indigenous initiatives was cocoa, and the evidence that had shaped African opinion was that this industry had developed though appropriate producer incentives in prices, marketing and transportation. Capital had played an important role but capital accumulation had been the result of the involvement of private profits from farmers and farmers' labour rather than financing from public sources or from other sectors. The emphasis in African thinking was on a reduction in public sector spending by government, resource transfers to traditional (rural) areas, and the removal of rural taxes.[60] The retention of farmers' profits was required to support development at the rural level.

African ideas on development were greatly influenced by what the African leaders regarded as indifferent and irresponsible attitudes towards indigenous producers. In their analysis of what a government should do to maximize producer confidence, the leaders ranked producer price and output stabilization very highly. They criticized the government's continued passive policy towards farmers, which they argued could 'no longer find support in the realm of efficient administration of the affairs by the government'.[61] The general desire of Africans for a development strategy that had an active promotional content and witnessed to the interest of the government was later confirmed in the Report of the Watson Commission that, in the field of economic development, 'the government had not formulated any plans for the future of industry and agriculture, and that indeed it was lukewarm about any development apart from production for export.'[62]

A summary of the issues on which African leaders focused in the inter-war period, therefore, would include the following. First, the recognition that, though primary exports were important in economic growth, a development approach focusing on broader modernization, from the grassroots, was more relevant. Second, the knowledge that, though capital was important in economic development, its role should not be overrated; of greater relevance to development were producer incentives to maximize productivity and retain profits for further investments. Third, African opinion stressed the importance of the promotional role of government: the interest which the government needed to show in the problems of the producer, at the farmgate level, and the efforts it should make to promote the interests of the producer at the industry and national level.

Development Ideas on the Eve of Decolonization

The ideas of African leaders in the Gold Coast summarized above were based on the practical knowledge, experience and wisdom of the period. Alongside these was a valuable input of ideas by academic economists who did not have the local experience, but who possessed experience from other regions of the world as well as the theoretical and analytical tools to distinguish the more important development issues relevant to the Gold Coast from the less relevant. The ideas analysed below relate to the period of decolonization from the mid-1940s to the latter part of the 1950s, and are attributable to Arthur Lewis, Dudley Seers and C.R. Ross.

As explained in the Introduction, Seers and Ross visited the Gold Coast early in 1951 at the request of the Colonial Office to enquire into the costs and organization of building resources in relation to the economy of the colony. Their Report, published in July 1952, proved controversial, but was also a landmark in development thinking in the country, and in the Colonial Office. It brought forward three important ideas. It was the first to use the concept of fragility as a limitation on the country's ability to cope with any major attempt at accelerated economic development. Seers and Ross observed that the economy was inflation-prone because 'it over-responds to any acceleration and could get out of control'.[63] They therefore suggested that strategies with inflationary tendencies had to be avoided if stable growth was to be achieved in the process of modernization.

Informed by the inflationary effects of the cocoa boom of 1948–9, they developed the theory that cocoa producer price increases should be limited to the rate of price increases for imported consumer goods. This was a valid anti-inflationary argument but its usefulness for economic development must be viewed in the context of retaining maximum producer incentives in relation to general price levels and producer prices of competing agricultural products. On the other hand, structural 'fragility' was an important concept for development, even though it was defined by Seers and Ross only in the limited inflationary sense, as we shall see later. In a wider sense encompassing the structural limitation of productive responses and organization, it was a major constraint on development *ab initio*.

The second major contribution made by Seers and Ross was the observation that the rate at which the non-agricultural sector could grow was limited by the rate at which productivity in the agricultural sector increased. Their principal argument was that if labour were to be released into the construction industry in the process of industrialization, then agricultural output needed to grow faster than the rate at which people were leaving the land if inflation, or loss of foreign exchange on the importation of food, was to be avoided. They observed that real increases in agricultural productivity were, in the short term, constrained by primitive methods of cultivation, while in the long term there were serious inadequacies in research, soil surveys and the scope of agricultural mechanization. These opinions corresponded well with the views of African leaders who had suggested more agricultural education and extension work among farmers. The third idea of Seers and Ross in the context of development was that industrial expansion was constrained by shortage of skills and a lack of savings.

These ideas met with a mixed reception. Some members of the Colonial Office criticized the Report for providing only a 'superficial and ... mistaken analysis of the Gold Coast development problem'.[64] Some thought that the analysis was static whereas 'any realistic appraisal of an expanding economy should be ... dynamic'.[65] The concept of development was not thought to have been well defined. The Report was criticized as being rather theoretical, focusing on Keynesian demand and cost push ideas, and employing a national accounting technique, derived from Keynesian economics, that was not altogether relevant. Others in the Colonial Office felt that the Report had ignored the subsistence sector and argued that 'the extent to which the subsistence sector is brought into association with the cash side of the economy depended upon the increase in incomes to be gained from such a course'.[66]

Others, however, found the analysis on inflation useful and thought that 'it led to a simple but fundamental question concerning future policy. *How can the cocoa buying price and development expenditure be influenced so that, taken together, they make sense?*'[67] [emphasis added]. In the context of future development, this was an important point raised on the Report by the Colonial Office, which was not pursued.

The reaction to the Report by the incoming African politicians, led by Nkrumah, was both lukewarm and instructive. Lukewarm, because the Report contradicted the aggressive industrialization policy submitted in the 1951 Manifesto of the Convention Peoples Party.[68] Instructive, because it suggested ideas for the financing of the ambitious development programme of the immediate post-independence period. One idea that particularly sowed seeds in the minds of the incoming African government was the capping of cocoa producer prices, as a fiscal strategy for public sector spending. Another was the use of the Cocoa Marketing Board surpluses for financing development, given the presumed shortage of domestic savings.[69] What the Nkrumah government actually did, however, was very much at odds with the spirit of the Seers and Ross Report (see Chapter 5).

To summarise, the most significant contribution of Seers and Ross to development thinking in Ghana was their introduction of the concept of 'fragility' and the severe constraint it places on development from the underdeveloped state. With hindsight, the probability of over-response to fiscal pressures was a good prediction, given the periods when the economy was to suffer massive bouts of inflation. The erosion of producer incentives in the cocoa sector, in the course of the attempted modernization, and against the background of primitive peasant agriculture, is another result which could be said to vindicate the predictions of Seers and Ross.

Arthur Lewis was invited to the Gold Coast in 1953, the year following the Seers and Ross Report, and after Nkrumah had settled in his new position as Prime Minister. His brief was to design a programme of accelerated industrialization in response to the Party's programme. His 'Report on Industrialization and the Gold Coast' was influential in the evolution of development ideas in Ghana for a number of reasons. First, even though his major publications had not yet begun, he was already an eminent theoretician in the field of development. Second, the Gold Coast was then a small country (population 5 million) which had such material wealth, natural resources and dynamic leadership as to offer the best ground for testing Lewis's 1944 theory and subsequent ideas on accelerated balanced agriculture and industrialization as a theory of development. Third, Lewis's work was to be undertaken against the background of the contradiction between the caution of Seers and Ross and the ambitions of the political leadership in the country. Fourth, Ghana was the underdeveloped country which absorbed most of Lewis's attention during the 1950s, in work that was to include the preparation of a Development Plan.

Lewis's Report, for our purposes, may be summarized under three headings, in relation to the principal conclusions which were set out in order of priority. Lewis stated the number one priority for Ghana's industrial growth as 'a concentrated attack on the system of growing food, so as to set in motion an ever increasing productivity' (Lewis, 1953: para. 253). In his view this was the way to provide the market, the capital and the labour for industrialization. The second priority was to strengthen the public services by the creation of a machinery of government services to facilitate the process of industrial development. These included industrial research, advice to foreign investors and local industrialists, the provision of financial assistance, the administration of industrial estates, and direct state initiatives in the ownership of factories. As a third priority, Lewis recommended a small programme of industrialization, in a small range of commodities, for the domestic market and not for export. As far as a major programme of industrialization was concerned, he stated (para. 255):

> very many years will elapse before it becomes economical for the government to transfer any large part of its resources towards industrialization, and away from the more urgent priorities of agricultural productivity and the public services.

Unlike the Seers and Ross Report the ideas in the Lewis Report were favourably received in the Colonial Office. This was largely due to its moderation and the abandonment of earlier ideas of agricultural and industrial revolution. The Report was thought to be educative for the public and a vindication of the colonial government's slow approach to industrialization. It was strongly supported by the Governor[70] and the colonial civil servants in the Gold Coast.[71]

If the colonial authorities so embraced the *new* ideas of Arthur Lewis, then had his ideas on development changed that radically since 1944? And what were his contributions to Ghana's ideas on economic development? Basically, Lewis's theory of balanced agricultural and industrial growth had not changed. But by insisting more rigidly on an order of priorities, with agriculture leading industrialization, Lewis was able to draw attention to the fact that the state of agricultural development in the Gold Coast, on the eve of decolonization, matched none of the ambitions of the incoming government for accelerated industrialization. Secondly, he drew attention to the formidable impediments in the way of agricultural modernization and also in the management of viable industrialization. Third, he recognized what Seers and Ross had stressed – the inflationary propensities of the fragile economy. None of these were compatible with any ideas of a revolutionary approach to development or with any goals that could be achieved quickly.

Thus Lewis's contributions to economic development thinking in the period just before independence were: 1) that the programme of initial post-independence development could not be hastened beyond the pace at which agriculture for food production could be modernized in the context of the maximum incentives and facilities for productivity increases; 2) that the proper machinery for the organization and management of development had to be put in place; and 3) that the maximum programme of manufacturing for the domestic market had to be carefully planned and implemented in a manner that matched the programme of agricultural modernization.

However, there were important omissions in Lewis's analysis of Ghana's development problems. His conception of *ab initio* economic development did not distinguish between the constraints imposed by the fragmentation of peasant production and those resulting from a lack of modernization. Writers who are not familiar with peasant production and marketing have difficulty in assessing the degree of fragmentation that exists in the supply of produce between the farmgate and the market, or in recognizing that farmgate prices are often lower than the equilibrium. This problem relates to transport costs and market access. Its implications for the first-stage improvement in peasant output and for long-term agricultural modernization are important, and are best illustrated by empirical analysis and then by the heuristic presentation in Figure 2.1.

Table 2.2 Roads Maintained by the State 1959–68

Year	Total mileage	Gravel surfaced (miles)	Bitumen surfaced (miles)	Funds provided for normal maintenance (000 cedis)
1959	4,923	2,473	1,820	1,850.2
1960	4,420	2,509	1,912	1,839.9
1961	4,792	2,778	2,014	1,964.0
1962	5,396	3,345	2,051	2,240.0
1963	5,514	3,388	2,131	2,276.9
1964	5,565	3,383	2,182	2,244.0
1965	5,575	3,380	2,195	2,264.0
1966	5,575	3,380	2,195	2,264.0
1967	6,238	3,794	2,444	6,660.8
1968[a]	5,925	3,590	2,335	7,000.0

a = Reductions in 1968 were due to inundations of roads due to the formation of the Volta Lake
Source: Economic Survey CBS, Accra, 1968

Three levels of transport network have to be considered in the discussion of feeder roads. The first is the road network from the urban market to the rural market town. This would usually be a first-class road, generally bitumen-surfaced and maintained by the state. In 1959 there were approximately 1,820 miles of such roads in Ghana, comprising approximately 42% of the total available road mileage in the country.

At the second level are secondary roads, which are generally gravel surfaced and connect the rural market town with the smaller village market. There were estimated to be 2,473 miles of such roads in 1959, again maintained by the state. Table 2.2 shows that the mileage of bitumen-surfaced and gravel roads had virtually ceased to increase in the latter years of the Nkrumah era. At the third level are numerous, not so well charted footpaths and bush roads. These are communally constructed and maintained access roads linking peasant farmers to villages. The bulk of the peasant food producers use the third category of roads and face a multitude of transportation problems. The farmer usually carries his produce in head-loads to the nearest village. The supply of produce to the market is therefore determined not only by what the farmer can produce, but also by what he can carry. 'The traders find it convenient to buy at places where they can arrange transportation to go and collect what they have purchased' (Nyanteng and Apeldoorn, 1973: 270). A farmer therefore must ensure that his produce reaches a transport-favoured village if he wishes to sell at a satisfactory price. In most cases where produce has to be left at an unfavoured village the farmer is forced to accept an arbitrary lower price from the trader in view of the higher transportation cost the latter has to bear. In the many cases where a farmer can only head-load his produce to the nearest roadside, he faces the problem of unreliable transportation. As a result 'some farmers rarely make the effort to take their produce anywhere to sell, except on market days when they hope that transport would be available where they head-load their produce' (*ibid.*).

Table 2.3 Transportation Charges on Urban and Rural Roads in Asante 1972: Pesewas Per 100 Kilo Bag of Produce

	Miles	Charge	Pws/mile
1. Urban to town roads Class I			
1.1 Mampong–Ejura	25	30	1.20
1.2 Amantin–Ejura	16	20	1.25
1.3 Akokoa–Amantin	5	10	2.00
2. Town to village roads Class II			
2.1 Ebuom–Ejura	10	20	2.00
2.2 Kokofu–Attebubu	8	25	3.13
2.3 Babaso–Ejura(tractor route)	2	20	10.00
3. Village to village roads Class III			
Nokwaresa–Ejura (tractor)	5	40	8.00
Sataso–Ejura	10	50	5.00
Daudakrom–Ejura	20	100	5.00

Source: Nyanteng and Apeldoorn (1973), p. 276

A further transportation problem, illustrated in Table 2.3, was also identified by Nyanteng and Apeldoorn (1973). Their survey of the Mampong Asante farming district emphasizes the distortions in transportation costs between the better roads and the poor rural roads. It would sometimes cost six times as much for the farmer to take his produce to the village market as it would for the trader to convey it from the village to the urban centre. This cost is in addition to the even more difficult method of taking the produce to the roadside. Another factor is the shortage of goods vehicles. In an analysis of this problem in the period 1956–67, Ewusi (1973) found that the average age of goods vehicles had increased by 46.7% and that the ratio of such vehicles to the population had declined by 32.7%. The available vehicles were getting too old and too few for the increasing food transportation needs of the larger population concentrated in the urban areas. For the rural peasant, there were fewer available vehicles, higher costs and lower output earmarked for the village, town or city market. The feeder road problem and the associated problem of transportation were therefore quite formidable in the 1950s.

The theoretical explanation of the fragmentation phenomenon is as follows. In Fig. 2.1, Dr and Sr represent the normal demand and supply curves at the farmgate under the conditions in which the farmer is able to produce at his present peasant capacity, and to supply all his output to the village market or at his farmgate. The diagram describes the different equilibrium conditions: Ea for the sub-optimal condition, Eo for the optimum

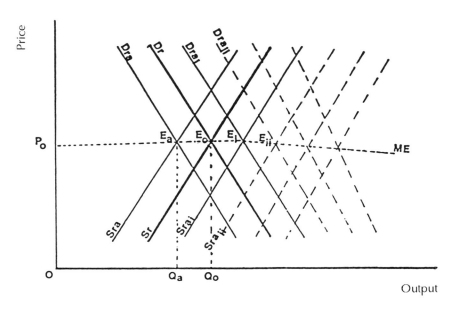

Fig. 2.1 Fragmentation of Peasant Production in the Pre-Modern State and Subsequent Modernization

peasant equilibrium and E1, E2 ... for expansion in the modern state. The equilibrium situation, Eo, is possible if farmers are able to respond fully to the real price structure for their output at the farmgate. However, the farmgate is not as accessible as it could be, because of the many structural problems that face both farmer and trader in peasant agriculture, such as transportation and storage. These structural problems are represented by a downward shift in the supply curve to Sra. A similar downward structural shift in demand occurs. This is typically induced by urban demand moving away from local staples if the supply becomes unreliable, or if they become more expensive than imported substitutes due to overvalued exchange rates. The trend towards the consumption of subsidized wheat-bread made from imported wheat is a standard example. Bread, in most cases, becomes cheaper than the equivalent local staple and volumes of imported wheat rise (Akoto, 1985: 50). This is also the case with imported rice. Dra and Sra therefore represent the sub-optimal demand and supply curves and Ea the sub-optimal equilibrium. If it is assumed that the elasticities of Dr and Dra and of Sr and Sra are unchanged and equal, the farmer will receive the same price at Ea as at Eo but his output would have dropped to Qa, the sub-optimal output level. The effect of this is to reduce output without increasing the farmer's price. The farmer's total income is therefore reduced.

We can now introduce the curves Drai ... to illustrate the upward shift in demand resulting from such situations as increased urbanization, and the supply curves Srai ... representing increased supply resulting from increased productivity due to modernization, after fragmentation and price distortions have been removed. These are denoted by the broken upward shifting demand and supply curves which plot output and farmer's price in the long-run modernized state of technical advancement and changing demand and supply structures.

It will be noted that the curve ME traces the probable long-run price trend during the process of technical advancement. An upward price trend, the more preferred (Lewis 1955) but less likely in the initial stages of growth, will be indicated by rising price elasticity of demand.[72]

This heuristic presentation helps us to identify two distinct processes in the development of agriculture from the peasant state. The first is the elimination of the sub-optimal equilibrium, Ea, by the provision of facilities, chiefly transportation, storage and marketing, so that output can be increased from Qa to Qo. This process concerns the raising of peasant supply to the pre-modernization maximum capacity.

The second is that of modernization in response to technical advancement. The peasant agricultural system cannot be modernized until it has been set on a path towards its maximum capacity. The acceptance of better methods of farming, including high-yielding seeds, fertilizers, etc., is dependent upon the removal of bottlenecks in storage, transportation and marketing. It is unrealistic to expect farmers to accept modern methods of producing goods they cannot store or transport to the market because of the existing fragmentation. It is after the arbitrary pricing and fragmentation have been removed and the small farmer is producing at close to his maximum capacity that the idea of using modern methods can be sold to him. Lewis's ideas relate mostly to technical progress on curve ME, and not in the period of arbitrary pricing and sub-optimal peasant production.

Writing in early 1953, Lewis significantly did not emphasize the role of the cocoa industry in Ghana's future development. He did recognize the heavy taxation of cocoa farmers, but observed that 'even with taxation, earnings in the cocoa industry still exceeded earnings in other industries' (Lewis, 1953: para. 227). He made this point to strengthen his argument that new industries other than cocoa should not be established unless they could, at least, pay their way without subsidy. The problem that he recognized with the cocoa industry was that it set an unsustainable wage level for rural agriculture. Moreover, the government resorted to heavy taxation rather than exchange-rate devaluation because there was no pressure on the external reserves. Using the familiar factoral terms of trade argument, Lewis would have preferred the enhancement of productivity, and therefore higher per capita rewards in other forms of agriculture to match those in the cocoa industry, in the process of initial economic development.[73] In this way, he would argue, the rise in cocoa farmers' incomes would be the result of a shift of labour and material resources to the non-cocoa agricultural sector. This, according to him, was a better way of protecting cocoa farmers' (international) terms of trade in a long-run equilibrium.[74]

Conclusions

The conclusions that follow are structured to address the issues on which the discussion in this chapter has been based. The intention is to identify the principles, deriving from Ghana's experience and development theory, that should have been of significant influence in initial modernization.

The characteristics of the Ghana economy on the eve of independence may be summarized as follows: first, a high degree of fragmentation in peasant production and marketing, which imposed a limitation on the value of new technology. Second, a weak productive base in food agriculture. In the period of rapid cocoa development, increased food production was observed but it was not permanent; it was linked with cocoa planting to provide shade for the young trees.[75] Otherwise food production, organized on a primitive peasant system, had remained unchanged for centuries. Cardinall observed this weak productive base; so did Seers and Ross, and Arthur Lewis. African political leaders in the inter-war period were also very concerned about this primary weakness of the economy. It was Lewis who was able to place the problem appropriately in a development model; the Lewis approach would indicate that this weakness was a serious brake on economic development.

The third significant characteristic of the Ghana economy on the eve of independence was its fragility. Seers and Ross described this problem as an important constraint on accelerated development: the pace of economic development could not exceed that at which the monetary system was modernized. Effective monetary instruments, such as interest rates and credit policies, were underdeveloped. Another implication was that accelerated economic development was possible only in so far as supply-side constraints, i.e. those on productive capacity, were overcome. Seers and Ross therefore drew attention to the constraints on economic growth without inflation. Factors on the demand side would include the control of deficits on savings, budgets and trade. The promotion of the supply side would include improvements in skilled labour, social and economic overhead capital, technology and productivity, energy resources and stability of the exchange system. In managing development, the problem was how to solve the supply-side constraints without inflation and without eroding the major sources of capital. In the case of Ghana, the kind of development management called for was that which squeezed some savings from the established cocoa and minerals sectors to develop productive capacity in other sectors without destroying the productive capacity of the primary sectors themselves.

The fourth characteristic of the Ghana economy was the excessive dependence on a single agricultural product and a few minerals. At the initial stages of development the solutions to be aimed at were export deconcentration and diversification. Deconcentration implied the shift of emphasis to other established products such as palm oil and rubber, which the War Council had demonstrated was possible given the adequate incentives. Diversification meant the introduction of new products. In the agricultural field, the attempt made by Guggisberg in the 1920s was not successful. [76]

The fifth characteristic was the weakness of public sector services to support economic modernization. This was manifest not only in low productivity in the public services but also in inappropriate orientation from the development management point of view. On the eve of decolonization, the large majority of public servants were in the administrative class. There was a limited number in the technical classes. For the government to play the role of a promoter of development, particularly industrialization, specially trained officers were needed to initiate research into new areas of development, to attract and advise industrialists, and to recommend to government various forms of assistance for investors (Lewis, 1953: 21). Higher budgetary costs were implied and therefore higher taxation in the period before productive responses were achieved. Usually public-sector expansion creates a momentum of its own, and the problem would then become one of excess taxation of the established sectors. Again the problem was how additional resources could be squeezed out of cocoa and the minerals sectors to administer modernization without destroying those sectors. This danger was even more pronounced as new ambitious actors prepared to enter the political scene.

Notes

1. See also a number of reports and addresses delivered to the Legislative Council in his capacity as Governor of the Gold Coast, 1919–27.
2. Nkrumah's contributions to development thought are contained in several books written between 1957 and 1973; see Bibliography.
3. Guggisberg wrote six volumes on the Gold Coast economy in the period he was Governor, all styled as 'The Governor's Annual Address to the Legislative Council' The most memorable was *Post-War Gold Coast*, the 1924 Address.

4. An itemized list of projects is in Guggisberg (1924).
5. The identity is derived from combining the growth identity $Y = C + I + G + (X - M)$ with the savings identity $S = Y - T - C$. C is private sector consumption. Other symbols are explained in the text.
6. On Colonial Office file CO852/503/3 is an exchange of correspondence between Clauson and Keynes confirming Treasury policy on this subject (though at a later period). Chapter 4, note 38.
7. Sufficient to more than offset Guggisberg's predicted fall in the barter terms of trade.
8. This was the source of the acrimony between Guggisberg and the expatriate companies throughout most of his term. See Guggisberg (1924), p. 44: 'I believe that the members of an Inchcape Enquiry would see for themselves that the cocoa industry has comfortably borne such duties, that local conditions are against the collection of direct taxation except at prohibitive cost, and that an export duty on cocoa is justifiable in view of the demands for education and other facilities of a similar nature by an enlightened, progressive, and prosperous race.'
9. It is important to note here that Kumase was the capital town of Asante and Mampong the next largest. In the hierarchy of the Asante Kingdom, the Chief of Mampong was second in rank to the King of Asante, and also the Chief of Staff of the Asante Army. Kumase was, and still is, also the second largest city in the country. It is justifiable to refer to Kumase and Mampong as urban areas in Asante in the 1921–31 period. Asante Akyem was a fast growing cocoa area in Asante in this period. The Asante gold mining industry was centred at Obuase, (currently, the Ashanti Goldfields Corporation, the Lonrho-Ghana Government partnership).
10. Lewis (1955: 337) states: 'Because economic growth reduces the importance of agriculture in the economy, it is necessarily associated with urbanization.' This would appear to contrast with the economic growth observed in the Gold Coast associated with the development of cocoa and mining during the early development period, and not with industrialization.
11. Lewis (1955: 275) argues that 'at low levels of economic activity, production for the foreign market is usually the turning point which sets a country on the road to economic growth.' This statement would be truer for manufactured exports than for peasant agricultural exports since the thrust of the argument is that it is 'foreigners who bring the new ideas' (p. 276). No foreigners were involved in cocoa production in Ghana.
12. Bateman (1971) ascribes this phenomenon to a number of factors, including the problem of managing too many cocoa estates and the shortage of suitable land. Also important was the tendency of the migrant 'capitalist' farmer to invest in real estate in his home town or village as a symbol of his success. This was almost mandatory among the Akan ethnic groups, particularly the Asantes and Kwahus.
13. Particularly Hill (1956, 1963, 1986), and Beckett (1944).
14. *Survey of the Gold Coast Economy, 1936* on Colonial Office file CO862/92/3, p. 108.
15. These characteristics of the cocoa farmer were studied in the contemporary period by Beckett (1944) and in a later period by Hill (1956, 1963). Their results largely confirmed the entrepreneurial character of the farmer. Beckett, for example, found a very negligible number of farms at Akokoaso of less than one acre in size. About two-thirds of all farms were between one and three acres (Beckett, 1944: 67–8), considered large, by peasant standards.
16. Ingham (1987) is a pioneering effort in this regard.
17. Crook (1986: 105) argues the 'externality of the state from local society'.
18. A comprehensive collection of official statements on decolonization is on Colonial Office file CO847/20/47139.
19. Final Report of the Royal Commission on *The Natural Resources, Trade and Legislation of Certain Portions of His Majesty's Dominions*, Cmd 8462, HMSO (Chairman, Lord D'Abernon), p. 163.
20. See Colonial Office file CO852/482/8.
21. House of Commons, Hansard, 26 November 1942.
22. Sir Sydney Caine may not agree that MacDonald played a pioneering role, as gathered by the author in a recent discussion on the subject with him (July 1988). He ascribed a much more significant role than is customarily accorded to Colonel Oliver Stanley, Colonial Secretary in the early 1940s.
23. Also on file CO847/20/47139.
24. Clauson's classic memorandum on the subject is in Colonial Office file CO852/1003/3 in which he wrote about the need for 'generations to debunk the charms of idleness [and] to think out more or less unscrupulous or disingenuous methods for discrediting leisure and stimulating the desire for money' on the part of the African (1944).
25. Flint's hypothesis is that the decolonization movement was initiated by Britain, albeit as a reform programme to be concluded in the long term. Planned decolonization failed when the nationalists discovered that if they confronted the British Government with 'organized mass nationalist parties the entire house of cards of colonial reform could be brought to the ground' (Flint, 1983: 405).
26. Sydney Caine, Colonial Office file CO852/588/2.
27. The minutes of this meeting are on Colonial Office file CO967/13.
28. Discussion with Sydney Caine, July 1988. Arthur Lewis, however, indirectly acknowledges the influence of Rosenstein-Rodan's ideas when he refers in Lewis (1984: 127) to 'balanced growth which we all owe to Rosenstein-Rodan'.

29. Colonial Office file CO852/1003/3. In a memorandum in this file, supported by Cohen, Sydney Caine stated: 'It will be remembered these subjects were brought up in a theoretical way in memoranda circulated to the CEAC largely written personally by Dr Arthur Lewis when he was Secretary of the Committee .... The general purport of the answers [to the questions raised by Lewis] was such as to persuade the Committee that there was little advantage in pursuing the discussion of revolutionary economic change any further. I suggest that the whole subject should be reconsidered now.'

30. On Colonial Office file CO852/1003/3.

31. Admitted by Lewis in Lewis (1984: 121).

32. The Clauson ideas are on Colonial Office file CO852/1003/3.

33. Colonial Economic Advisory Committee, minutes of meetings ,CEAC (43) 7 and 8, 1944.

34. W.A. Lewis, memorandum on 'Colonial Economic Development' submitted to the Colonial Economic Advisory Committee, Agenda Sub-Committee, CEAC (44) 38, 14 September 1944. Colonial Office file CO852/588/2

35. *Ibid.*, para 14.

36. *Ibid.*, para. 15.

37. This took the form principally of chartered companies to promote the private businesses of British citizens in the colonies. In Africa, the chartered companies were the Royal Niger Company, the Imperial British East Africa Company, and the British South Africa Company. 'The direct contribution of these companies to mining, plantations and factories, in the form of capital was small. They rather played the role of governments establishing the legal framework and providing the public works which are essential preliminaries to economic development' (Lewis, 1944b: 5).

38. The detailed questions on the Lewis ideas and the official Colonial Office answers are on Colonial Office file CO852/588/2.

39. Lewis (1955: 280) for the upward twist hypothesis. Also Myint (1958), Caves (1965), Fei and Ranis (1964).

40. Legislative Council Debates, 1930–31, pp. 380–4 contain full details of Governor Slater's statement on the dispute between the Federation of Farmers and buying companies. See also Dr Nanka-Bruce's speech, Legislative Council Debates, 1931–2, pp. 380–5. The details of the Fund and its objectives are in an official document, *Memorandum on the Creation of a Fund for Improving the Quality and Marketing of Cocoa* (Government Printer, Accra, 1930). The memorandum suggested a cocoa cess of 10 shillings on each ton of cocoa exported. The cess was described not as an export tax, but for the creation of a fund 'for the benefit of the industry which would provide the money, and not as an addition to general revenue'.

41. The full text of the despatch is on Colonial Office file CO98/57.

42. *Report on the Marketing of West African Cocoa*, Cmd. 5845. 1938.

43. *Ibid.*

44. *Ibid.*

45. Colonel Oliver Stanley, the new Secretary of State for the Colonies, in a note on the speech by Lord Listowel on economic assistance for the colonies to enable them to make their military and economic contribution to the war effort. See CO852/482/7. A longer memorandum on this subject is on file CO852/506/2.

46. Minutes of the War Council, CO554/133/33819/3.

47. *Work of the Department of Agriculture in the War Years* (Government Printer, Accra, 1946), p. 5.

48. Report on Food Production, quarter ending 30 September 1942, by the Director of Agriculture, Accra, see file CO852/469/1.

49. Viscount Swinton, *Economic Policy in West African Colonies* 24 February 1943, WAWC (CM) (4), file CO554/132/23712/1. Comments on the memorandum are on file CO852/480/11.

50. Caine's hypothesis was that a major civilizing influence could come from the actions of the élite, provided that social structures enabled them to emerge from the average ruck. It appeared to him that traditional social customs did not give enough scope for the emergence of the more enterprising in the community. He did not link the process firmly with rural productivity as Steuart or Lewis did.

51. At least in the British colonial territories. More evidence is, however, required to be able to study the influence of the War Council in the French territories during and after the war.

52. One of Ghana's greatest scholars, Ph.D from the University of London in 1927, recipient of the J.S. Mill Prize for the Philosophy of the Mind and Founding Fellow of the Ghana Academy of Arts and Sciences.

53. Asante representation on the Legislative Council in this period was not possible because of the constitutional position of that state as a defeated nation and a protectorate. There were advantages, such as greater respect by the British Government for Asante traditional institutions and customs, and therefore a greater measure of regional autonomy in local government, compared with the Colony. Non-representation in the Legislature, however, implied imposition of laws and regulations. An example was the enactment on 26 July 1928 of an Ordinance providing for the establishment, constitution and management of Stool Treasuries under which 'the Chief Commissioner of Ashanti could at any time compel any Head Chief in Ashanti to establish a Stool Treasury' (CO98/63, p. 30).

54. *Financing of Stools*, Memorandum of the Gold Coast and Asante Delegation to London, 1934, p. 34.

Material on this delegation is on Colonial Office file CO98/63. The memorandum discussed aspects of economic development, such as financing at local government level and appropriate indigenous capacity building. It also requested that some of the advantages of autonomy which Asante and the Northern Territories appeared to enjoy, 'as a conquered territory' (p. 30), should be extended to the Gold Coast Colony. The membership of the delegation was: Nana Ofori Atta I (Akyem Abuakwa), Nene Mate Kole (Manya Krobo), Nene Awah II (Shai), Togbe Sri II (Anglo) and Nene Larbi Agbo II (Prampram).

55. This was an aspect of governance which might have been expressed with greater force if there had been Asante and Northern membership of the Legislative Council as the larger agricultural interests were in those regions. The political economy implications of the non-representation of Asante and the Northern Territories in the Legislative Council, in this period, are yet to be researched.

56. Memorandum of the Gold Coast and Asante, p. 42.

57. A copy of this statement is on file CO98/76 (1937–9).

58. Governor Sir Ransford Slater, speech to the Legislative Council, 1 March 1932.

59. Legislative Council Debates, Accra, 1931–2, pp 380–5.

60. The rural taxes were *Ntokua too* (window tax), a form of poll tax determined by the number of windows on a dwelling.

61. A comprehensive memorandum on these government omissions was presented by the four chiefs of the Southern Provinces in June 1932. File CO98/63.

62. The Watson Commission Report (Commission of Enquiry into Disturbances in the Gold Coast, 1948).

63. Seers and Ross (1952: 5).

64. Full texts of the various comments on the Seers and Ross Report are on file CO554/747.

65. P. Selwyn on *ibid.*, p. 2.

66. A useful note by P. Selwyn on this subject is also on file CO554/747.

67. W.F. Searle on *ibid.*, p. 3.

68. The Party Manifesto for the 1951 elections stated, *inter alia:* 'The industrialization of the country is one of the principal objectives of the Party, and under Dominion Status it will be carried out with all energy.'

69. Writing in 1957, Nkrumah stated (1957: 179): 'about this time [1954] it became clear to me that further steps were necessary to control the price paid locally to the cocoa farmer, otherwise we would shortly be faced with inflation.'

70. Governor Arden-Clarke to Secretary of State for the Colonies, dated 25 October 1953: 'this moderate and useful Report can make an important contribution to public understanding of the problems of industrialization and therefore it should be published forthwith', CO554/202.

71. Armitage (colonial Minister of Finance, Gold Coast) to M. Smith, Colonial Office, file CO554/202: 'when the Report was published, it would prove useful in helping many people in the Gold Coast to see that the slow pace of industrialization there was not due to the wicked imperialist but arose out of the nature of the country and its state of development.'

72. Lewis argues that the way to stop the factoral terms of trade moving continually against LDCs is to raise the productivity of LDC farmers producing for the local market and thereby to increase the supply price of export crops. Arnold Harbeger's interpretation of Lewis's idea is that 'if perhaps through technical advances farmers can earn higher incomes in producing, say, truck crops for the domestic market, then market equilibrium will require that those left producing export crops also earn higher incomes.' Harberger argues that a price elasticity of demand greater than unity is what is likely to attract more resources to the domestic food crop sector, but this is highly unlikely (Meier and Seers, 1984, p. 140). See further notes 73 and 74.

73. Lewis later argued (1954) that, in the long run, it was the 'factoral terms of trade' that determine the commodity terms of trade and not the other way around. The argument is that the factoral terms of trade will continue to fall unless a method is found 'to raise the productivity of LDC farmers producing for the domestic market, thereby increasing the supply price of export crops' (Lewis 1984: 124).

74. Harberger (comment on Lewis 1984, p. 140 of Meier and Seers, 1984) disagrees with this argument. Harberger argues that the assumption implied in the Lewis analysis, that technical advance would shift the supply curve to the left to increase the world price, was invalid. He argues, as we do in Figure 2.1, that 'technical advance itself shifts the supply curve to the right, producing a downward pressure on price. Technical advance in the production of a domestic crop would actually draw resources to its production only if the price elasticity of demand for it were greater than unity – a rather unlikely event in the case of agricultural goods produced just for the local market.'

75. Hammond (1962: 262–6) has shown that food production in the cocoa areas has been positively related to cocoa planting. Medium-term perennial crops, such as plantain, are planted among young cocoa trees to provide shade. Thus increased food output was associated with periods of heavy cocoa planting.

76. Guggisberg's several attempts to diversify agriculture included sisal on the Accra plains, banana exports, tobacco and cotton, all of which were unsuccessful.

3 A Theory of Economic Decline

Rule over them with dignity and they will be reverent; treat them with kindness and they will do their best.

Confucius (*Analects*, II.20)

Chapter 2 ended with an account of the factors influencing economic development on the eve of independence, the combination of a weak productive capacity and monetary fragility, a structure inhibitive of accelerated development. This was a typical feature of underdevelopment in Africa, which even the rise in primary agricultural and mineral export production over several decades had not been able to cure. Rather than promoting an export-led development, the export sectors had introduced an imbalance that masked a fragile economic structure.

The organization of the public services was also weak. The development ambitions of the incoming politicians pointed to a situation in which a weak administration could be rapidly expanded and driven beyond its capabilities.[1] Such an event could create a political/bureaucratic state that would exhibit predatory tendencies against the more successful economic sectors quite early on in the post-independence development phase.

The professional economists had indeed drawn attention to the lack of capital for development on the eve of independence.[2] However, writing on the Gold Coast in the early 1950s, they do not appear to have regarded financial capital as a principal constraint on development in Ghana immediately post-independence. The savings rate was high in the 1950s for an underdeveloped country (18%). There was also an abundance of external reserves. Towards the end of the colonial era, the external reserves of the Gold Coast stood at $336m, which were 35.3% of GDP (Ghana Government 1955, Annex I, Table A6.3, Col. 8). The principal exports, particularly cocoa, had just experienced the post-war and the Korean war booms. Ghana was thus in a peculiar situation in which there was considerable underdevelopment together with large financial reserves. This enabled the professional economists to depart from economic orthodoxy.

The lack of concern on issues relating to financial capital had some disadvantages. It encouraged economists and politicians alike to ignore the incentives needed for the preservation of the financial base in the initial stages of growth. It gave the impression that the accumulated external reserves were adequate for a long process of development. It imparted to the incoming administrators more financial authority than was actually warranted for aggressive modernization (Bauer, 1981: 183; Apter, 1972: 184). It even dissuaded later writers on the Ghana economy (eg., Birmingham *et al.*, Chazan, Roemer) from investigating closely the assumed potential for modernization on the eve of independence.

From our analysis of development ideas in Chapter 2, it was concluded that the reduction of fragmentation in peasant production and marketing and the provision of producer incentives were key requirements in the initial stages of the country's economic growth. Also, the fact that financial capital was not a constraint did not imply that the economy could easily overcome the major constraints of monetary fragility and weakness in productive responsiveness in agriculture. Massive capital expenditures on development in an economy constrained by such weaknesses could lead to the rapid erosion of the external reserves and to the destruction of incentives in the sectors on which development should be based. The scenario that emerges from our analysis is one which, rather than conferring confidence, predicts pitfalls for development on the eve of independence in Ghana.

The Economics of the Political Process

From the above reasoning, the model to be developed in this book lies in the general field of political economy. It has been observed by Keith Hart (1982: 14) that 'for the nations of West Africa, not even the appearance of a separation of state and economy is plausible.' Hart argues that the dilemmas of the countries in the region derive from the synthesis of politics and economics in the colonial period, which has been made even more explicit since independence. This fact does not come out clearly in the works of neo-classical scholars, who have had a tendency to view orthodox economics as able to deal with factors relating to economic development without emphasis on the role of state, class structure or the distribution of power or wealth.

By contrast, classical economists (from Steuart and Adam Smith to Mill, Ricardo and Marx) did recognize the conflicts and interrelationships in the economy, and hence emphasized the political economy discipline. In so doing they made no distinction between positive and normative theory. Their definition of economics (or political economy as it was generally called) was almost synonymous with economic policy. Thus Marx emphasized the conflict between capital and labour, while Ricardo did not conceive of a positive or normative distinction in the theory of comparative advantage.

The significant departure of contemporary economic thought from both classical and neo-classical strands of economics lies in the greater attention paid nowadays to the factors influencing the decision-making process. Thus the modern concept of political economy stresses the influence of interest groups on the state in the way an economy is managed. It also stresses the nature of the power of those controlling the state and how it affects the welfare of the governed. In this modern definition of political economy, economic activity ceases to be autonomous of the sphere of government and of politics.

As the present book concentrates on public policy as it affects the incentives of producers, the definition of political economy that is considered appropriate is that of the 'economic approach to the governmental process' (Brennan and Buchanan, 1980: 13). The Brennan and Buchanan model, which they refer to as the 'Leviathan Model of Political Process', is not based on the conventional policy framework of orthodox fiscal theory which implicitly accepts the model of the ethically benevolent or efficient government. Thus, by following Brennan and Buchanan, the interpretation developed here does not utilize the concept of a well-behaved and efficient politician bureaucrat. Rather it is assumed that such Platonic guardians have been rare in present-day Africa, in both the colonial and post-colonial periods. The focus, therefore, is on a process which recognizes that the motives of governments and of the governed can be in conflict, and that the ideas and interests of the constituents of the state should at least carry equal weight.[3] This approach frees the mind and facilitates the examination of the economic behaviour of governments and of the governed in a more realistic and practical manner.

Brennan and Buchanan (1980: 26-30) assume that the government is both a revenue and a surplus maximizer and that there must be methods to accommodate the maximum benefits of the taxpayer or tax beneficiary in the objectives of government. By defining the maximand of government (Y) as equal to (1 - a)R, where R is tax revenue and a is the proportion of tax allocated to provide public goods and services, they argue that government will seek to maximize revenue available to itself by maximizing R and minimizing a, if a and R are unrelated. If, however, a and R can be positively related, then Y may be maximized without minimizing a. This recognition provides a rationale and a strategy for devising tax instruments beneficial to the taxpayer and the taxbase and therefore to economic development.

The benefit to this study of the Brennan-Buchanan Leviathan model is that it enables us to analyse the process of incentives to production in a real-world context of development from the primary nascent state, when a government's principal objective is to squeeze as much as possible from a limited tax base in order to attain development at the fastest rate possible. In this case we have a visible target of aR (equal to the size of public goods out of taxation). Under conditions in which the two variables are positively related, aR should be stable or increasing throughout the development process.

The Leviathan model has other ingredients. It argues that the political process of the post-constitutional state[4] is not effectively constrained by electoral competition, and can be arbitrary or even indifferent and malevolent. The constraints on government must therefore be additional and imposed at the constitutional level. As there has been a general absence of constitutional or democratic process in most of Africa, what may be more important from the standpoint of this book is that it enables us to include the lack of constitutional process as a variable in our analysis and thus take explicitly into account a degree of arbitrariness and malevolence.

The Leviathan model also draws attention to the monopolistic character of government in which there is the tendency to self-interest implied in the monopolistic model or indeed in the hypothesis of economic man generally. In both colonial and post-colonial African settings in which constitutional constraints were wholly absent, the Leviathan model suggests an almost limitless potential of government predatoriness. This tendency would be further reinforced, in the African situation, by the urgent desire to make a quick transition to industrialization from the overwhelmingly rural economy. The self-interest and monopolistic tendency dictate the character of a variety of political processes underlying this transformation.

For a number of African countries the different processes have been well documented (Bates, 1981, 1983). There are commonalities of 'repression, co-optation, organization and the promotion of factional conflict'[5] to demobilize the rural economy and promote the ascendancy of an industrial era by a variety of coalitions centred around governments. Bates (1981) concludes that the coalition of 'revenue-starved governments, price-conscious consumers, profit seeking industries, and dependent farmers will persist in seeking their individual, short-run, best interests, and will continue to adhere to policy choices that are harmful to farmers and collectively deleterious as well.'[6]

Deepak Lal, in his model of the predatory state, attempts to theorize this malevolent political phenomenon of development (Lal, 1984, 1986, 1988). The Lal model, like the Brennan-Buchanan Leviathan model, assumes government to be a revenue maximizer. An aspect of the model which is useful is that, like Bates's coalition theory, it divides the economy between a revenue-hungry state (the predator state) and the bulk of rural producers (the prey). The government is, however, postulated narrowly as seeking a tax structure that maximizes its revenues and not the welfare of its constituents.

Other assumptions underlie the Lal model. The ruler is a dictator or a charismatic leader: Lal includes, in this definition, a colonial state ruled by a colonial governor whose actions are not much affected by those of domestic interest groups, such as traditional rulers or farmers. He also includes several African states in the post-independence period, in which the colonial powers were replaced by charismatic or autocratic life presidents such as Nkrumah in Ghana, Nyerere in Tanzania, Kaunda in Zambia or Mobutu in Zaire. The state is in a rudimentary state of development, and the absolute ruler provides public goods: law and order, and basic economic infrastructure, such as roads, to facilitate production. Thus, despite the revenue the state derives from these services, overall production is expected to increase.

Bates's analysis, however, offers a wider dimension. By introducing the concept of coalition, Bates postulates a wider definition of the state and therefore a more pervasive condition of predatoriness. By characterizing the government as revenue-starved rather than revenue-maximizing, he argues that the policies to exact revenues from the prey are bound to result in increasing scarcity of resources to underpin the political order. This implies that the costs inflicted on the prey are eventually transferred to the predator to erode the basis of existing equilibrium, force changes in policy choices and induce new coalitions. Bates also introduces the idea of variations from the general rule such as those resulting from historical factors and the characteristics and power of the effective claimants of available resources. Thus the policy change must include appropriate methods to admit the prey into the governing coalition if economic decline and political disintegration are to be halted and reversed, and must also recognize impediments from entrenched powerful interests within the coalition.

A Model of the Political Economy of Decline

Brennan and Buchanan's Leviathan model, Bates's Deleterious Coalition Theory and Lal's Predatory State model all provide useful insights into the economics of the political process and supply building blocks for the analysis of the political economy of decline. However, for the purposes of this book, they suggest that an appropriate model must take specific account of the particular characteristics of an economy like Ghana's on the eve of independence and recognize the relevant aspects of incipient decline. This book therefore introduces concepts which include the passivity of the colonial state and the weak economic structure for accelerated economic development. It also takes account of the weak organization of the public services and the aggressive ambitions of the indigenous state.

Following, particularly, the historical variation suggested by Bates, a distinction must be drawn between the nature of the colonial predatory state, the immediate post-independence indigenous state and the more recent indigenous state. The colonial predatory state was able to break the barrier to entry by virtue of the underdeveloped military technology of the indigenous African states in the nineteenth century. The coalition in the colonial state included mining interests, trading companies and trading firms but excluded the bulk of indigenous sectors outside the export farmers. Thus the colonial predator, once installed, was faced with high internal costs in terms of its legitimacy, as compared with potential indigenous rivals. The colonial coalition, moreover, was in no hurry to introduce manufacturing into the colonies if this conflicted with the export to the colony of products of higher social value.[7] The colonial predatory state therefore maintained economic modernization at a relatively slow pace. It preferred to build up external reserves even if this implied a sub-optimal level of employment in the colonial territory (Ingham, 1987: 255). A colonial predatory state would be wary of promoting policies that raised the rural agricultural wage and therefore the wages of government employees and other urban labour.

It is possible also to conceive of another type of state, which for some 'political' reasons would not emphasize revenue maximization and would therefore push employment towards the socially optimal level and even beyond the point where no surpluses are theoretically available to it. This could be an immediate post-independence indigenous state which would not wish to accumulate the same levels of external reserves as the imperial trade gains of the colonial state. By whatever means the indigenous rulers employed to replace the colonial states (Flint, 1983; Crook, 1986),8 they achieved their initial legitimacy through popular arguments against colonial neglect and promises to purge backwardness, assumed to have been created or fostered by colonialism. The initial coalition therefore consisted of nationalist politicians, indigenous businessmen, mostly small-scale traders, the mass of urban labour and a number of demobilized and dependent farmers. The indigenous government, therefore, was subject to more popular pressures than the colonial rulers; an expansion of patronage was to be expected, leading to larger employment; depending on the ambitions of the political leadership, international and regional aggrandizement was also to be expected, with the creation of diplomatic missions, and in some cases, such as Ghana, ambitions for continental leadership. More ambitious attempts at modernization, including industrialization, were also to be expected, leading to efforts to raise larger state revenues. The expectation would be a new equilibrium with higher government employment beyond the theoretical state surplus maximization point. The popularity of the independence movement, however, would confer on the immediate post-independence rulers considerable legitimacy. Thus in terms of other indigenous contestants, whether civil or military, the barrier to entry would be high, and costly to scale.

Another characteristic of the post-independence indigenous state is the high probability of expenditures increasing due to the action of a rent-seeking political bureaucracy of hangers-on (Krueger, 1974; Buchanan *et al.*, 1980). The state may no longer be a revenue-maximizer but it could become an involuntary spender and inevitably become revenue-starved. As Findlay and Wilson (1984) put it, in such circumstances: 'Government expenditure expands to absorb all the resources available to finance it.' In such a situation government employment could move well beyond the socially optimal level.

Finally, exogenous factors, such as international prices, interest rates on debt, climatic factors, etc., could result in export and domestic revenue instability which, in the medium term, could lead to substantial losses of revenue without corresponding adjustments in expenditures because the state would be unable to adjust employment or wages when revenues fall. For the indigenous state, the compelling desire to promote development, respond to popular desires, and provide greater employment, is reason enough for the state to go beyond the socially optimal levels of government employment and also to forgo all state revenue surpluses (Lal, 1984). In the new theory of the political process, state objectives would have been achieved without real long-term benefits to the economy. This theoretical description of the economics of the political process would be applicable in many countries in Africa in the euphoria of the immediate post-independence period.

For ideological or other reasons, however, the state may continue to expand public sector employment and public-funded industrialization beyond the point where state expenditures have significantly exceeded revenues; as a result, large fiscal and balance of payments deficits may be sustained. Depending on relevant demand elasticities, tariff revenues will fall because as expenditures rise the government will make efforts to exact more revenues from the existing limited sources of a weak peasant export sector and a burdened minerals sector. Tariffs on final consumer goods will also become more and more prohibitive; larger ratios of imported capital goods will be allowed in with low to zero tariffs to support ailing and inefficient public and private sector industries. The direct and indirect tax burden on the export sector will increase and there will be a fall in production and consequently in revenue (Bhagwati, 1978). The state, at this stage, ceases to be a mere predator and mutates into a vampire.

The effect of such a scenario on a fragile economy could be devastating. There are established interrelationships between export taxes (direct and indirect),[10] export production, the rural-urban terms of trade, and the subsistence-based supply price of peasant labour (Lal, 1984). Where these interrelationships work consistently against peasants in the export crops, with ever-increasing direct and indirect adverse effects[9] (Krueger, Schiff and Valdes, 1987[10]), it should be expected that producers will move to sectors beyond the taxation range of the state coalition. At this stage, total incomes from employment in the primary export sector would be inadequate to support production in the inefficient import substituting sector and hence employment in that sector. If the state, for whatever reasons, is unable to seek appropriate remedies such as monetary stabilization and economic restructuring, the minerals and other export sectors become uneconomic and the external deficit worsens. The collapse of export supply (Svedberg, 1991) leads to import compression (Besley and Collier, 1987; London, 1988), and hence to a contraction in fiscal revenues and in general economic activity.

The state may then be described as having entered a fiscal, foreign exchange and domestic production crisis.[11] If stabilization and economic restructuring are not embarked upon quickly, the economy will be set on a path of economic decline. But why should a patriotic indigenous government follow the irrational course of self-destruction?[12] Why should a patriotic indigenous government foster such a harmful ruling coalition and seek to create such a vampire state with the potential to destroy absolutely the primary productive sectors of the economy? What are the factors in the economic and political process that induce a condition that inevitably leads to economic decline in which both the state and its constituents face long-term economic and social decay and political instability?

The most plausible answer is to be found in the structural weakness of the pre-industrial state (discussed in Chapter 2). Public policy appears not to recognize that the weak and fragile peasant-dominated economy is unable to bear the burden of aggressive modernization. Errors in management can then have extreme and protracted effect, including inflation and curtailing production. Another answer is that domestic political processes, dominated by the predatory coalition, become so entrenched that they gain the upper hand over rulers and block the implementation of appropriate economic policies. A further answer is that protracted low producer prices, particularly for export tree crops and minerals, lead to long-run producer withdrawal which requires equally protracted and unaffordable price incentives to restore. In these circumstances, adverse exogenous factors tend to have an amplified effect on the external credibility of the state. Another answer is ineptitude in economic management: economic advice has not always been correctly given (Lewis, 1968: 83); many misconceptions in economic development have prevailed (Killick, 1978); good economic advice is often intercepted by the ignorance and self-interest of 'friends' and businessmen with vested interest.

The fragile nature of the productive sectors also provides insights in assessing the state of decline of the political and economic process. For peasant export production, the arguments suggest the need to measure the trends in optimum and minimum producer incentives. It is also necessary to estimate the short- and long-term supply elasticities with respect to the productive base and to producer prices and with competing non-taxable agricultural products. These indicators help in assessing the degree of erosion of the economy's fragile productive base that occurs in the process of decline. For the minerals sector, the analysis points to the effect of the gap between the nominal and real exchange rates on producer incentives. It is known that ore reserve development and exploitation strategies in periods of exchange-rate overvaluation are adversely affected by loss of revenue. The quality and quantity of ore reserves are expected to decline with protracted exchange-rate overvaluation. In terms of macroeconomic policies, the trends in fiscal policy provide the principal measurements of decline induced by the collapse of the primary export sectors. The most relevant indicators are the degree of erosion of the tax base, the trends in the ratio of fiscal revenues and expenditures to the gross domestic product, and the expansion of the informal sectors leading to the lowering of the authority of the state over fiscal and domestic policies.

These aspects of a model of the political economy of decline should provide an appropriate framework within which to explore the conditions under which economic reforms aimed at reviving the productive sectors of the economy might be instituted. The model should assist in gauging matters such as the authority of the state to effect change – its ability to enforce change, the credibility of the process of change, and the economic dimension of the reform process.

Conclusions

In developing this approach, one objective will be to gauge its contribution to the study of economic development *ab initio* through the facility it provides for assessing public policy towards the primary productive sectors and, in particular, the degree to which their incomes can be squeezed to finance development without destroying producer incentives in the initial stage of development. Another objective will be to monitor the conflicts between the government and powerful interest groups on the issue of mobilization of the primary sectors and their admission to the reformed coalition during the process of economic recovery.

There are thus four working hypotheses to be tested. First, it would seem that the constraints imposed on development from the nascent state by the fragile and weak structure of the underdeveloped economy cannot be overcome merely by large development expenditures in a new modern sector dominated by a deleterious alliance. Second, the political imperatives that dictate modernization under these conditions could lead to higher taxation of the incomes of the primary sectors and to lower incentives in those sectors. Third, this process, incorporating an all-important political dimension, results in lower and lower production levels, economic stagnation and decline rather than economic growth. Fourth, the management strategies that can assure economic growth would be those that guard against powerful and unhealthy coalitions and protect incentives in the primary sectors. They recognize that these are the sectors that ultimately provide the structural foundations for a viable transition from the predominantly rural and peasant economy to industrialization and, ultimately, to sustained economic growth.

Notes

1. Development Progress Report (Government Printer, Accra, 1955), para. 22.
2. Such as Lewis in his 1944 memorandum to the Colonial Office.
3. J.M. Keynes *General Theory*, particularly p. 384.
4. Brennan and Buchanan define a constitution as a 'set of rules that establish the setting within which the whole range of individual interaction takes place'. The post-constitutional state is that in which a constitutional choice has been made whether or not behind a 'veil of ignorance' (Brennan and Buchanan, 1980: 3–4).
5. Bates (1981: 120)
6. Bates (1981:132).
7. G.L.M. Clauson, Colonial Office file CO967/13.
8. Flint argues that Britain initiated the process of planned decolonization which got out of control. Crook, on the other hand, argues that the imperial alliance with traditional rulers in indirect rule was basically unworkable, and that it crumpled as the nationalist movements grew.
9. Direct effects are those transmitted to the producer by direct taxation, often through the fixing of producer prices so that they remain significantly below border prices. Indirect effects are those transmitted through exchange-rate overvaluation. Krueger *et al.* (1987) define indirect nominal protection as the 'ratio of (i) the difference between the relative producer price and the relative border price, and (ii) the relative adjusted border price measured at the equilibrium exchange rate and in the absence of all trade policies.'

10. The paper provides research results suggesting direct and indirect adverse effects of nominal effective protection on the production of cocoa in Ghana of between 55% and 65% in 1954–85.
11. Lal (1986: 21), would describe this situation as that in which 'the predator will have a problem of survival as it has virtually destroyed its prey'. Or as in Bates (1981: 130) 'The basis of the equilibrium erodes.'
12. It would be difficult to accuse Nkrumah, Nyerere, or Kaunda, for example, of not being patriotic.

Part II
Ghana's Economy in the Twentieth Century

Part II tells the long-run story of the Ghana economy in three phases: the colonial era, the immediate post-independence period, and the period of protracted economic decline from 1961. The approach is two-fold. The first is to use the interpretative tool developed in Chapter 3 to tackle some of the major questions raised by the long-run development of the Ghana economy that have yet to be fully answered in the literature. In this task, a secondary objective is to test the principal hypotheses of the model of decline, namely 1) that the colonial predatory state would seek to maximize its gains at the expense of socially optimal employment and development, 2) that the post-independence indigenous state would seek and exceed socially optimal employment and development at the expense of efficient economic management, and 3) that the vampire state would tend to destroy the principal productive sectors and place the economy on a long-run path of economic and political decline. The second approach is to identify one principal economic sector on which Part III of the study will concentrate its in-depth analysis of the decline of the Ghana economy and the conditions for economic recovery.

4 The Colonial Economy

> Unless the Gold Coast spends every penny it can justifiably afford on extending its present lamentably inadequate facilities for transport, education and sanitation, its progress must, and will, be so hopelessly retarded as to give real cause for discontent, unrest and failure.
>
> Guggisberg, 1922[1]

In this chapter, an attempt is made to reconstruct the performance of the colonial economy from the beginning of this century to 1951, the year when internal self-government was attained and an indigenous government was installed. Between that date and 1957, when full independence was achieved, a colonial Governor remained. The period up to 1951 has been chosen as the period of the colonial state, as it was the period during which the administration of the country was fully in the hands of the colonial government.

The period under study has not been researched in sufficient depth by economists to provide a reliable statistical basis for rigorous analysis. The information that is available is fairly reliable on international trade and production relating to the interests of the colonial administration. It is rather weak on the economic activities of the rest of the population, and therefore economy-wide analysis is not possible. Based on Szereszewski's (1965) estimation of the Gross Domestic Product (GDP) for the period to 1911, Teal (1984) has estimated data for the period 1919-50, but the results are not sufficient detailed for our analysis. For a more reliable data base, this chapter draws heavily on Colonial Office records, such as those gathered by Ingham (1987), for long-term trends in fiscal policy and policies relating to trade, output and employment, wages and prices. Data on production relating to some specific industries in the export sector, and on road and rail communication and labour migration, are drawn from Cardinall (1931). Due to data limitations some of the analyses start in 1919, the beginning of the Guggisberg era.

The trends in the series in Tables 4.1 and 4.2 enable three distinct periods to be identified for the purposes of our analysis of the interaction between the economic and political processes in the colonial period. These demarcations are based on fiscal performance and external sector trends and prices, particularly trends in the real cocoa producer price. The first is the period up to 1928 in which there was considerable economic expansion built around a fast-growing mineral and primary agricultural export sector. In this period international trade expanded rapidly and with it government revenues and expenditures. This was the period that culminated in the Guggisberg Ten Year Development Programme (discussed in Chapter 2). The second period is 1929–42 which was generally the period of economic contraction in which the post-war aggressive policies were curbed at the dictation of British Treasury policy (Ingham, 1987). In this period, the economy took on the character of a colonial predatory state with strict fiscal discipline, and an accumulation of external reserves in Britain. There was also minimum state intervention in production.[2] The third phase, 1943–50, was one in which the influences of the Second World War were felt on production and international trade. It has been shown in Chapter 2 that during the war new

Table 4.1 Government Revenues and Expenditures, Prices, Wages and Cocoa Producer Prices, 1918–50

Year	Adjusted[1] govt revenues £'000 (a)	Adjusted[1] govt expenditures £'000 (a)	Surplus and deficit £'000	Govt wage index Base:1918 (b)[2]	Retail price index Base:1918 (c)[3]	Cocoa export price £/ton fob (d)[4]	Cocoa producer price nominal £/ton (e)[5]	Cocoa producer price constant domestic prices (1918)(f)[6]	Cocoa producer price constant import prices (1918)
1	2	3	4	5	6	7	8	9	10
1918	845.0	1086.0	−241.0	100.0	100.0	45.0	39.5	39.5	39.5
1919	2276.5	1730.6	545.9	85.0	160.0	47.0	31.5	37.1	23.2
1920	2935.1	3135.7	−200.6	101.7	136.8	81.0	75.5	74.2	54.2
1921	1910.5	4908.8	−2998.3	116.2	90.6	35.0	20.5	17.6	22.6
1922	2228.1	3161.1	−933.0	110.5	89.0	36.0	23.0	20.8	25.8
1923	2325.7	2217.1	108.6	121.6	95.0	32.0	25.5	21.0	26.8
1924	2578.8	4316.1	−1737.3	112.3	93.6	32.0	23.0	20.5	24.6
1925	2544.5	3799.3	−1254.9	118.1	88.6	37.0	33.0	30.7	37.2
1926	2492.2	3615.3	−1123.1	128.4	83.2	39.0	39.0	22.6	34.9
1927	3515.9	3943.6	−427.7	113.4	83.4	55.0	43.0	37.9	51.6
1928	3741.1	4252.0	−510.9	100.8	75.6	49.0	48.5	48.1	64.2
1929	1928.9	2156.5	−227.7	175.7	65.2	40.0	35.0	19.9	53.7
1930	1959.5	2562.2	−602.6	135.9	50.0	36.0	32.0	23.5	64.0
1931	1587.5	1827.2	−239.7	143.5	48.2	22.0	15.5	10.8	32.2
1932	1992.5	1783.0	209.5	133.2	44.4	23.0	17.0	12.8	38.3
1933	2126.6	1737.2	389.4	124.8	41.6	21.0	16.5	13.2	39.7
1934	2178.4	1739.5	438.8	126.7	44.8	17.0	10.5	8.3	23.4
1935	2731.2	2029.6	701.6	118.3	45.4	19.0	14.0	11.8	30.8
1936	3139.6	2392.8	746.8	118.9	53.0	24.0	15.5	13.0	29.2
1937	3123.3	2661.7	461.7	120.0	48.2	42.0	38.0	31.7	79.2
1938	3295.2	2961.0	334.2	112.8	42.0	17.0	17.4	15.4	41.4
1939	2480.9	2398.5	82.4	149.3	55.6	18.0	13.0	8.7	23.4
1940	2250.6	2259.4	−8.8	170.8	63.6	20.0	15.9	9.3	25.0
1941	2295.4	1977.1	318.3	179.4	66.8	18.0	13.1	7.3	19.6
1942	2180.9	2158.8	22.2	189.6	70.6	19.0	14.9	7.9	21.1
1943	2335.7	2454.5	−118.8	183.5	70.6	18.0	13.1	7.1	18.6
1944	2665.0	2189.9	475.2	203.3	78.2	19.0	13.1	6.4	16.8
1945	3346.6	2790.2	556.4	213.5	82.1	30.0	22.4	10.5	27.3
1946	3256.3	2828.9	427.4	231.4	89.0	40.0	27.1	11.7	30.4
1947	4116.5	3992.7	123.8	248.0	95.4	92.0	51.3	20.7	53.8
1948	5370.8	5279.6	91.2	216.0	102.2	197.0	74.7	34.6	76.3
1949	7677.7	5977.5	1700.3	235.2	119.8	129.0	121.3	51.6	101.3
1950	8336.0	7100.0	1236.0	250.0	141.4	204.0	84.0	33.6	59.4

(a) 1 Adjusted by railway wage index in lieu of appropriate price index

(b) 2 Railway wage index used in preference to import price index used in other literature, e.g., Bateman 1971

(c) 3 Index of import prices used for period 1918–39, remainder is Accra index

(d) 4 Source for 1919–50, Ingham 1987, page 235

(e) 5 Source: Bateman 1971, Table II 5

(f) 6 Adjusted by railway wage Index

Sources: Ingham (1987), unless otherwise stated

Table 4.2 International Trade, Output and Employment, 1918–50

Year	Imports ú'000 Current Prices	Exports ú'000 Current Prices	Balance of Trade ú'000 Current Prices	Net Barter Terms of Trade	Railways Number of African Workers 000	Goldmining Number of African Workers 000	Gold Exports Volume oz'000	Cocoa Exports Volume Tons'000	Cocoa Price ú/ton FOB Current	Cocoa Exports Ratio % of Total Exports
1	2	3	4	5	6	7	8	9	10	11
1918	3256	4472	1216	54.8	2.5	10.8				
1919	7946	10814	2868	61.1	2.8	11.0	360	176	47.00	0.76
1920	15152	12352	−2800	81.4	3.5	9.8	230	124	81.00	0.81
1921	7661	6942	−719	48.6	3.7	10.3	221	133	35.00	0.67
1922	7900	8335	435	68.0	4.0	12.1	228	159	37.74	0.72
1923	8448	8959	511	57.7	4.1	10.0	225	200	33.17	0.74
1924	8315	9914	1599	55.5	4.9	10.3	232	223	32.51	0.73
1925	9782	10890	1108	65.4	4.9	9.1	218	218	37.72	0.76
1926	10285	12104	1819	72.0	4.6	8.2	220	230	39.74	0.76
1927	13770	14350	580	82.8	5.3	7.8	189	210	55.85	0.82
1928	12220	13824	1604	88.0	6.1	7.8	179	225	49.91	0.81
1929	10082	12677	2595	75.0	3.5	7.4	225	238	40.77	0.77
1930	8953	11287	2334	78.3	4.6	7.4	272	190	36.49	0.61
1931	4804	9301	4497	55.0	4.0	7.9	273	244	22.51	0.59
1932	5605	8349	2744	68.4	3.8	8.8	286	233	23.55	0.66
1933	5543	8049	2506	57.1	3.8	10.4	294	236	21.06	0.62
1934	4849	8117	3268	58.9	3.7	15.1	351	230	17.57	0.50
1935	7376	9315	1939	66.7	4.0	23.5	371	268	19.35	0.56
1936	8531	12337	3806	77.8	4.1	27.0	434	311	24.63	0.62
1937	12307	16124	3817	95.7	4.2	27.3	558	236	42.33	0.62
1938	7651	11276	3625	60.9	4.6	30.5	677	263	17.27	0.40
1939	7318	12944	5626	68.2	4.7	33.7	793	280	18.15	0.39
1940	6878	13657	6779	68.9	4.7	33.8	858	223	20.07	0.33
1941	6137	13039	6902	56.3	4.7	34.5	815	218	18.30	0.31
1942	8732	12122	3390	59.0	5.1	30.1	786	123	19.24	0.20
1943	8598	12619	4021	39.6	5.2	21.7	630	187	18.68	0.28
1944	8580	12259	3679	33.3	6.1	22.7	534	202	19.16	0.32
1945	10207	15596	5389	37.7		25.4	475	232	30.79	0.46
1946	12861	20142	7281	50.0		30.1	646	236	40.20	0.47
1947	21843	27181	5338	64.2	5.4	31.1	568	180	92.42	0.61
1948	30114	55543	25429	98.7	5.8	30.1	671	214	197.04	0.76
1949	44434	49573	5139	74.0	5.5	29.5	656	263	128.86	0.68
1950	47979	76386	28407	107.5	5.7	31.0	705	267	204.51	0.71

Sources: Ingham (1987: 234), for employment, gold, cocoa, and 1918–30 trade data
Cardinall (1931) for Gold mining employment for 1930
Metcalfe (1964: 751–2) for 1931–4 trade data
Ministry of Finance, Accra (1951) for trade data 1935–50
Blue Book of Statistics, various issues, and Legislative Council Debates Accra (1932) for cocoa export prices (fob)

demand was generated both for exports and domestically consumed goods, and for certain specific needs of the colonial government. In the immediate post-war period, there was a relative increase in producer prices resulting from higher demand. This was also the period in which perspectives on colonialism were changing in favour of greater activity in development.

The discussion in this chapter is structured around the economic events of the three historical periods. Within the framework of the colonial predatory state, our enquiry is guided by the following questions:

1. Do the distinguishing features of the three periods assist a better understanding of colonial development strategies in the Gold Coast?
2. Of what value was the pre-1929 economic development effort to the long-run economic growth of the country? If there were positive factors, why were they not sustained in the period that followed?
3. How did colonial imperialism really work? What were the predatory aspects, and did they contribute to any long-run weaknesses of the Ghana economy?

Before 1928

The period from the turn of the century to about 1928 showed characteristics associated with the colonial ideal of promoting primary production for export. This was the development period that saw the beginning of the cocoa industry and the emergence of the country as the world's number one producer of cocoa in a little over two decades (Table 4.3). The same period saw Ghana's emergence as a leading producer of diamonds and manganese, in addition to gold, of which it was already an established major world exporter (Table 4.4). As the data in Table 4.4 indicate, the colony experienced phenomenal growth in production of manganese and diamonds in the 1920s, the Guggisberg era. The trend in gold production does not relate to the development strategies of the period. The history of gold dates back to the sixteenth century, when the Gold Coast produced 35.5% of the world's total.[3] Production fell as attention shifted to new discoveries in other parts of the world, particularly in South Africa. Production in the development period under discussion significantly recovered from the low levels of the eighteenth and nineteenth centuries. In the Guggisberg period, gold, being a high-value, low-volume product, did not benefit directly from the transportation programmes targeted towards the new heavy products.

The latter part of the period, however, was not typical of the colonial model in two ways. A principal partner of the colonial government was the merchant trader who had thrived on spectacular expansion in imports in the initial years of export growth.[4] He saw himself at variance with Guggisberg, the colonial Governor who was the principal architect of the phenomenal expansion of imperial production and trade. From the available evidence (Guggisberg, 1924: 24, para. 41), the chief reason for this change was the aggressive programme of modernization which had imposed a burden of taxation on the merchant class in order to finance development (see Table 4.5). Hitherto, taxation had been concentrated on imports. Taxation on exports began with the Guggisberg development programme but did not rise to the level of import taxes. The government considered that the level of export taxation was not a disincentive to producers. Improved facilities in the road and rail network, opening up the country for the rapid movement of cocoa and bringing head-loading to an end, was believed to have increased output (Guggisberg, 1924: paras. 113–18). The government was of the view that a reduction in the newly created export tax would 'be an injustice to the farmer. He is not likely to get any more benefit out of a fresh reduction than he did out of the last, whereas he did get the benefit of the railroad and the roads constructed out of the duty' (*ibid.*: 28, para. 49).

Table 4.3 The Early Growth of the Cocoa Industry

Year	Vol.'000 tons	Year	Vol.'000 tons	Year	Vol '000 tons
1905	7	1914	53	1923	200
1906	8	1915	78	1924	223
1907	10	1916	73	1925	218
1908	13	1917	92	1926	230
1909	21	1918	115	1927	210
1910	22	1919	176	1928	225
1911	41	1920	124	1929	238
1912	39	1921	133	1930	190
1913	52	1922	159	1931	244

Sources: Guggisberg (1924), Cardinall (1931)
Blue Book of Statistics (CO100/90) 1941
Ingham (1987)

Table 4.4 The Growth of the Mineral Industry of the Gold Coast

Year	Gold		Manganese		Diamonds	
	Numbers employed '000	Fine oz produced '000	Numbers employed '000	Tons produced '000	Numbers employed '000	Carats exported '000
1921	10.6	203.4	0.8	7.2	0.1	1.8
1922	10.3	207.8	0.6	66.5	0.2	6.7
1923	10.3	200.7	1.2	181.6	0.8	30.4
1924	10.6	210.3	2.0	276.9	0.8	61.4
1925	9.3	198.1	3.2	361.8	1.0	152.1
1926	8.4	189.1	1.4	398.6	1.2	340.0
1927	8.0	168.9	1.6	334.5	1.4	501.4
1928	8.0	167.1	1.6	376.9	2.0	686.1
1929	7.6	218.5	1.8	496.5	3.1	716.9
1930	7.3	246.1	1.6	396.0	3.4	848.2

Source: Cardinall (1931)

Whatever the reason, for most of this period the programme of export expansion saw greater cooperation with the farmers and traditional rulers, and less with the merchants, than was customary. Such an atmosphere of mutual cooperation and confidence between the government and the producers, in which the government made the effort to provide the incentives for increased production, was untypical.[6] This was a situation where the traditional alliance between the government and the expatriate trading classes, in which the latter dominated public policy, was not regarded as the appropriate way forward. The colonial government was not, as we might have expected, distanced from the economic sector from which it derived its imperial trade benefits. This period may be described more positively, a point which Nkrumah (1957: 38) reluctantly acknowledged.[7]

The relevant characteristics of the period from the point of view of this study are the following:

• Government economic activity was considerable. Budgetary revenues and expenditures quadrupled in real terms in the period 1918-28. Budgetary deficits were common, resulting from the development programme, and were financed by external capital inflows (Table 4.1, cols 2 and 3). Both these developments were contrary to British Treasury philosophy.

Table 4.5 Taxation of International Trade, 1910–31 (£'000 current prices)

Year	Imports[a] Commercial imports	Import duty	Average tax rate(%)	Exports[a] Commercial exports	Export duty	Average tax rate(%)
1910	2,619	609	23.2	2,614	–	–
1911	2,853	663	23.2	3,471	–	–
1912	3,141	735	23.4	4,004	–	–
1913	3,252	780	24.0	5,027	–	–
1914	3,160	766	24.2	4,470	–	–
1915	3,117	828	26.6	5,815	–	–
1916	4,382	1,099	22.5	5,576	33	0.5
1917	2,964	632	23.0	5,529	212	3.8
1918	2,738	489	17.9	4,025	131	3.3
1919	6,896	1,252	18.2	10,729	419	3.9
1920	13,074	1,700	13.0	12,300	583	4.7
1921	4,748	891	18.8	6,457	656	10.2
1922	5,221	1,299	24.9	7,589	674	8.9
1923	6,901	1,757	25.5	8,427	475	5.6
1924	6,336	1,800	28.4	9,624	389	4.0
1925	8,023	2,274	28.3	10,648	276	2.6
1926	7,800	1,920	24.6	11,863	302	2.5
1927	11,041	2,764	25.0	14,223	280	2.0
1928	10,505	2,679	25.5	13,731	303	2.2
1929	8,847	2,040	23.1	12,487	318	2.5
1930	7,770	1,860	23.9	10,050	259	2.6
1931	4,074	992	24.3	7,687	309	4.0

a) Excludes government trade

Source: Blue Book of Statistics, Accra, 1936

Table 4.6 Export Growth in Response to Increased Rail and Road Mileage, 1921–30

Year	Total exports (£'000)	Gold exports (£'000)	Exports Less gold (£'000)	Index of non export expansion	Rail mileage	Road mileage	Total mileage	Index mileage increase
1921	5,532	864	4,668	100	276	2,241	2,517	100
1922	6,632	883	5,750	123	334	3,287	3,621	144
1923	7,544	853	6,691	143	379	3,561	3,940	157
1924	8,715	893	7,822	168	394	3,977	4,371	174
1925	9,786	841	8,945	192	394	4,801	5,195	206
1926	10,999	803	10,196	218	457	5,110	5,567	221
1927	13,459	712	12,747	273	480	5,527	6,007	239
1928	12,944	710	12,016	257	495	5,941	6,436	256
1929	11,531	923	10,603	227	500	6,111	6,611	263
1930	8,855	1,045	7,810	167	500	6,738	7,238	288

Source: Basic data from Cardinall (1931)

- Despite some annual variations, wage levels remained relatively stable in the period while import prices generally fell. The isolation of the indigenous sector from the urban economy is indicated by the lack of direct relationships between the import price index and the wage index (Table 4.1, cols 5 and 6).
- The farmer's cost of living basket was significantly different from that of the urban sector. When adjusted by the domestic (wage) index, real producer prices for cocoa were much lower than when adjusted by the retail price index. The latter was, in fact, an import price index, which tended to exaggerate the real producer price of cocoa. On the basis of the domestic (wage) index, the real earning of farmers are shown (Table 4.1, col. 9) to have been significantly higher in the period to 1928 than in all the following years until the post-war boom of the late 1940s.

Production indicators have been shown in the preceding tables to have responded well to the socio-economic and political policies of the period. The following features of the growth in production during the period are worth mentioning:

- In all cases of mineral production, not only did total output increase, but also labour productivity, which increased at a very rapid rate. While this result for diamonds and manganese may reflect nascent development, the same cannot be said of gold (Table 4.4), which was a product dating back to Portuguese–Gold Coast trade in the fifteenth century and earlier.
- Despite greater activity in the export sectors of cocoa and minerals and in construction, food production did not decline in the initial period of growth. It has been argued that food crops are positively related to cocoa planting (Hammond, 1962: 252–6).[8] This accounts for the absence of inflationary signs in the initial development period.
- There is also considerable evidence of the effort to diversify production. Crops such as cotton, tobacco, bananas and oil palm were attempted both at the peasant and plantation levels. All the efforts failed.[9] In discussing Cardinall's observations in Chapter 2, the reasons for the failures were attributed to the relative ease with which cocoa could be cultivated (Cardinall, 1931: 99) and the larger monetary reward compared with other industry (Lewis, 1953: 20, para. 277). The long-run disadvantages for the economy of the successes in the initial years were also discussed.

An important feature of this early growth period was the development of the infra-structure, which began at the turn of the century, even though greater efforts were made in the Guggisberg period. In the initial period the emphasis was on infrastructure to tap the mineral resources of the Western Province and Asante and link them with coastal points for ocean transportation. The additional effort in the Guggisberg period was the introduction of economic and social infrastructure on a large scale.

The principal focus was on the construction of railways. In total 495 miles of new rail permanent way had been constructed by 1928, compared to 276 miles in 1921 at the early stages of the Guggisberg programme (see Table 4.6). An extension planned to the north of the country was later abandoned. The initial efforts had been directed at the newly established cocoa areas some fifty miles to the north-east of Accra. In the Guggisberg period more extensive construction took place, completing the link from Accra to Kumase, and improving the southwestern route from Sekondi to Kumase.

The long-term viability of the railway system came rather quickly into question even before Guggisberg's departure. Road transportation appeared to be more efficient, cheaper and more versatile. This applied to the principal trunk roads that were in competition with the railways (treated in greater detail later in this chapter). However, the feeder roads, which were almost wholly constructed by the farmers themselves, served a useful purpose throughout the colonial period and into independence.[10] Road mileage tripled in the ten years 1921–30 (Table 4.6).

Also relevant in this period was the importance attached to the social infrastructure in matters such as education, health, good drinking water and electrification. The capital city of Accra received electric power (Guggisberg, 1924: 96, para. 75), Achimota College was built and plans laid for making it a university (ibid.: 69, para. 136). Korle Bu Hospital in Accra was acclaimed as having the best facilities in Africa when it was opened (ibid.: 79, para. 150), and facilities for basic medicine and hygiene were introduced in a large number of towns throughout the country.

These characteristics of the early colonial development show the predatory state in a positive light, in the sense that the colonial government saw the advantage of promoting indigenous exports for which a comparative advantage appeared to exist. New taxes were introduced but not such as to destroy incentives; efforts were made to share some of the benefits by improving the welfare of the general population; and there appeared to be harmony between the prey and the predator. However, Guggisberg, the colonial Governor who inspired these positive attitudes, was removed from office before completing his development programme, though it appeared to have been continued for a while by his successor. In what way did he deviate from the appropriate model of colonial development? What were the advantages and disadvantages of his policies for the colonial predatory state? These questions are taken up, with others, at the conclusion of this chapter.

1929–42

The second colonial period, 1929–42, was characterized by a marked reversal of the strategies of the initial period.[11] With the ending of the Guggisberg Programme, budgetary expenditures were cut back and remained stagnant until 1941 (see Table 4.1), reaching the lowest point in 1934. Budgetary revenues declined drastically from 1929 for three years, but recovered from 1933 to 1938 before falling off again to another low in 1942. In nominal terms, the 1938 level was lower than that reached in 1928. The contraction of the budget in the first half of the 1930s was very much related to poor international trade performance (see Table 4.2).

The recovery in exports after 1936 was due to cocoa and also to the increased production of gold, which had been least affected by the development strategies of the earlier period. As may be observed in Table 4.2 (col. 11), the ratio of cocoa to total exports declined throughout the period, and in 1942 was only 20% from the peak of over 80% in 1927 when it was the backbone of the country's international trade. This decline in the importance of cocoa was due to stagnant and declining production as well as to falling export prices (Table 4.2, cols 9 & 10). If cocoa was the focus of the early development strategy, and particularly of the Guggisberg programme, then by 1942 its importance vis-à-vis other exports had been reversed. The value of the early development strategies, which focused on cocoa exports, must therefore have been completely eroded from the minds of policy-makers. Various 'vent for surplus' arguments (e.g., Myint, 1958) suggest reasons why, despite its falling price and declining importance, producers continued to retain interest in the industry. A further reason is that in this period the industry, which had moved into the Asante region in its second development phase, was still young and productive, and therefore could respond better to short-term changes in price (see Chapter 7 for a more detailed treatment). The farmers' faith in the industry contrasted significantly with official indifference.[12]

The above observations suggest that a close study of the political economy of the cocoa industry provides an example of a key primary-producing industry in a colonial predatory state in the period 1929–42. The aspects singled out for study are the following: the peculiarities of the labour market facing the cocoa industry; the nature of property rights in the industry, particularly cocoa land; the characteristics of transport costs facing the industry; the nature of the market for capital available to the industry; and the characteristics of the market for the industry's output, particularly state and non-state intervention, and the determination of producer prices.

Much has been written about the peculiarities of the labour market in the Ghana cocoa industry but not much in the way of actual records of that market exist in the literature.[13] Despite the commercialization of production, the farmers largely retained their peasant identity. Hired and seasonal labour had in the past come from the countries to the north of Ghana specifically for the cocoa industry (Hill, 1956). The planting and harvesting seasons were complementary rather than competitive with other agricultural crops.[14] Cocoa production in its development phase was not in competition with food crop production in the sense, noted earlier, that food crops were grown among young cocoa trees for protection (Hammond, 1962: 252-6 and Bates, 1983: 63). Furthermore, the tree crops, oil palm and rubber, that cocoa replaced grew wild rather than in organized plantations.

The fact that cocoa has coexisted comfortably with other occupations and commercial activities has meant that labour has had neither the need nor the incentive to organize itself. The cocoa industry in Ghana has suffered labour market isolation compared with other industries in the country or other agricultural sectors elsewhere. The disadvantage of such isolation is that the industry did not have the support of the labour movement during this period of stagnation. Such support would have provided a sympathetic counterweight to the predatory advances of the colonial state or of merchant buying companies during the difficult period of the 1930s.

The evidence suggests that the traditional rulers have been the only real allies of the cocoa farmer.[15] The relationship of the traditional ruler to the cocoa farmer has usually been that of a landlord, often a farmer himself, and political leader of a rural community. The evidence suggests, however, that the authority and influence of the traditional ruler was steadily eroded in this period (Crook, 1986).

In the development of the cocoa industry the availability of suitable land and the cost of such land have been key factors. In other parts of Africa, particularly in Eastern and Southern Africa where commercial agriculture in the colonial period was the monopoly of the settler farmer, a principal strategy in increasing agricultural profitability was to facilitate, through state patronage, access to suitable land at low cost. An example of such a strategy was the alienation of land from indigenous jurisdiction in Kenya, allowing the confiscation of peasant land without compensation and its subsequent transfer to commercial farmers at very low cost.[16]

In this period of decline, such state patronage was not forthcoming. The evidence indicates that the cocoa farmer, in all cases, has had to compete for land at market rates and, because of his general poverty, has often had to pool resources with others or borrow to acquire land (Hill, 1956, 1963). In the climatically ideal forest zones of Ghana, by traditional law in most cases and particularly in Asante and Brong Ahafo, cocoa land is held as a collective property by the 'stool' (i.e., by the traditional ruler). Normally such land is available to any citizen for the cultivation of food crops. With the advent of the commercial cocoa crop, and on the advice of Southern lawyers, private property rights gradually emerged (Kimble, 1963; Sampson, 1969). The Ghana cocoa farmer, in terms of land input, faced a market-oriented price structure (Hill, 1963: 50) which, in economic terms, should have led to productive efficiency. Throughout this period, however, the cocoa farmer faced a distorted market on the demand side.

The literature on the sources of financial capital for the cocoa industry in its formative and later phases is not vast. Again Polly Hill (1963) is a major source and so is the Colonial Office's *Report of the Commission on the Marketing of West African Cocoa.*[17] According to these two sources, this capital comprised loans either from local purchasing agents or from other established cocoa farmers against the pledge of future production. Hill's analysis (1963: 56) suggests a competitive market for loans from numerous sources. The general thrust of the analysis, however, shows that the cocoa farmer was a rural capitalist,[18] in the sense that investment in the industry was largely derived from farmers' earnings. One can conclude that the market for financial capital in the cocoa industry was not large, though probably competitive.

If it is accepted that the market for capital was competitive, then it follows that the interest rate should have been close to the market rate. But the evidence is complex. For example, the Report of the Quaidoo Committee states that 'the impression gained during the Committee's Field Surveys tends to suggest that, by and large, perhaps three quarters of farmers of Southern Ghana and Ashanti are indebted in one form or another' to professional money lenders.[19] It further states that loans are 'commonly obtainable at a rate of interest of 100% per annum or season', plus a letter-writer's fee for preparing a receipt.[20] Loans arranged between farmers attracted lower interest rates and usually ranged between 0% and 50% per season.[21] Polly Hill's results and the findings of the Quaidoo Report would suggest that the majority of Ghana cocoa farmers faced interest rates much higher than those available through financial institutions for other commercial activities. This is a strong indication that the cocoa farmer required the most favourable market conditions for his output to enable him to retain an optimum incentive in further investment.

The evidence in the 1930s and early 1940s suggests that cocoa farmers in Ghana 'appear to have been compelled to pay a price for transport services that lay far above the competitive market rate, with the result that the relative profitability of farming declined' (Bates, 1983: 66). The cocoa industry was not yet established when the idea of the first railways was conceived in the early 1890s. The decision to develop the rail links with the mining centres in the Western region rather than a network into the potential cocoa areas in the forest zone of the Asante was therefore logical (Church, 1936). Bates argues that the decision in 1926 to develop the new harbour at Takoradi rather than in the east (a part of the Guggisberg Programme) was due to the superior influence of mining over cocoa interests, and that shipping cocoa through Takoradi raised the transportation costs (Bates, 1983: 67; Kay and Hymer, 1972). Bates further argues, on the basis of an analysis by Church (1936), that the government deliberately closed down some smaller ports in the eastern half of the shore line in order to force the use of rail transportation to Takoradi at the expense of the emerging cheaper road network (Church, 1936: 137).

The problems of transportation offer further insight into conflicts within the political economy in the 1930s. When Guggisberg constructed the major trunk roads in the 1920s, and mobilized the local chiefs and farmers to build the feeder roads, it was not contemplated that the trunk road network would rapidly render the railways uncompetitive.[22] It would appear that the railway tariff structures, beneficial to the British mining interests, were possible only if cocoa was also transported by the railroad and not by the motor road network.[23] During the Guggisberg era, the British authorities were to question him about encouraging the import of American trucks that were able to use the comparatively poor-quality roads to convey cocoa for long distances, obviously to the detriment of the mining interests.[24] After his departure, the response of the colonial government was dramatic. Rules were introduced prohibiting the transportation of cocoa by long roads that ran parallel to the railroads. Works that were in progress on such roads were suspended.[25] Thus the cocoa farmer was prevented from using the most competitive means of transport available, and was forced by various methods and regulations to depend on forms of transport at above-market prices. Clearly the government's objective in the 1930s was to subsidize the mining interests at the expense of cocoa.

The above analysis suggests the need for favourable market conditions for cocoa farmers if producer incentives were to be preserved. Instead, 'the Ghanaian cocoa farmers faced cartels organised by purchasers and shippers of their products – cartels which sought to depress the prices received by the producers of cocoa' (Bates, 1983: 71). The conflict between farmers and buying agents reached its peak in this period. The efforts by the large purchasing companies to form cartels for the regulation of producer prices were, however, not successful during the depression of the cocoa market in the 1930s and early 1940s. The evidence suggests that a number of agreements to set up cartels were reached by the major buying companies (Report of the Commission on the Marketing of West African Cocoa) but were all subverted by smaller companies prepared to offer higher prices (Hancock, 1942: 185; Bates, 1983: 74). The government's passivity towards the efforts of the trading companies to gain final control of producer prices through the formation of cartels incited the resentment of the traditional rulers (Memorandum of Four Southern Chiefs)[26] and fuelled the cocoa boycotts of the period.

As for the cocoa producers, in the period 1929-42 their interests had ceased to be a paramount influence on the objectives of the colonial government. In the principal markets for inputs, the cocoa farmer was forced to purchase at the competitive market price (or above, as in the case of transportation). In the market for his output, he remained unorganized and constantly faced a better organized group of buying agents, who thus found it easier to establish a monopsony. It is not difficult, therefore, to explain why the cocoa industry experienced stagnation in this period. That there was not a major withdrawal from the industry was due to the faith the farmer retained in his investment in tree stock.

Other conclusions may be drawn from the analysis of the predatory colonial economy in this period. The passive fiscal policy may have conformed to Treasury policy. Following closely on the Guggisberg policy of cooperation, the impression could not be avoided, however, that public policy was set against indigenous development. There was also the continued accumulation of external reserves, despite falling world prices for cocoa. Producer price stabilization cannot be imputed because that policy did not exist at the time. It can be assumed that this accumulation was designed for the benefit of the colonial predatory state and not for the bulk of the population producing tradeable goods.

1943–50

This was the period which marked the end of colonial rule in a *de facto* sense, and which also produced unprecedented economic and political activity. It was a period of intense war activity and fiscal expansion. Both export prices and cocoa producer prices significantly recovered. The role of cocoa in exports and in general economic activity was reasserted.

Budgetary expenditure, stagnant at around £2m annually since 1928, rose at an average annual rate of 16% to over £7m in the eight years from 1942 to 1950. Revenues rose at a slightly faster rate of 18%, thus ensuring budgetary surpluses in this period of greater activity. Nominal cocoa producer prices rose over five-fold and real producer prices four-fold, to levels higher than those attained in the early development period (Table 4.1, col. 9). This was enough to revive the short- and long-term interest of farmers. The long-term response took the form of a search for new lands for cultivation. Mineral production was also sustained at its previous high levels, with gold remaining the dominant non-cocoa export product (see Table 4.2, col. 8).

It was also a period when considerable debate took place in Britain on self-government

(Flint, 1983; Crook, 1986). In the Gold Coast, nationalist political groups also emerged to demand self-government. These events were associated with those new ideas on economic development in the colonies generally which have already been discussed in Chapter 2.

The creation of the Cocoa Control Board was an important policy initiative that was to have significant influence on the cocoa industry and the Ghana economy as a whole. The Board, later renamed the West African Produce Control Board, was created to prevent the collapse of the cocoa industry after the loss of European markets during the war, and to engage in producer price stabilization (Bates, 1983: 75). Some writers (e.g., Bauer, 1984) take the view that ideology associated with a progressive group that gained influence in the latter period of decolonization played a major role in promoting economic controls, of which the marketing board was one effective instrument. Other instruments, it is argued, were restrictive trade licensing, where the 'progressive' group in the Colonial Office, aided by influential commercial interests in the country, actively promoted the 'role and power of ambitious civil servants, creating influential and lucrative positions and helping many of them to secure honours ranging from OBEs to august GCMGs and peerages' (Bauer, 1984: 95).

These views support the argument that, in responding to popular pressure to provide long-term protection to the producer, the creation of the marketing board and its actual operation in later periods provided the vehicle for the attainment of an imperial objective: to gain greater control over the industry, and to ensure for the British government substantial convertible currency reserves. The marketing board can therefore be seen as consistent with the strategy of a colonial predatory state. The rapid recovery of cocoa, viewed in the context of the previous period of depression, had two further effects. It produced considerable wealth which could not be absorbed into the peasant economy in its underdeveloped state and therefore found its way to the urban economy to support the creation of a new urban élite.27 This process was particularly fostered by the expansion in the budget. Unlike the Guggisberg period, when expansion favoured the rural economy, most expenditures were to the benefit of the urban sector. This had the effect of creating articulate contestants to the authority of the colonial government. In addition, the new investors in cocoa were largely absentee landlords who invested most of their wealth in urban activities and in real estate. The villagers invested, particularly, in school buildings.[28] The full benefit of the cocoa boom therefore did not accrue to the rural peasant producer.

One effect of the war was the imposition of monetary and exchange restrictions that bore no relation to the economic conditions in the country at the time: in particular, the existence of a foreign-exchange surplus.[29] In terms of macroeconomic management, it had the effect of needlessly bottling up demand. Without an external deficit, the devaluation of the pound sterling in 1949 was theoretically unjustifiable. It also wiped out a large portion of the country's reserves in terms of non-sterling currencies and increased the cost of non-sterling imports for no economic reason. The restrictive trade and exchange policies, at a time when they were not desired, introduced a culture of macroeconomic management which was later relied upon extensively. These factors sowed the seeds for an economic management style, later in the post-independence period, that was anti-sterling, anti-exchange rate adjustments and pro-restrictions.

The Colonial Predatory State

There are both common and distinguishing features in the three colonial phases. The colonial policy of concentration on international trade, to the exclusion of the wider development needs of the indigenous population, was preserved, especially in the period immediately after Guggisberg. The state made little contact with producers engaged in domestic development, such as food crops.[30] The result was that on the eve of independence the country suffered from a skewed economy with relatively intense activity in the international trade sector. The social effects were typified, on one hand, by growing urban trading and administrative centres, concentrations of population in the mining districts, and wealthy indigenous farmers in the forest cocoa belts. On the other hand, backward and passive systems of agriculture still existed, with 'a peasant and his wife and children working in a small area with primitive tools, and only a limited traditional knowledge, scratching a living from the soil' (Lewis, 1944a: 2, para.7).

These economic conditions were observed during the war by British soldiers who, from the success of international trade and the standards of welfare at home, had believed that there was a broader and more balanced development in the colonies.[31] The problem was also worrying to the younger members of the British colonial service. As minuted by Cohen in 1943:[32]

> The principal reason for putting forward the idea [rural development] is the extreme importance of rural development in the West African territories which are primarily agricultural.... A number of officers on leave, and particularly the younger ones, have given me and others who have talked to them the impression of being extremely depressed because they feel that the governments ... have no policy in these matters.

As Nkrumah put it, characteristically emphasizing industrialization, when he became Leader of Government Business in 1951:

> it was when they [colonial government] had gone that we were faced with the stark realities ... there were slums and squalor in our towns ... there was much ignorance and few skills ... of industry we had none ... we made not a pin, not a handkerchief, not a match (Nkrumah, 1963: xiii).

This was the common result of the colonial predatory state and was to be an important influence on the development policies of the post-independence indigenous state.

The distinguishing features of the different phases of government policy were also important for the future development of the country. They point to some explanations of how colonial imperialism really worked and why the programmes of the pre-1929 period were not sustained and failed to generate long-term economic growth. From the indigenous point of view, Guggisberg, and Clifford before him who pioneered the early development of the country, were the most respected and among the best contributors to the country's economic progress. The ending of the Guggisberg programme, his removal from office, and the policies of economic contraction that followed, point clearly to how colonial imperialism was designed to work. Economic management was to be concentrated and carefully undertaken so that the colonies did not become a financial burden;[33] no development programmes were to be undertaken which committed the colonial governments to management other than simple administration;[34] a colony's ability to develop must be based not only on its own ability to save but on the lucky accident of having a governor who could defy colonial policy and accelerate development;[35] as much savings as possible should be accumulated and invested in Britain; and policies in all the above respects need not take into consideration the real trends in the macroeconomic conditions of the colonial state.[36] Questions continued to be raised up to the 1940s whether the development programmes in the years after the First World War were wise. In 1943 an influential Colonial Office memorandum expressed the view that:

> the period immediately after the last war saw a great deal of uncoordinated and badly conceived development in the colonial empire. Large sums of money were borrowed at high rates of interest to construct public works of various kinds - railways, harbours, etc. – some of which

have been a burden to the territories which constructed them ever since. It is obvious that this must not occur again.[37]

Thus we have a situation in which the early development policies, particularly those of Guggisberg, satisfied the colonial test on some points but failed on many others. From the point of view of the colonial state, it was successful in expanding export production of minerals and cocoa, and it made unsuccessful attempts to produce other crops. But the Guggisberg policy failed, from the point of view of the colonial state, because it created colonial debts rather than accumulating reserves in Britain.[38] It failed also because it levied high taxes on the merchant collaborators of the colonial predatory state, and promoted indigenous welfare by creating an excessive social infrastructure such as hospitals, schools, water supplies, etc., pushing government employment towards the more socially optimal level. The Guggisberg development strategy therefore reduced the gains of the colonial state in a period when there were no contestants to challenge the power of the colonial government.

The fact that the Guggisberg programme was allowed to continue briefly after his departure, and that its benefits contributed significantly to the accumulation of external reserves after the depression, may thus point to a significant aspect of the colonial predatory state. Was Guggisberg removed so that the advantages of his programme could be better concentrated to imperial advantage by governors more dedicated to the colonial cause? Guggisberg's friendly relation with the people, and his greater cultural identification with the country (he always referred to the Gold Coast as *our country* in all his official addresses, which no other governor did), does suggest that if benefits had accrued from his development programme a substantial part would have been earmarked for improvements in welfare in a manner more characteristic of an indigenous than a colonial state. His Farewell Message to the people of the Gold Coast, delivered from the first vessel to dock in the newly completed Takoradi Harbour, testifies to his personal commitment to the country: 'The fruits of your labours so plainly to be seen on every side, must give a pleasant feeling of satisfaction at work well done.'[39]

The value of the pre-1929 development effort to the colonial state and to the Gold Coast indigenous state was substantial, but it had little potential for generating long-term economic growth in the context of the colonial predatory state. The worldwide depression and major falls in commodity prices provided a plausible excuse for a revision of policy from development to consolidation.[40] The depression also provided arguments against aggressive approaches to development.[41] The contrast between Guggisberg's relations with the people and those of the administrations which followed did not help in educating the farmers about the effects of the depression. The post-Guggisberg passivity increased the farmers' hatred of the colonial government, as was demonstrated by the rejection, in 1930, of the cess for cocoa producer price stabilization, aimed at 'improving the quality and marketing of cocoa.'[42] The colonial government needed no encouragement to remain indifferent to the problems of the cocoa farmer.[43] In a series of confrontations, hatred of the government increased. A failed attempt by Governor Slater to introduce direct income taxes led to acrimonious exchanges in the Legislative Council in which African members demanded full representative government and 'the control of our finances for the people of this country.'[44]

The colonial government remained indifferent to economic development and to the welfare of the citizens of the country in the period of decolonization, as the notes of Sydney Caine and Arthur Lewis testify. To quote Caine:

> quite simply, the trouble I see is that not enough schemes are produced in the first place. There is not enough thinking, above all not enough original and coherent thinking about the possibilities of development. Machinery for that kind of thinking for the colonies is virtually non-existent.[45]

It was left to the indigenous government in the post-independence state to conceive and structure a development strategy with the large inherited external reserves, against the background of the skewed economy and in the context of its own ambitions.

Conclusions

Does the analysis so far offer insights into any primary weaknesses in the economy of the Gold Coast on the eve of independence, and how were they likely to be repaired or further weakened by an indigenous state? Any rudimentary peasant economy is weak by comparison with an advanced modern economy. But such underdeveloped states have for centuries endured many adverse economic circumstances and natural calamities without permanent damage to their economic and organizational structures. The small states within the present boundaries of Ghana survived for centuries before colonization in this way. Their efficiency in production of goods traded with North Africa (gold) and later with Europe (gold and palm oil), the drawn-out Asante Wars with the British, and the successful adoption of cocoa at the end of the wars, all point to socio-economic and political structures and organizations that had evolved and matured over long periods. The fact that the country was economically underdeveloped in the 'modern' sense could not *per se* disqualify it from becoming developed.

The concept of a primary weakness must therefore be relative to other factors. The factors constraining development which the literature has surveyed, such as capital, technology, labour and land, have been assumed here as relevant to Ghana's case at independence. Too much importance cannot, however, be attached to them. In fact, what marked Ghana out at independence from other African countries was its wealth in discovered and exploited natural resources, human resources and external reserves. The search for a primary weakness, if there was one, must therefore be made with less orthodox tools. This is where the models of the economic approach to the political process are useful.

A significant conclusion from the analysis of the activities of the colonial predatory state was the creation of a dual society with a prosperous export sector superimposed on an impoverished peasant economy. One danger for the Ghana economy at independence was that the existence of the impoverished and underdeveloped peasant economy was masked by the wealth of the export sector and would be ignored, thereby worsening the already skewed economic structure. Another danger was that the incoming indigenous state would be tempted into thinking that the financial resources at its disposal could be employed to modernize agriculture quickly and to replace the peasant economy with large-scale modern systems. The viability of such an approach was doubtful. A further danger was that relative financial wealth would tempt the new state to undertake development ventures too ambitious for both the underdeveloped peasant sector and the export sector to bear. This could set development back several decades. Given the primary weakness, a critical factor in the success or failure of the Ghana economy in the post-independence period would inevitably be the way in which the political process coped with the demands of economic development.

The contemporary literature (see Chapter 1) frequently mentions the 'potential' of the Ghana economy at independence, which later governments squandered – referring no doubt to the natural, human and external resources and the goodwill that Ghana inherited. These descriptions would, however, need to take full note of weaknesses in the economy and the dangers inherent in the impending political process, in order to determine the real potential that existed and the proper tools for converting it into lasting economic growth.

Notes

1. Despatch from Governor Guggisberg to the Secretary of State, August 1922.
2. Bauer (1981, 1984) would prefer such government non-intervention in this period to the 'activity' in the later period which resulted in the creation of marketing boards, etc. He states that 'the centralization of decision-making in the Colonial Office and in Secretariats, and the diminution of the powers of governors and district officers, promoted the diffusion of controls in the late colonial period. Restrictive licensing spread from the East African to the West African colonies, while export monopolies spread from West to East Africa.... Numerous honours, however, flowed from the establishment and operation of Marketing Boards whose activities impoverished the farmers and promoted tension and corruption' (Bauer, 1984: 94–5).
3. Kesse (1985) gives the following gold production data:

Period	Fine ounces	% of world total
1493–1600	8,153,426	35.5
1601–1700	6,430,146	22.8
1701–1800	5,465,626	8.9
1801–1900	2,543,294	9.7
1901–1934	7,837,087	1.1

4. Lewis (1944b) describes how the Colonial Office, through various chartered companies, had supported British merchant traders. The Royal Niger Company and the United Africa Company are listed among companies that received state patronage. It is the gold mining companies in West Africa that are said to have developed 'outside the sphere of the trading companies'. Mimeo, 1944, Colonial Office file CO852/482/2, pp. 5–6.
5. See also Governor Slater's Address to the Legislative Council, 17 February 1930, p. 88.
6. Legislative Assembly Debates 1931–2, pp. 241–2. Nana Ofori-Atta I was referring to Guggisberg's last statement in 1927 when he said 'I make one claim, and that is, the Government of 1919–1927 has been a Government of Cooperation, as far as any government can justifiably be of that nature'.
7. He refers to the colonial government developing a communications network which was, however, more for the benefit of imperial trade than for the welfare of the natives.
8. This supports the 'vent for surplus' argument of export expansion without reduction in peasant production of food for domestic consumption (Myint, 1958).
9. For example, on sisal Governor Slater stated in his Address to the Legislative Council on 17 February 1930, p. 22: 'The receipts of this plantation [sisal] fall short of the costs of maintenance...and it would need further extension of the plantation to make this venture a profitable one. The chiefs who own the surrounding land are, however, resolutely opposed to any further concessions. In the circumstances, I have decided to close the plantation and the factory forthwith.' Evidence of other attempts are in various issues of the *Bulletin of the Imperial Institute*, London, 1924 and 1925. Also on Colonial office file CO99/53.
10. Governor Slater stated in his Address on 17 February 1930 that: 'except in the most remote parts of Northern and Western Ashanti, almost every village is connected by its own motor road with the main trunk roads, and head carriage is now a rare sight. The village feeder roads have been constructed by the chiefs and people on their own initiative and at their own expense'.
11. Governor Slater, shortly after taking office, declared that the difficult financial position of the country imposed a check on the rate of expansion and called for 'consolidation and stabilization of government services for the time being'. Full text of his statement on Colonial Office file CO98/57.
12. A comprehensive memorandum by chiefs to the British Government on this subject is on Colonial Office file CO98/63 (already referred to in note 54, Chapter 2).
13. The classic accounts are by Hill (1956 and 1963).
14. Cocoa does not require maximum labour for weeding once it is established (after ten years). Maximum price of labour is required for the main crop harvesting which is October to January. Most food crops, particularly cereals, require maximum labour for planting, weeding and harvesting during the period March to July.
15. Colonial Office file CO98/63 documents some interventions by the traditional rulers on behalf of farmers.
16. The Law of 1899 was followed by the Lands Ordinance of 1915 which authorized the transfer to private individuals of land leased by the state. Bates argues that economic rent accrued both from the cheap transfer price and from the future sale of land freely acquired (Bates, 1983: 64–5).
17. Cmd. 5845, HMSO, 1938.
18. The farmers, according to Polly Hill, held as rigid a view as many old-fashioned communities or capitalists about the wastefulness of consumption expenditures. See testing of this hypothesis in Ingham, 1973.

19. *Report of the Committee on Agricultural Indebtedness* (Quaidoo Report), 1957, p. 22, para. 4.3.
20. *Ibid.*: 24, para. 5.1.1.2.
21. *Ibid.*: 26, para. 5.1.3.3, p. 25, para. 5.1.2.2.
22. Guggisberg (1924: 60) cites the example of the people of Kwahu collecting £5000 from their own resources and engaging an Italian contractor in 1923 to 'blast and link a motor road up the hitherto unconquered Kwahu scarp'.
23. Ormsby-Gore (1926) among others states that 'cocoa and cocoa alone made the railway pay its way'.
24. Guggisberg's reply, perhaps naively, was to invite British manufacturers to come and view the graveyard of unsuitable British trucks (Guggisberg, 1924: 61, para. 119).
25. There is considerable literature on this subject. See particularly Church (1936: 146), Dickson, (1969: 233), Kay and Hymer (1972: 194) and Bates (1983: 68).
26. Colonial Office file CO98/76.
27. Bateman (1971) has argued that there is a limit to the investment a farmer would be prepared to make in cocoa, given an increase in the producer price. This is treated in detail in Chapter 7.
28. *The Times* (London), 4 May 1949 reported from a correspondent in Kumase, the Asante capital: 'Londoners will be envious to know that, although the total population is only 70,000, there are 500 taxis licensed for hire ... the country is flooded with gramophones, bicycles and motor cars.... The whole Ashanti has gone education mad and vast sums are being subscribed in the villages for building schools.'
29. This was an extension of the British exchange control regime during the war to the scheduled territories (the Sterling Area).
30. That the promotion of local food production was possible is illustrated by the work of the West African War Council which promoted the production and storage of food for British, American and indigenous military personnel. The possibilities for the promotion and modernization of production, transportation and marketing of food crops by the Colonial government were discussed in Chapter II. See also Colonial Office files CO554/132/33712/1 and CO852/480/11.
31. Intercepted letter from the London *Daily Mail* West African Correspondent, Graham Standord, 11 October 1943, quotes a British District Officer: 'For years, we have drained West Africa of her wealth without putting anything back. We have allowed vested interests to do much as they liked.' Standord then goes on: 'I believe the fault lies back at home with those Members of Parliament who have no knowledge of the colonies, make the wildest statements in the House of Commons, and fundamentally the elector who for so long has remained in abysmal and apparently comfortable ignorance of what happens in our possessions overseas. Maybe he does not bother because he believes that everything British is bound to be the best. If that is so, I should like to take him to Freetown [or Accra or Lagos] and then fly on down to some wilder outposts of French Ivory Coast. Freetown makes the neat well designed outposts seem like health resorts and then can you wonder that at first anger and then frustration grows in the minds of men [British soldiers] who can see for themselves how apathy at home is rotting our colonial system.' Colonial Office file CO554/133/33738.
32. Colonial Office file CO554/132/33718/3.
33. Exchange of correspondence between G.L.M. Clauson and J.M. Keynes, Colonial Office file CO852/503/6, see further note 38.
34. Note to this effect by Clauson on file CO967/13.
35. Sydney Caine's statement that it is a lucky accident if a colony had a Governor capable of conceiving and carrying out development has already been referred to in this context. (CO852/588/2).
36. Such was the trend observed in the period 1929–42 when domestic conditions did not correspond to the contractionary policies (Ingham, 1987).
37. In the same Colonial Office memorandum, dated 31 March 1943, Clauson also states that 'After the last war [1914–1918], economic forces were broadly left unchecked, and primary producers in the period immediately after the war reaped a rich harvest owing to the high prices which they received for their goods. The consequences, so far as most colonial producers were concerned, were almost wholly evil. They received more money than they knew what to do with ... exaggerated ideas of the value of their products and numerous expensive tastes were acquired.' CO967/13.
38. Keynes, in his letter from the Treasury to the Colonial Office (2 March 1942), stated: 'The balance of payments of the rest of the Empire, including the Protectorates and Mandates ... was adverse by 25.2 Million in 1938 and adverse by 7.4 Million on the average of the years 1923–1929. This indeed is what one would expect, namely that the colonial empire was on balance an importer of capital. It shows, however, that if this continues, *we cannot hope to gain much exchange from the colonies* except in so far as U.S.A. take over the task of providing them with their capital requirements.' Agreeing with Keynes 'general thesis', Clauson was at pains, in his reply, to state '*I do not think the colonial empire is going to be a drain on the United Kingdom* except to the extent that the colonial governments want some money for ordinary capital works and under the Colonial Development and Welfare Act.' [emphasis added] Keynes/Clauson correspondence, CO852/503/6.

39. *Gold Coast Gazette,* 25 April 1927. Guggisberg was transferred to British Guiana, but died within two years of leaving the Gold Coast. The stone on his grave, at a cemetery near Brighton, has the inscription: 'From the People of the Gold Coast and Ashanti'. It is believed that a visiting delegation from the Gold Coast was disappointed that his grave was not marked and ordered the stone. It is relevant to note that Guggisberg was born a Canadian, of Russian-Jewish ancestry.
40. Governor Slater on Colonial Office file CO98/57.
41. Clauson on Colonial Office file CO967/13, to the effect that 'works were designed in the period of boom, and under the influence of boom prices, but did not come into existence until the slump had set in.'
42. See *Memorandum on the Creation of a Fund for Improving the Quality and Marketing of Cocoa,* Government Printer, Accra, 1930.
43. As illustrated in Governor Slater's statement on the dispute between buying companies and the Federation of Farmers. Slater states: 'in the controversy as to what is, and what is not, a fair price for the cocoa farmer to receive ... the government cannot take part.' Legislative Council Debates, 1930–1, pp. 380–4.
44. A full account of the debate is in *Legislative Council Debates,* 1931–2, pp. 380–5.
45. Strongly worded by Sydney Caine in his memorandum on Colonial Office file CO852/ 588/2.

5 Development in the Post-War Indigenous State

> An individual who based his personal expenditure programme on his needs, without regard to his resources, would soon be written off by his fellow men as irresponsible.
> W. Arthur Lewis (1959: 5)

At the end of the preceding chapter, the Ghana economy on the eve of decolonization was shown to have a weak and fragile structure. It was necessary that initial development should be focused on food agriculture. It was also important that the primary export sectors should not be deprived of incentives to produce at their optimum, in order to contribute capital for development. In this context, the nature of the political economy, particularly the ambitions of, and demands on, the incoming indigenous state, was a critical factor in the success or failure of the initial economic development.

This chapter focuses on the characteristics of that political economy by defining the development model of the crucial transitional state under Nkrumah and specifying the factors determining its conception and influencing its implementation. We also review its financing, its successes and its failures. Finally, we discuss its legacy for governance and for development in the period after 1960.

The period of the immediate post-independence indigenous state is 1951–60. The Kwame Nkrumah era began in 1951. The Convention Peoples Party (CPP) had an executive majority in the transitional government, and Nkrumah was Leader of Government Business and later Prime Minister in the period up to independence in 1957.[1] The Nkrumah period lasted until February 1966, but the period up to 1960 was that before the Republican Constitution.

The Nkrumah State

Nkrumah's development philosophy belonged to the mainstream 'Big Push' ideas of the period. Nkrumah (1963: 167) defined his idea as follows:

> One thing is certain, unless we plan to lift Africa up out of her poverty, she will remain poor. For there is a vicious circle which keeps the poor in their rut of impoverishment, unless *an energetic effort is made to interrupt the circular causation of poverty*. Once this has been done, and the essential industrial machine has been set in motion, there is a snowballing effect which increases the momentum of change. [Emphasis added.]

The ultimate goal, logically, is industrialization, but the development model conforming to this philosophy must recognize that development is constrained by an underdeveloped peasant system, in the context of the Lewis thesis (1953);[2] that a certain rate of investment can permit a transition from the peasant state to a modern agricultural and industrial state;[3] and that such a transition is possible within the limits of existing and borrowed resources. In particular, it must be assumed that the state will be able to squeeze domestic resources from the primary sectors during the long period of modernization, and that conflicts in the political economy will not hinder the process of initial development. The analysis that follows examines these factors.

A number of economic, social and political pressures in this period dictated a development strategy that was possibly contrary to that recommended by Seers and Ross, and also by Lewis (see Chapter 2). Conflicts within the state, and between the state and the primary sectors, were likely to occur. The factors responsible may be placed in three categories: those concomitant with the rise to power of Nkrumah; the political pressure to accelerate development; and the wider Pan-African objectives of the leadership.

It can be argued that Nkrumah's rise to power, defeating the more conservative nationalists, implied a development direction that would bring fundamental economic and social change, and a sharper break with macroeconomic management in the past than would otherwise have been the case. Nkrumah was a leader in the West African National Secretariat, a radical political group then in London.[4] It is argued that he was reluctant to accept the invitation from the nationalists in the Gold Coast, in 1947, to become the General Secretary of the United Gold Coast Convention (UGCC), stating that

> it was quite useless to associate myself with a movement backed almost entirely by reactionaries, middle-class lawyers and merchants, for my revolutionary background and ideas would make it impossible to work with them. [5]

He gave as his reason for eventually accepting the invitation that

> the time had come to come to grips with imperialism on the soil of Africa, and by working for the UGCC I would at least be actively engaged in the national liberation struggle to end colonial rule. I knew, however, that it might not be long before the basic differences between our long term objectives might make it impossible for me to continue to work for them (Nkrumah, 1973: 51).

He defined his long-term differences with the nationalists as their lack of contact with the masses, their lack of ideas in bringing about fundamental economic and social change, their belief in the capitalist approach to development, and their narrow view of African liberation.[6]

Nkrumah therefore saw his work in Ghana in a much wider perspective than the nationalists, his followers or the average Ghanaian did. He was inclined to conduct his development strategy with his sights on a socialist state with far more government involvement than might have been necessary at the time, considering the fact that indigenous large private capitalists had not yet emerged. Those that could, with some justification, be described as capitalists were the expatriate companies.[7] The colonial restraints in the 1950s prevented nationalization, however. Furthermore, the Lewis Report of 1953 had brought to the surface British sensitivities on nationalization which Nkrumah could not afford to inflame during the prelude to independence.[8] Nkrumah therefore selected the option of creating state enterprises to compete, with government support, against the existing large expatriate organizations, namely, the Ghana Commercial Bank, the Ghana National Trading Corporation,[9] the State Insurance Corporation and the State Gold Mining Corporation.[10] Thus Nkrumah did not nationalize any major enterprise in his socialist programme.[11] With state support, these companies grew rapidly.[12] However, in productive terms, they were less efficient than their rivals (Killick, 1978).

The other major aspect of Nkrumah's rise to power was the radical change in macro-economic policies. Ghana was the first to break away from the West African Currency Board in 1958 in order to attain maximum monetary and fiscal sovereignty. It was also, in 1961, the first to introduce currency inconvertibility, exchange restrictions and import quotas. These policy changes removed the direct relationship between growth of demand and growth of export production. The alternative approach was to use exchange rate policies that recognized changes in the nominal exchange rate; in this case, trade policies would promote development within the constraints of domestic capability and the international trading system. Rimmer, writing on this period, regarded the shift in policy as a transition from 'development without loss of innocence' to development with sin (Rimmer, 1966: 19). For Nkrumah, development in the liberal environment of 'innocence' would not offer enough scope for self-determination.

Nkrumah's ideological inclinations and commitments were transmitted into development programmes not necessarily because there was an established economic need for them, but because they satisfied a political ambition. They also had a sense of urgency and impatience about them that was difficult to justify on economic grounds. For example, the Second Development Plan was an annual plan three times the size of the First Plan and the Consolidated Plan combined. It contradicted the experience gained in the earlier plans. An official review of the First Development Plan had stated that there was 'reason to believe that an annual programme of £15 million is the most and, if the effort has to be sustained over a long period, may well be more than the present administrative machinery can deal with'.[13] No evidence has been found of staff strengthening or capacity building to ensure that the larger amount would be managed efficiently.

Politics and the Pace of Development

Nkrumah had to mobilize the support of the grassroots constituents in order to win leadership from the nationalists. In so doing, he alienated a large number of people who lost their political influence to the so-called 'verandah boys'.[14] Nkrumah's urban followers were not so independent of the state as the peasant farmers. His greatest problem was satisfying their demands for an increased manifestation of development, for larger expenditures on less productive industries, and for more publicly financed jobs.

The best tools for urban political mobilization were those that equated colonialism with poverty and underdevelopment, under such slogans as 'Paradise in one decade after independence', and 'Seek ye first the Political Kingdom and everything else will be added unto you'. The immediate post-independence state therefore came under intense pressure to deliver more results of development than were necessary or feasible. These results were not only increases in personal incomes; also important were social and community services such as schools, dispensaries, water supplies and community centres, which did improve public welfare, particularly in the urban areas. These increased government expenditures, but the urban beneficiaries did not contribute adequately to production in the immediate term. Indeed, in some cases more schools reduced youth labour on the farms and thus total production. The educated also tended to drift into the towns.

Development also meant more government jobs. 'Jobs for the boys' were created in existing state enterprises like the Cocoa Marketing Board (CMB) and in new public enterprises such as the Industrial Development Corporation (IDC). Observing such employment in the IDC in 1958, Arthur Lewis wrote:

> The IDC has greatly suffered from outside interference, in the shape of Members of Parliament and other influential persons expecting staff appointments to be made irrespective of merit, redundant staff to be kept on the payroll, disciplinary measures to be relaxed in favour of constituents, businesses to be purchased at inflated prices, loans to be made irrespective of security, etc. [15]

In discussing the difficulties that Ghana faced in this period, some researchers have warned that unbiased analysis is 'hindered if the question is posed in terms of "capitalist" or "socialist" paths of development' (Teal, 1984). One argument is that an alternative nationalist leader could have found himself under the same pressures for development. Another is that there are fundamental problems of growth that are common to both approaches. The validity of these arguments is recognized. It should, however, be emphasized that, with the benefit of hindsight, the nature of the transition in macroeconomic management at independence has been a factor in determining the pace and viability of economic development. In Ghana the radical and abrupt change leading to restrictive policies, on whatever ideological pretext, considerably reduced the range of policy options available for economic management (see Chapter 6).

Pan-African Objectives

Nkrumah is mainly remembered today for his Pan-African initiatives and his pioneering work in African liberation. It is best so because that was his real political ambition. In concluding his autobiography, he wrote (1975: 240):

> I have never regarded the struggle for the Independence of the Gold Coast as an isolated objective but always as a part of a general historical pattern.... Our task is not done and our safety is not assured until the last vestiges of colonialism have been swept from Africa.

This ambition was noble and appropriate. It was, however, not without its direct and indirect costs to Ghana's economic development. The direct costs were the expenditures actually made in promoting liberation movements in most of Black Africa, particularly to foster African unity and approaches to a more radical break with the past. Other costs were incurred in supporting former French colonies that lost French financial support at independence and in UN peace-keeping operations in the civil war in the Congo (later Zaire). For example, Ghana loaned £10m to Guinea and Mali at independence. The indirect costs were those of urban development deliberately designed to impress other African states and to encourage them to fight for independence. For instance, in defence of maintaining an unviable national airline, Nkrumah wrote (1963: 113): 'we certainly experience a glow of pride in seeing our flag flying on planes and ships travelling to other countries'.

Much of the African liberation expenditure was made through a special consolidated account for which expenditure records are not available. There are therefore no reliable estimates for the period of the 1950s.[16] They would, however, be contained in the figures for defence and foreign affairs in Table 5.2, col. 7 and in central administration expenditures. The indirect costs cannot be estimated as they also come under the category of factors creating pressure for development that was not needed or was not productive. A familiar admonition to the population by Nkrumah was that 'every African who visited Ghana in the 1950s should be made to see the fruits of independence', in visible manifestations of development.[17]

Britain and the Transition

Britain was able only to a limited extent to play a mitigating role in the period of transition. The work undertaken by Seers and Ross was designed to encourage less than radical change in macroeconomic policy in this period. Their report, particularly after the terms of reference had been widened, was to educate the indigenous administration before it attempted to implement its full intentions. The widened terms of reference included discussions and suggestions on the mechanics of inflation in a poor agricultural economy, the role of capital accumulation in development, foreign investment in a developing economy, the financing of development, and the selection of priority areas for development policy (Ingham, 1987).

As noted in Chapter 4, Seers and Ross concentrated on the mechanics of inflation. They reported that the machinery of ordinary income taxation was not efficient and could not be relied upon for development resource mobilization; that for development reasons public expenditures could not be cut; and for inflationary reasons a ceiling should be placed on cocoa producer prices. Combined, these ideas provided intellectual justification for higher cocoa export taxes for development. For Nkrumah 'it became clear that further steps were necessary to control the price paid to the farmers otherwise we would shortly be faced with inflation' (1957: 179). He observed, quite reasonably given supply-side constraints in terms of the availability of imports and inelasticities in the supply of domestic goods, that if the international price of cocoa continued to increase, and farmers were paid higher prices proportionate to the increases, this would lead to domestic inflation and wage increases detrimental to the development strategy.

British colonial policy in this period also offered some indirect encouragement to the development strategies of the 1950s. From adverse experience elsewhere in Africa, there was strong opposition to foreign interest in agriculture on a large scale. 'Plantation development was at variance with land policy ... and would be resisted by Africans.'[18] This left indigenous agricultural technology to underpin modernization. Also a major factor in the strategies of the 1950s was the existence of the CMB. In the literature there has been extensive discussion of the Board's advantages and disadvantages. The existence of the cocoa price stabilization fund and a state-controlled marketing system provided the vehicles for cocoa taxation (Bauer, 1954, 1971; Helleiner, 1964; Killick, 1965).

The greatest caution, surprisingly perhaps, came from Arthur Lewis in his work on the review of the First and Second Development Plans, and in his general role as a UN Economic Adviser to Nkrumah in the period 1957–60. Caution was also the hallmark of his 1953 Report (Lewis, 1953). He was concerned that expenditures on social and economic infrastructure should not outpace the responses in productivity. This was a difficult task considering the generally low state of economic development. The greatest problem was to persuade the new indigenous government that results should be expected only in the long term. To ensure some productivity, his recommendation was that the state should involve itself less with direct investment and instead promote policies that would stimulate private investment in the production of commodities (Lewis, 1953: 9, para. 104):

> Most governments ... need all the money they can raise, whether by loans or by taxes, for the urgent purpose of expanding the public services.... *Even the Gold Coast Government, which seems rich to its citizens, is really very poor....* There is no doubt in the writer's mind that the Gold Coast Government can do more for development by spending its money on expanding the public services ... and on quadrupling that part of its agricultural services which relate to food production for the local market, than it can do by operating factories. *If the Government is determined to exclude private foreign capital, it would be better to postpone industrialization rather than divert money to it from more urgent purposes.* [Emphasis added.]

Lewis also attempted to ensure that, in the allocation of development funds in the economic sectors, there was an equal share between agriculture and industry: 'In writing about the Gold Coast, I laid emphasis on the need for an agricultural policy that would have equal priority with import substitution' (Lewis, 1984: 122). The total expenditures on agriculture in the First Development Plan (1951–7) and the Consolidation Plan (1957–9) were £7.047m (5.2%) compared with £7.654m (5.6%) on industry. Total expenditures for the 1951–9 period were £136.048m. For the Second Development Plan, in whose preparation Lewis assisted, the expenditures on agriculture and industry out of the total plan nearly doubled to become £24.668m (9.9%) and £25.331m (10.1%) respectively.[19] Lewis's primary objective, that these expenditures should stimulate private investment and greater productivity, did not materialize, however. The policy of the government was to develop through state initiatives in both agriculture and industry,[20] largely due to its socialist orientation.

Priorities of the Indigenous State

Given its declared intentions, the government's development strategy in the 1950s was aggressive. This is well illustrated by the budgetary expansion that took place. In 1951, government revenues doubled from the 1950 level; by 1955 they had trebled in real terms, while expenditures were four times the 1950 levels in real terms. These trends were a major departure from the colonial tradition and reflected a major change in macroeconomic policy (see Tables 5.1 and 5.5).

All government services benefited from the increases. Of particular interest to this study are the increases in development spending, which throughout the post-Guggisberg period and until the mid-1940s had been completely neglected. The new emphasis is shown in Table 5.1, col. 5, with sub-divisions in cols 6, 7, 8 and 9. The evidence in Table 5.2 points to defence, foreign affairs, justice and police as the government's greater priorities. Next were the organs of the state at the regional level and at the centre. Financial administration, whose endowment was somewhat smaller, nevertheless was on average nearly forty times its size in the old colonial administration.

The government's priorities in economic administration are illustrated in Table 5.4. There were significant increases over the old era. Agriculture, significantly, is given high priority in terms of amounts spent. Manufacturing and commerce, which previously were not regarded as areas of government financial involvement, benefited from large government expenditures, and direct participation from 1951. In typical Guggisberg tradition, harbours, transport and communications received priority treatment in very large amounts. The mines received greater attention than in colonial times, though expenditures on this sector were significantly less than on the other economic sectors.

Social construction, roads and power were of the greatest importance in social services (Table 5.3). Following this was education, and then health. General social services, which had been ignored by the colonial government, became an important area of interest to the indigenous government.

The larger expenditures in all departments of government do not, of course, imply that the objectives of such spending were justifiable or that the results benefited development. Lewis, observing these expenditures in 1959, put it succinctly (1959: 4): 'policy is more important than expenditure'. This analysis draws a sharp contrast between colonial policy and the early post-independence policy. It confirms that the leadership of Ghana in this period shared the belief in 'the efficacy of a big investment push' which was then current.[21] It aimed at a fundamental structural change before productive economic modernization was undertaken.

The difference between the Guggisberg Development Plan of the 1920s and the Nkrumah strategies of the 1950s is therefore clear. Guggisberg's programme was designed for a specifically identified need. That of Nkrumah was for general long-term modernization for unspecified needs. It was dictated by the desire of a nationalist leader seeking rapid general economic advancement for his country. The size of expenditures could not, however, be maintained without significant increases in productivity.

Table 5.7 shows that the 1951–7 Development Plan kept expenditures on agriculture at previous levels, while the major emphasis was on the modernization of the social and economic infrastructure. The two plans were regarded as the first phase of economic and social modernization only, and were undertaken 'without recourse to overseas borrowing'.[22]

Table 5.1 Government Expenditures with Functional Breakdown of Development, 1951–60 (With comparable data for period 1900–50 – £'000 constant 1920 prices)

Year	Total	Ordinary	Extra-Ordinary	Develop-ment	General Services	Community Services	Social Services	Economic Services
1	2	3	4	5	6	7	8	9
1900	3532	986	1029	1518	0	0	0	1518
1905	1861	1692	169	0	0	0	0	0
1910	2998	1879	255	863	0	201	0	663
1915	3746	2545	790	411	0	64	0	344
1920	3190	1845	571	774	0	21	0	753
1925	3994	2311	348	1335	0	608	0	727
1930	2562	1992	553	18	0	0	0	18
1935	2030	1892	138	0	0	0	0	0
1940	2250	2115	135	0	0	0	0	0
1945	2790	2072	489	230	24	70	119	25
1950	7100	4901	1313	886	12	367	274	233
1951	8585	5250	936	2398	286	943	800	369
1952	14279	8276	834	5168	518	1659	1749	1243
1953	17869	10454	1624	5791	274	1638	1592	2285
1954	18312	10716	581	7015	461	3644	1652	1258
1955	28074	15375	1266	11433	1244	5114	1888	3188
1956	21978	13601	771	7606	1028	3893	1110	1575
1957	21276	13963	0	7313	1028	2881	1137	2266
1958	28133	17131	0	11002	1507	3492	1245	4729
1959	30201	20280	0	9921	2665	2828	1469	2216
1960	36346	22323	0	14022	3299	3350	2807	4566

Source: Kay and Hymer (1972), Table 29

Table 5.2 Government Priorities in General Service Administration, 1900–60 (£'000 constant 1920 prices)

Year	Organs of state		Financial admini-stration	Tax admini-stration	General economic regulation	Defence & foreign affairs	Justice & police	Other	Total
	central	regional							
1	2	3	4	5	6	7	8	9	10
1900	39	137	35	125	0	606	153	39	1138
1910	45	322	48	175	0	258	210	115	1176
1920	40	130	41	85	0	117	193	112	716
1930	30	93	27	66	0	69	201	202	689
1940	26	83	31	117	0	358	183	207	1005
1950	120	833	430	138	4	413	656	790	3384
1955	162	1786	608	180	10	931	1192	1546	6414
1956	93	1814	890	121	24	1278	868	1155	6223
1957	122	1722	506	138	23	1351	1215	742	6190
1958	280	1690	1192	157	38	1298	1580	895	7130
1959	381	1110	677	171	13	2279	1297	1506	7434
1960	382	2133	589	188	20	4119	1532	1233	10196

Data for 1900 to 1955 are averages for five subsequent years including year in question
Source: Kay and Hymer (1972), Table 26b

Table 5.3 Government Priorities in Community and Social Services, 1900–60 (indicated by expenditures in £'000 constant 1920 prices)

Year	Construction, roads, power	Scientific services	Education	Health	General social	Total
1	2	3	4	5	6	8
1900	231	74	27	110	4	446
1910	1064	38	70	258	0	1430
1920	848	53	95	230	0	1226
1925	1185	65	175	258	0	1683
1930	392	42	180	225	0	839
1940	505	29	194	244	5	978
1950	3203	102	2207	879	468	6858
1955	6212	244	4147	1612	683	12898
1956	5396	127	2784	1235	825	10367
1957	3342	136	3379	1241	573	8671
1958	5074	190	3478	1431	717	10891
1959	6305	278	4448	1555	260	12846
1960	7139	396	5261	1971	557	15325

Data for the years 1900 to 1950 are annual averages for the five years following those years inclusive of the years
Source: Kay and Hymer (1972), Table 26c

Table 5.4 Government Priorities in the Provision of Economic Services, 1900–60 (indicated by expenditures in the economic sectors – £'000 constant 1920 prices)

Years	Agriculture	Mines	Manufact. and commerce	Railways	Harbours	Transport and communication	Other economic services	Total
1	2	3	4	5	6	7	8	9
1900	12	0	0	1412	0	254	0	1678
1910	54	10	0	226	175	134	0	599
1920	78	13	0	915	249	156	0	1411
1930	9	8	0	18	2	133	0	252
1940	158	9	0	2	6	163	0	338 .
1950	1569	35	131	554	146	632	4	3070
1955	3150	56	655	56	1720	1780	376	7793
1956	2562	52	338	71	773	1134	0	4930
1957	2463	51	608	0	1369	1097	0	5590
1958	2710	38	875	0	2916	1561	196	8295
1959	2842	43	583	0	1354	1927	1030	7779
1960	3970	62	983	223	1242	2722	770	9972

Data for the years 1900 to 1950 are annual averages for the five years following the respective years
Source: Kay and Hymer (1972), Table 26d

Table 5.5 Government Revenue by Principal Sources, 1951–60 (with comparable data for 1900–50 – £'000 constant 1920 prices)

Year	Total revenue	Import duties	Export duties	Other taxes	Income taxes	Profit taxes	Mineral duty
1	2	3	4	5	6	7	8
1900	1498	1099	0	0	0	0	0
1905	2106	1200	0	0	0	0	0
1910	3208	1946	0	0	0	0	0
1915	3912	2225	0	0	0	0	0
1920	3722	1711	571	0	0	0	0
1925	3665	1928	244	0	0	0	0
1930	1965	1050	218	9	0	0	0
1935	2762	1571	456	32	0	22	0
1940	2265	707	778	18	0	36	0
1945	3359	871	666	23	689	49	0
1950	8344	2889	1980	45	1696	1	84
1951	14459	3615	7271	48	1770	0	153
1952	15958	3545	6250	39	2516	0	587
1953	17988	4461	6897	291	2112	0	829
1954	32235	5178	19708	69	2391	0	483
1955	25640	7312	9876	123	2459	0	543
1956	18387	6078	4675	297	1939	0	747
1957	22257	5565	8444	742	2022	0	865
1958	24781	5983	9567	1111	2235	0	653
1959	24347	6552	7751	1049	1956	0	523
1960	27109	8405	5251	1029	2138	0	662

Revenues excluded are interests on investments, rents and royalties
Source: Kay and Hymer (1972), Table 24a

Table 5.6 The Burden of Cocoa in Total Export Taxation, 1900–60 (£'000 current prices)

Calendar year	Cocoa	Diamonds	Gold	Manganese	Wood and timber	Kola nuts	Palm kernels	Total	Cocoa ratio to total %
1	2	3	4	5	6	7	8	9	10
1900	0	0	0	0	0	0	0	0	
1905	0	0	0	0	0	0	0	0	
1910	0	0	0	0	0	0	0	0	
1915	159	0	0	0	0	0	0	159	100.00
1920	580	1	0	0	12	6	1	555	104.50
1925	262	20	0	0	14	0	0	296	88.51
1930	265	29	44	0	3	5	0	344	77.03
1935	320	35	265	0	3	10	0	633	50.55
1940	412	39	681	31	12	11	0	1188	34.68
1945	702	53	394	91	44	14	0	1298	54.08
1950	17084	271	0	204	101	15	0	17675	96.66
1955	28785	270	0	0	135	10	0	29200	98.58
1956	13951	390	0	0	188	11	0	14440	96.61
1957	12511	453	0	0	172	8	0	13144	95.18
1958	26812	450	0	0	213	17	0	27492	97.53
1959	23976	437	0	0	296	24	0	24733	96.94
1960	18077	380	0	0	478	32	0	18967	95.31

These data are for financial years, not calendar years as in other tables
Data for years 1900 to 1950 are averages of five subsequent years inclusive
There were no export duties before 1916. Gold export duty was replaced by production duty in October 1948. Duty on manganese was similarly replaced in 1952 (the Mineral Ordinance, 1952)
Source: Kay and Hymer (1972)

Table 5.7 Amounts Spent on Development, 1951–59 (£'000)

Ministry	First Development Plan 1951–7		Consolidation Plan 1951–7		Total development	
	Amount	%	Amount	%	Amount	%
Agriculture	4,820.5	5.2	2,226.5	5.2	7,047.0	5.2
Education	13,648.5	14.6	4,304.7	10.0	17,953.2	13.2
Health	4,644.9	5.0	680.6	1.6	5,325.5	3.9
Interior	2,189.4	2.3	675.9	1.0	2,865.3	2.1
Defence	2,689.5	2.9	408.6	1.0	3,098.1	2.3
Local government	3,032.5	3.2	1,861.5	4.4	4,894.0	3.6
Trade/industry	3,113.9	3.3	4,540.6	10.6	7,654.5	5.6
Transport	18,180.0	19.5	13,015.8	30.5	31,195.8	22.9
Works/housing	39,245.9	42.1	12,738.8	29.8	51,984.7	38.2
Other	1,746.0	1.9	2,284.3	5.3	4,030.3	3.0
Total	93,311.1	100.0	42,737.3	100.0	136,048.4	100.0

Source: Digest of Statistics, Office of the Government Statistician, Accra, various issues 1961

The analysis also indicates that a second objective of the Second Development Plan was to increase administrative capacity.[23]

It was inevitable that this should be so, for the development of the Gold Coast economy, whether in terms of agriculture or industry, could not have been possible without extension and consolidation of government services and public utilities to form a nationwide structure.

By 1959 some significant results had been achieved: power supplies had 'at best caught up with urban demand and were at the point of becoming freely available for industrial development.'[24] The educational system had been expanded, with free primary education and a national system of secondary and higher education. The quality of rural life had also been improved field units delivered medical care and water supplies were provided in many areas. Systems of local participation in government through District Councils and Regional Development Committees had also been established.

Table 5.8 Urban Indices of Market Prices of Locally Produced Foods, 1948–62

Years	Weighted index	Accra	Kumase	Sekondi Takoradi	Tarkwa	Tamale	Keta	Ho
1	2	3	4	5	6	7	8	9
Weights	100	42	25	14	8	5	4	2
1948	100	100	100	100	100	100	100	100
1949	145	116	158	183	145	159	136	132
1950	145	128	153	154	160	182	166	158
1951	186	200	157	178	165	239	217	201
1952	190	197	170	178	176	249	219	197
1953	186	185	182	181	172	244	177	199
1954	184	188	177	172	167	235	185	204
1955	199	207	184	170	174	230	198	228
1956	212	237	193	177	185	233	207	206
1957	213	218	207	189	200	270	207	257
1958	208	216	202	170	195	294	196	233
1959	219	227	221	173	197	298	200	241
1960	215	227	212	170	190	296	198	224
1961	241	244	253	205	204	320	235	294
1962	261	276	257	212	225	338	268	326

Source: Quarterly Digest of Statistics, Office of the Government Statistician, various issues

Despite the heavy expenditures incurred in these development programmes and the use of much labour on development work, there appeared to be an adequate supply of locally produced food (Table 5.8). Inflation grew at a moderate average annual rate of 4% throughout the period.[25] These results did not imply an increase in agricultural productivity. The moderate price trends in the towns of the forest belt (Kumase and Takoradi) indicate that production of local food increased in conformity with the development of new cocoa farms in this period (Hammond, 1962).

Modernization and Agricultural Development

Following Lewis's thesis (Lewis, 1953), it is on the viability of agricultural strategies that the development efforts of the 1950s should be judged. It has been argued in this book that the initial modernization of agriculture is best studied within the framework of fragmentation, which impedes it as a result of inadequate feeder road networks, storage and marketing facilities, and arbitrary producer pricing (see Chapter 2). It was correctly acknowledged in the development programmes of the 1950s that improved farming practice along modern lines was to be considered a long-term policy and that in the meanwhile 'improvements of output within the existing agricultural system' were to be government policy. It was proposed, however, that 'if the two problems of increased output of foodstuffs and diversification of production for export [were] to be solved, a second method of approach, apart from the assistance to existing agriculture ... [was] necessary.'[26]

The efforts to improve the existing peasant systems, however, concentrated on second-stage ideas, such as the introduction of better seeds and fertilizers, and not the first-stage removal of fragmentation. Thus the government, like most theoreticians and policy-makers unfamiliar with the problems of the rural economy, confused the two processes, and imagined that it was possible to skip the first phase and proceed to the stage of modernization without bringing the peasant and small-scale farmers to their full producing capacity. The attempts to improve the peasant system did not relate to the arbitrary pricing and sub-optimal peasant production typical of this period.

Efforts in large-scale mechanized agriculture were also largely unsuccessful. The government created the Agricultural Development Corporation (ADC) in 1951 and, within it, the Gonja Development Corporation (GDC) with a licence to introduce mechanized farming in the northern savanna belt of the country. The company was given an initial 30,000 acres of land and the following three objectives: to develop a system of mechanized farming suitable to the Northern Region and to carry out experiments in large-scale agriculture; to utilize tracts of empty savanna land to raise the output of foodstuffs in the region; to initiate schemes of settlement, by shifting populations from the over-populated Frafra district to the empty areas of the thinly populated Gonja district.

The attempt failed on all three counts. The particular types of heavy machinery brought in were not suitable for the hard soil conditions; they suffered frequent breakdowns and maintenance was poor. Skilled operators were lacking and the initial land preparation often took away the fertile top soils. Suitable managerial and supervisory staff were lacking. The farmers thought they had better traditional knowledge of farming methods than their supervisors. There was generally very limited knowledge regarding the new technology and the production programme (Dadson, 1973). By 1953 only 1,200 acres had been cultivated. It was generally considered that several years of experimentation and modification would be required before the most appropriate and applicable technology could be evolved.

The government persevered with a further attempt under the Second Development Plan in 1959. The new programme was nation-wide and covered a broader selection of crops than the Gonja experiment. For the small farmers, specific provisions were made for a wide range of farm and non-farm incentives. Farm incentives included improved seeds, mechanization at subsidized rates and the loan of breeding stock. Non-farm incentives included credit and capital grants as well as guaranteed prices for selected commodities. For plantation agriculture, rubber and oil palm were specified for the Western Region, and cattle and cereals for the North. Still using the vehicle of the ADC, the government was determined to pursue its efforts in large-scale agriculture. Introducing the Second Development Plan, Nkrumah stated:

> Although our emphasis is on helping the small Ghanaian farmer, we have also had no difficulty in deciding that it would be helpful to have some sort of large scale modern agrarian projects in this country, partly to demonstrate to the farmers the profitability of new crops and new methods and partly because this is the quickest way to develop some of the empty spaces in our large and under populated country.[27]

Three years later the ADC was dissolved after a series of failures and losses; the reasons given were similar to those which led to the failure of the Gonja Scheme. The failure of the second larger attempt would suggest that methods of introducing agricultural modernization, while fragmentation persisted, were bound to be difficult and slow. Given the primary weakness of the economy, general modernization, which was to begin appropriately enough with agriculture, was not to be achieved as quickly as the government had expected.

Financing Modernization

The financing of the Nkrumah development attempt in the initial post-independence phase created conflicts between the state and the primary producers. It also depleted the external reserves and brought about a major fiscal crisis.

The state and the cocoa farmers

Chapter 7 will show that the early 1950s saw the peak of cocoa producer incentives after several decades of neglect. In this period the country's external currency receipts, largely derived from the cocoa sector and, to a lesser extent, the mining sector, also reached a peak level (Annex I, Table A6. 3). Cocoa had become an important source of wealth for the state and for the farmers. It was to be expected therefore that interest groups in the industry, at the state and the producer levels, should protect their advantages.

Nkrumah (1957: 179), representing the new government's position, defined the role of cocoa in the country's future development as follows:

1. Cocoa was the mainstay of the economy accounting for 68% of exports in 1955. It belonged to the country and affected everyone, and so 'we had to think of the general public as well as the cocoa farmer'.
2. The reliance on the single crop of cocoa was disadvantageous to the long-term stability of the economy. A tax on cocoa was therefore justified, and 'the funds that accrued to the government would be used on expanding the economy of the country as a whole, with special reference to agriculture'.
3. The maintenance of a high producer price would not only deprive the government of direct revenue for development but would also indirectly, through inflation, raise the cost of development and thereby make it 'impossible to carry out [the Development Plan] owing to the greatly increased costs that had not been reckoned upon.'

For these reasons the government brought in the Cocoa Duty and Development Funds (Amendment) Bill of 1954. This legislation imposed a producer price ceiling of 72 shillings for a 60lb load (equivalent to 268.8 cedis per ton compared to the 1954 price of 637 cedis per ton) for five years.

It has already been noted that farmers' interests were linked to those of traditional rulers, most of whom were farmers themselves. In Asante, where cocoa growing was the major occupation, cocoa interests deeply penetrated local politics. The new government's policy therefore opened up old wounds. In particular, it aroused resentment in Asante against rule by Southern Gold Coast politicians. The Asantes publicly rejected not only the policy towards cocoa but also that of integrating Asante in a unitary state.[28] They demanded a federal constitution, citing the Cocoa Duty and Development Fund's Amendment as 'an eye opener', and federalism as 'the surest means of closing the avenues for dictatorship'.[29] Specifically on cocoa, Bafuor Osei Akoto, the chief spokesman of the Asantehene (King of Asante), spoke of the

> highhanded manner of pegging cocoa prices which affects Asantes more than any other group in the country ... an attitude of the present government to dismember and break up Asante (Andoh, 1984: 2–3).

The government in Accra responded to the Asante demand for higher cocoa prices and political autonomy by securing support from the traditional rulers in Brong and Ahafo, where the recent Asante investments in cocoa estates had been heaviest (Dunn and Robertson, 1973: 50). The government promised the Brongs independence from the Asantehene which had been lost in the Asante hegemony of the nineteenth century (Lewin, 1978: 168–74). They were joined by Ahafo.[30] The Brong chiefs (the Brong Kyempim Federation) thereafter publicly disagreed with the Asantehene in a declaration published on 18 September 1954:

> Certain groups of people in Asante have recently taken upon themselves to agitate against the government's Cocoa Duty Bill and the price of 72 shillings per load of 60lb ... these same people have been demanding a federal form of government which we feel will be detrimental to the aspirations of this country and to us Brongs in particular.... We resolve to register our unflinching support for the Prime Minister and the present government, to wholeheartedly support the price of 72 shillings for a load of cocoa.

This was the beginning of acrimonious relationships between the Asantes, on the one side, and the Brongs and Ahafos and the government on the other. The cocoa farmers who allied themselves with the Asante separatist National Liberation Movement failed to stop the Cocoa Duty and Development Funds (Amendment) Bill, which was passed on 13 August 1954 after only three days of debate. Nkrumah honoured his promise to the Brong Kyempim Federation by creating a separate Brong Ahafo Region. The victory of the government over the Asante farmers, however, did not have the intended effect on the cocoa industry and on economic development. It gave the government a full mandate to use the resources from the cocoa industry to undertake economic development in other sectors of the economy. Its value, however, depended on the strategies to maintain cocoa production at levels that would optimize producer savings – a function of market conditions in which optimum, and not arbitrary and distorted, producer pricing is the key.

It can also be argued that the climatically most suitable lands for cocoa were not in the Brong area (see map, p. xvi), but in Ahafo, Asante, Akyem, Kwahu and the Western Region. The Brong Kyempim victory led to a producer pricing policy which shattered the confidence of farmers in the more productive areas, and had a far more devastating effect on future production than was anticipated at the time. What was overlooked was that the cocoa farmer was a rational entrepreneur, whether he was Ahafo, Brong or Asante. His decision to plant was determined by his judgement of market conditions, not by politics. Ultimately, all farmers would react in the same way, and would withdraw or remain in the industry on the basis of their rational expectations of the reward from their investment.[31]

Another effect of the state's victory over the farmers was the authority provided by the Cocoa Duty and Development Fund's (Amendment) Act, 1954, for the government to reorganize the management of the cocoa industry. The Cocoa Purchasing Company (CPC) was created, and the government proceeded to reorganize the management of the CMB also. It injected into both a considerable amount of party political activity. The CPC foundered very rapidly after losing large sums of farmers' money on political spending (Jibowu Commission).[32] Through the reorganization of the CMB, the government was able to infuse a political style of management which later resulted in the creation of the United Ghana Farmers Council Co-operatives (UGFCC), which succeeded the CPC as the sole buying agency. It was also the political arm of the CPP in the cocoa industry.[33] The producer price stabilization fund was transferred from the CMB to the Treasury and integrated with government fiscal policy. In this way, it effectively linked the producer price to the ability of the Treasury to pay, and not the market. This policy has had far-reaching adverse implications for the producer price and production since the early 1960s.

Modernization, fiscal policy and the external reserves

The available evidence indicates that the new development was financed by taxation of the export sector and by the drawing down of external reserves. The data in Tables 5.1 and 5.5 show large budgetary deficits from 1954, indicating that a substantial part of the new capital costs were financed from accumulated external reserves and domestic borrowing. The data in Tables 5.5 and 5.6 show that export duties rose significantly in the period under review. At their height, in 1954, they were, in real terms, ten times the peak reached in the colonial period (in 1950). The bulk of the export taxes fell on the cocoa farmer. Mineral duties were also heavily increased, and so was income tax. But as can be noted in Table 5.5, the increases in import duties and income taxes were not as high as those in the export sector.

Financing from external reserves has been discussed extensively in the literature, but there has been no agreement on the amounts involved. Published balance-of-payments figures for the period show many inconsistencies (Killick, 1978: 102). The data in Tables 5.9. and 5.10 are therefore meant to indicate the general picture rather than the exact amount of reserve loss. From the middle of the decade, the balance of visible trade, which had for several years been favourable, became negative. In the second half of the decade, adverse results occurred in the balance of payments (Table 5.10). The estimated deficit for the period 1956–61 was C350.4m. and, in the absence of any major capital inflows, the major burden was on the external reserves.

The large loss in reserves in this period included the payment of £10m to Guinea and Mali noted earlier and a transfer of £5.5m for the government's acquisition, on the London Stock Market, of British-owned gold mining companies in the Western Region of the country which were threatened with liquidation. The International Monetary Fund estimates the net loss in reserves in the period 1956–61 at US$176.5m (International Financial Statistics). On the other hand, Manu (1972) puts the loss in reserves in 1961 alone at £100m (US$280m) which compares with Killick's (1978: 102) estimate of an external 'liquidity' loss of £109.5m (US$306.6m) for the same year.

The financial situation in 1960 was therefore a crucial factor in the scope and pace of further development. We ask whether there were additional sources of domestic and foreign financing to sustain any future increases in development spending.

Government revenue was rising at an average annual rate of 8.8% over the period, and nominal capital expenditures were rising at an approximate average annual rate of 23.5%

Table 5.9   Imports, Exports and Balance of Visible Trade, 1950–60 (£'000 current prices)

Year	Imports	Exports	Balance of visible trade
1950	96.2	154.8	58.6
1951	127.6	184.0	56.4
1952	133.2	172.8	39.6
1953	147.6	179.9	32.3
1954	142.1	229.2	87.1
1955	175.8	191.3	15.5
1956	177.8	173.2	− 4.6
1957	193.4	182.3	−10.2
1958	169.2	209.1	39.9
1959	226.0	226.7	0.7
1960	259.2	232.9	−26.3

Source: Statistical Year Book, Economic Survey, Government Statistician's Office, Accra, 1957

Table 5.10   The Capital Account of the Balance of Payments, 1956–61 (cedi million current prices)

Current account deficit		350.4
Capital inflow		−50.6
Deficit foreign investment	18.2	
Long-term investment	8.8	
Government transactions	23.6	
Charges in resources		−330.5
Errors and omissions		30.7

Source: Manu (1972), p. 20

Table 5.11 Budgetary Trends, 1951–60 (£'000 current prices)

Year end in	Total revenue	Current expend.	Current balance	Capital expend.	Overall balance	Capital ratio to revenue	Capital ratio to total expend.
1	2	3	4	5	6	7	8
1951	38,929	16,619	+22,310	6,457	+15,853	16.6%	38.9%
1952	42,965	24,529	+18,436	13,915	+ 4,521	32.4%	56.7%
1953	48,428	32,461	+15,967	15,591	+ 376	32.2%	48.0%
1954	80,587	29,143	+51,444	17,538	+33,906	21.8%	60.2%
1955	64,099	41,732	+22,367	28,582	−6,215	44.6%	68.5%
1956	49,502	38,694	+10,808	20,477	−9,669	41.1%	52.9%
1957	59,922	37,593	+22,329	19,688	+ 2,641	32.9%	52.4%
1958	66,719	46,122	+20,597	29,620	−9,023	44.4%	64.2%
1959	70,231	58,501	+11,730	28,617	−16,887	40.8%	48.9%
1960	83,413	68,688	+14,725	43,146	−28,421	51.7%	62.8%

Source: Tables 5.1 and 5.5

(Table 5.11). Taxation of international trade was a principal source of finance for the rapid increase in capital spending (Table 5.12). Cocoa, which accounted for an average of 62% of total export earnings in the period, was the key factor in direct taxation (Table 5.12, cols 5 & 6). Cocoa revenues also generated indirect revenues through the taxes on imports they helped to finance, and facilitated capital goods imports. Table 5.6 illustrates cocoa's burden by comparison with the principal exports that were taxable. The potential growth of cocoa was therefore the most important factor in the country's ability to maintain the tempo of development at the high pitch reached throughout the 1950s.

Table 5.12 Burden Sharing in Taxation, 1951–60 (£'000 current prices)

Year ending in	Total revenue	Import duties	Export duties	Cocoa taxes[a]	Ratio: cocoa taxes to total	Ratio: cocoa to total export revenues
1	2	3	4	5	6	7
1951	38,929	9,732	19,576)			65.6%
1952	42,965	9,545	16,827)	68,334	32.4%	60.8%
1953	48,428	12,010	18,570)			62.4%
1954	80,587	12,944	49,271)			73.8%
1955	64,099	18,280	24,690	20,009	31.2%	68.5%
1956	49,502	16,364	12,586	25,052	50.6%	59.0%
1957	59,922	14,983	22,734	13,516	22.6%	55.5%
1958	66,719	16,109	25,757	16,086	24.1%	59.6%
1959	70,231	18,900	22,358	26,103	37.2%	60.7%
1960	83,413	25,862	16,158	22,501	27.0%	53.7%

a) Includes farmers' 'voluntary' donations for development
Source: Table 5.5, Kay and Hymer (1972), Table 24C, Cocoa Taxes adjusted from calendar to financial year basis

Trends in the cocoa industry in the 1950s, however, did not point to an expansion in the long term, even if the short-term production trends indicated differently (Table 5.13, col. 2). Real producer prices were falling rapidly in the period (col. 6), and with them the long-term producer price incentive (col. 8) which governed farmers' decisions to invest in this long-term tree crop industry. It has been estimated that from the crop year 1950/1 to 1960/1, a total of £246.7m. was taken in taxes and 'voluntary' contributions. At the highest point, 60% of total farmers' gross incomes was taken in this way (Beckman, 1976: 279–80).

The evidence on the trends in external reserves towards the end of the 1950s also indicates some uncertainty about the country's ability to finance capital imports for development at 1950s levels from its own resources. Total reserves began to fall steadily from the mid-1950s, and the falls occurred with respect to all holders (Table 5.14). What appeared to be a recovery in Central Bank holdings was the result of a transfer from the CMB with the introduction of exchange controls in 1961. It was clear by the end of the decade that any major programmes of development would have to be financed by creating external debt.

The Nkrumah State and the Predatory State

In presenting his model of the predatory state, Lal (1986: 17–19) assumed that a fiscal crisis could occur in a situation of export price instability and that the state would resort to

Table 5.13 Trends in Cocoa Production and Producer Prices, 1951–60

Crop year	Production ton '000	Value fob £'000	Current producer prices £ 'ton	Price index 1963= 100	Real producer prices £ 'ton	Estd planting costs £ 'ton	Price[a] incentive £ 'ton
1	2	3	4	5	6	7	8
1950/1	262	60,310	130.7	70.7	186.7	81.0	105.7
1951/2	211	52,533	149.3	68.5	217.5	78.5	139.0
1952/3	247	56,143	130.5	68.1	191.6	78.0	113.6
1953/4	210	84,599	134.4	68.1	197.4	78.0	119.4
1954/5	220	65,559	135.0	72.3	184.2	82.9	101.3
1955/6	229	51,062	148.5	72.9	203.7	83.5	120.2
1956/7	264	50,813	149.2	73.7	202.4	84.5	117.9
1957/8	207	62,318	134.2	74.4	180.4	85.3	95.1
1958/9	256	68,719	131.9	76.5	172.4	87.7	84.7
1959/60	317	66,434	112.0	79.8	140.4	91.5	48.9
1960/1	432	69,521	112.0	86.1	130.1	98.7	31.4
1961/2	409	67,010	100.8	89.5	112.6	102.6	10.0

a) See Chapter 7 for method of estimating price incentive variable
Sources: Bateman (1971), Tables II-1 and II-5

Table 5.14 Trends in Gross Foreign Exchange Reserves by Holders, 1949–62 (£ million current prices)

End of year	Total	Central Govt.	Central Bank	Other banks	Marketing Board	Other
1	2	3	4	5	6	7
1949	84	18	29	–	32	5
1950	114	19	32	4	52	7
1951	138	30	34	3	64	7
1952	145	35	36	7	61	6
1953	158	37	35	10	66	10
1954	196	72	37	11	66	10
1955	208	82	38	14	63	11
1956	190	74	41	12	51	12
1957	171	59	38	11	49	14
1958	173	61	31	14	52	15
1959	167	60	43	11	37	16
1960	149	43	54	6	30	16
1961	73	11	48	3	7	9
1962	72	10	47	–2	8	9

Source: Digest of Statistics, Office of the Government Statistician, Accra, March 1963

different forms of action to insulate itself. Such action, he suggested, could include commodity stabilization funds, and import substitution industrialization which provides a higher level of stable employment, though not necessarily profitably. He also suggested tariff protection to expand local industrialization and therefore local employment. These solutions are merely necessary evils in the situation in which a 'predatory state' has reached the point where government has expanded its activity to absorb all the resources available to it and has no cushion left to sustain employment in the face of exogenous factors. The above strategies could therefore be designed to reduce the effect of these exogenous factors. Lal concludes that this seemed to be the case of 'Ghana till about 1961 during the Nkrumah regime' (Lal, 1986: 19).

The account of the Nkrumah state given in this chapter is different from that of Lal in a number of important details but confirms his account in others, though for different reasons. First, Ghana did lose large reserves between 1951 and 1961 (Table 5.14); this occurred when producer prices were falling. However, due to increases in production from earlier planting, total export revenues continued to rise (Table 5.9). Second, Ghana embarked on programmes of import substitution, not in response to the need to maintain employment at an unsustainable level after a fiscal crisis, but rather as part of a development strategy initiated in a period when resources were abundant. Indeed, the fiscal crisis was induced by the poor management of development and of import substitution, and not the other way round.

Third, the creation of the CMB and its stabilization fund took place well before independence. It was rather the expropriation of the Stabilization Fund by the Treasury that contributed to the fiscal crisis.[34] Fourth, much of the public expenditure that took place in the 1950s was not production-oriented, but infrastructural in nature, thus providing employment but not production for several years to come. In these respects, therefore, the Nkrumah state of the 1950s was the result of a patriotic drive for modernization rather than of fiscal crisis, reserve loss or failure of production.

The principal strategy of financial management in the Nkrumah state clearly separates (almost alienates) the state from its principal revenue source, the cocoa sector. Nkrumah stated (1957: 179), in defence of the government's tax policy on cocoa, that 'by using cocoa funds for development and for providing amenities, it would be possible to improve the general standard of living in the country as a whole at an early date'. Also, the post-independence indigenous government made a clear effort to push employment above the colonial predator's sub-optimal welfare level. Nevertheless, this was attempted in response to an uncontrollable desire to modernize, not to a fiscal crisis. This puts the Nkrumah state in a different category of predatoriness – one induced by aggressive nationalism. There were, also, obvious internationalist ambitions which exceeded the 'normal' financial resources and required some sectors of the economy to make larger contributions than they could sustain. In these ways the Nkrumah state must be differentiated from Lal's predatory state.

But there are also undeniable similarities. An indigenous state with large grass-roots support, which had defeated the only effective Asante opposition, constituted a high barrier against the entry of contestants for power. This was also a period of active suppression of political opposition.[35] A sure hold on power enabled the government to levy high taxes, particularly on cocoa and on imports. All these features resembled those of Lal's predatory state.

Further evidence of the increasingly predatory power of the Nkrumah state includes the strengthening and expansion of the defence forces (Table 5.2), the cooption of the Trade Union Congress and the Farmers' Council into the Party, the raising of the status of their leaders to ministerial rank (Chazan, 1988), and the steady reduction in the role and financial strength of the indigenous private sector. In the Lal predatory state model, these steps are designed to raise the authority of the state and to create charismatic leadership capable of exacting the maximum of taxation without effective opposition.

Thus the Nkrumah state comes closer to the deleterious coalition of Bates even if one cannot attribute to it the implied harmful intention. The form of Nkrumah's coalition was determined by his wider vision of Africa and was dominated by his personality. There were few real beneficiaries in Ghana. In terms of Pan-Africanism, the core combination was himself and the few dependents whom he had brought up from the grass roots. The greater beneficiaries were Africa and the Black races; the cost was paid by Ghana as a whole. The mass grass-roots movement ultimately benefited neither the masses who drifted from the countryside, nor the state enterprises he created, nor the membership of the CPP. Improvements in health and education and other infrastructure benefited both urban and rural dwellers.

Where the Nkrumah state conforms to Bates's deleterious predatory coalition is in its destruction of the rural agricultural sector, particularly the cocoa sector following the defeat of the National Liberation Movement, standard-bearer of the rural producer.

Conclusions

Because the development strategy of the Nkrumah state in the immediate post-independence period was moulded by Nkrumah's own philosophy with its wider African vision and ambitious aim of rapid progress in Ghana, it concentrated on much-needed social and economic infrastructure for both real and demonstrational effect, achieving some important successes. However, it could not claim ultimate success as a development strategy. It was too aggressive and demanding on the fragile peasant productive structure, whose weakness it ignored. The primary export sectors, in particular cocoa, were squeezed rather hard for finance. This led to conflicts that were bound to have long-term adverse consequences for the industry and for development. Resources ran out more quickly than productivity in the food sector increased. Peasant agriculture remained underdeveloped and fragmented, as it had been for centuries.

The approach to the modernization of agriculture was inappropriate and lopsided, so that fragmentation remained while unsuccessful attempts were being made to introduce better seeds, large-scale farming and advanced technology. State-initiated attempts at the introduction of large-scale mechanized farming were similarly unsuccessful for technological, managerial and sociological reasons.

Significantly, the economy did not have the financial ability to sustain development spending into the next decades at the tempo established in the 1950s. Any further aggressive development stood the risk of squeezing the cocoa sector even harder, which risked destroying the long-term foundation of the industry and therefore of the long-term development strategy itself. There were no alternatives, except heavy external borrowing, which ran the risk of serious indebtedness given the weak productive base and the fragile nature of the economy. A cautious approach to further development was therefore called for in the period after 1961. A substantial reduction in infrastructural spending and a shift of emphasis to known productive initiatives was urgently necessary.

This conclusion indicates that the weak and fragile economy at independence contained the seeds of it own destruction. Indeed one can postulate that, in the context of such a weak economy, access to large financial resources by a charismatic leader with aggressive development ambitions and predatory propensities can induce nascent economic decline.[36] If economic decline is defined as the setting in motion of factors inducing loss of production, then by the end of the 1950s these factors had been primed in Ghana. The analysis suggests that Ghana had to choose, in the years that followed, a path of development that emphasized appropriate methods of assuring maximum productivity by the most efficient approaches and in a macroeconomic environment that guaranteed domestic and external stability. Economic stagnation was otherwise inevitable. To avoid economic decline, it was necessary for the government to modify its political and economic ambitions substantially. Factors in the economic approach to the political process are therefore important in the search for explanations of the fate of the country in the years that followed.

Notes

1. Three key ministerial positions were held by *ex officio* colonial civil servants from 1951 to 1957. Nkrumah states: 'apart from my own nominations, the Governor nominated as *ex-officio* ministers Mr R.H. Saloway as Minister of Defence and External Affairs, Mr R. Armitage as Minister of Finance and Mr P. Brannigan as Minister of Justice and Attorney General' (Nkrumah, 1957: 118).
2. The Lewis (1953: 8) thesis postulates that 'the secret of industrialization is a rapidly progressing agriculture, and more particularly, since food is the major part of agriculture, the number one priority in any programme of economic development is the measures which increase food production per head. Without such measures, a country like the Gold Coast cannot spare the labour for industries, cannot find the capital for them, and has too small a market to support their output.'
3. Lewis (1955: 208), states that 'all the countries which are now relatively developed have at some time in the past gone through a period of acceleration, in the course of which their annual rate of investment has moved from 5 per cent or less to 12 per cent or more. That is what we mean by an Industrial Revolution.'
4. About the West African National Secretariat, Nkrumah states that one of the groups within the Secretariat of which he was the chairman 'became the vanguard group and we called ourselves The Circle. Membership cost seven guineas and only those who were believed or known to be genuinely working for West African unity and the destruction of colonialism, were admitted.'
5. Nkrumah (1957: 50–1) gives a detailed account of his reaction to the first invitation from Ako Adjei, in 1947. He concluded: 'I was very sure of the policy I would pursue and fully prepared to come to loggerheads with the Executive of the UGCC if I found that they were following a reactionary course.... I wrote and accepted the post. I also wrote another letter to Danquah explaining that I was without funds and that I would need about a hundred pounds to cover my passage and travelling expenses.'
6. (Nkrumah, 1973: 51). He states in particular that the 'sponsors of the movement were men whose political philosophy was contrary to the political aspirations of the Gold Coast.' He gathered from Tony Maclean (Extra-Mural Tutor at Oxford) before his return to the Gold Coast that William Ofori-Atta might be the one 'who appeared to him to have some ideas of the political and economic needs of the country.'
7. The United Africa Company, a subsidiary of Unilever, and the British commercial banks and insurance companies would have been the prime targets for nationalization.
8. Colonial Office sensitivities are documented in Colonial Office file CO554/202. Lewis had stated (1953: 8, para. 101) that 'foreign capital is unpopular in all countries which are or have been in colonial status', and in para. 135 that: 'every capitalist would like to have a guarantee that his firm will not be nationalized. In these days no government can usefully give a pledge that a subsequent government will not nationalize an industry.'
9. Previously A.G. Leventis & Co., a rebel outcast from the European merchant cartel.
10. This organization comprised a number of small mining companies which were acquired by the government when they were threatened with dissolution in the mid-1950s. They were operationally unprofitable at the then low and fixed gold price.
11. It has to be mentioned that the acquisition of the Gold Coast Insurance Company, owned by the American Robert Freeman, and A.G. Leventis & Co., owned by Mr A.G. Leventis, a Greek Cypriot, were purely commercial negotiations in which fair prices were paid. Freeman, a black American, stayed on as Managing Director of the State Insurance Corporation for several years. Sir Patrick Fitzgerald, retiring Chairman of UAC, was hired to manage the Ghana National Trading Corporation in its initial years.
12. In less than a decade the Ghana Commercial Bank grew to twice the size of Barclays Bank and Standard Bank combined (Bank of Ghana, *Quarterly Bulletin*, various issues 1963–70).
13. *Development Progress Report* (Government Printer, Accra, 1955), para. 22.

14. The term 'verandah boys' refers to the grassroots urban followers of Nkrumah in the initial years of his political agitation for independence. The description is of those who were too poor to be properly housed and who therefore spent the night on the verandahs of the richer classes.
15. Quoted by Killick (1978: 245).
16. Apaloo Commission on the Assets of Specified Persons, 1966.
17. The longer-term and perhaps greater benefits to development would be in agriculture from the grass roots, which could not be made immediately visible, and therefore was not preferred.
18. Lord Swinton, Memorandum by the West African War Council, Colonial Office file CO554/132/33712/1. 'The adoption of the plantation system would accelerate the creation of a landless class, which in times of depression will provide an unemployment problem. It is true that in the cocoa areas of the Gold Coast the formation of African owned plantations is already well advanced, but this provides no justification for the establishment of European owned plantations nor for hastening the perceptible movement from communal to individual ownership of land.'
19. Lewis confirmed his participation (1959: 3): 'I have played some part in drawing up the Second Development Plan - not by any means a decisive part'.
20. Lewis had put great emphasis in his 1953 'Report' on indigenous private investment also. He had relied on private domestic savings with 'farmers providing the wherewithal' (para. 98). For foreign investment he even suggested that its protection should be 'enshrined in the Constitution' (para. 135).
21. Killick (1978: 167) believes that 'Nkrumah shared with mainstream development economists in the necessity for fundamental structural changes if the economy was to be modernized'.
22. *Development Progress Report* (1955), para. 6.
23. *Ibid.*, para. 5.
24. *Ibid.*, para. 24.
25. An increasing rate of inflation was, however, observable towards the end of the period (see Table 5.8).
26. The Development Plan, 1951 (Government Printer, Accra), p. 4.
27. Gold Coast, The Second Development Plan, 1959–1964 (Government Printer, Accra, 1959), p. 6.
28. In the joint letter dated 29 December 1954 addressed to the Prime Minister by the Asanteman Council and the National Liberation Movement, the Asantes reminded 'Gold Coast politicians and students of Gold Coast politics that although Asante has during the past ten years sought cooperation with the rest of the country and played her full part in the march towards Gold Coast independence, she will not forgo her separate identity, forged with the sweat and blood of her ancestors and sealed by the Golden Stool, whose position is now threatened by the political set up of the country.'
29. On this issue, the Secretary of State for the Colonies appointed a one-man independent committee (British), designated the Constitutional Adviser, in 1955, to advise on the devolution of the regions before independence. The Asantes refused to attend any hearings of the Adviser because, just before his arrival, the government had passed the State Councils (Ashanti) Amendment Ordinance, 1955, by which the authority of the Paramount Chiefs and the Asanteman Council over their subordinate chiefs had been reduced. The Constitutional Adviser nevertheless stated in his Report: 'Whatever may be the outcome of the longstanding differences between the Brong States of Western Ashanti and the Asanteman Council, I cannot see any administrative justification for creating a separate region for this comparatively small area wherein local opinion on the subject is far from unanimous.'
30. The leading negotiator for Ahafo was B.K. Senkyire. Nana Agyemang Badu, Omanhene of Dormaa Ahenkro, was the leader of the Brongs in the negotiations with the government.
31. As observed by Dunn and Robertson (1973: 65) 'As an individual, any rich Ahafo farmer ... might contrive to maximise the returns of his political energies by aligning himself with the CPP ... as a group, with so much money potentially to lose, and such solid and available clientages to dispose, the rich farmers of the Ahafo forest combined the maximum of incentive with the maximum of opportunity in their belated resistance to the ... political entrepreneurs of the city and the coast.'
32. The Jibowu Commission produced serious findings on the corrupt use of public funds from cocoa taxation. It reported that the CPP had been involved in major malpractice which affected Nkrumah himself (Andoh, 1984:32).
33. The Secretary General of the UGFCC, Martin Appiah Danquah, a very able political organizer, was of Cabinet rank.
34. It introduced considerable instability into public sector revenues, relating them to world cocoa prices. These were previously absorbed by the stabilization fund.
35. By the close of the decade most of the members of the UGCC which had brought Nkrumah to Ghana were in prison, including Danquah, who died in prison in 1964.
36. Other examples are Guinea under Sekou Touré, Tanzania under Nyerere, Zaire under Mobutu, etc.

6 The Political Economy of Decline: Ghana 1961–1983

> And besides the violation of the law, it is a bad thing that many from being
> rich should become poor; for men of ruined fortunes are sure to stir up
> revolutions.
>
> Aristotle, *Politics* [1]

The worst of the scenarios outlined at the conclusion of the previous chapter came to pass
in Ghana in the two decades from 1961. The macroeconomic management and development strategies were of the inferior type. Central to the problem remained stagnant agricultural productivity and fragmentation in pricing and marketing. Stoces, observing the start
of decline, commented (1966: 10):

> Figures of the sample of 1,000 holdings taken in the Agricultural Census, Phase I, 1963 made
> it clear that the overwhelming majority of small scale private farmers used only simple tools
> and implements such as hoes, cutlasses, axes, etc., which they had been using for generations....
> All available figures show that output per man in Ghana's agriculture in the period 1960–1965
> did not change.

Food production, in the initial period of decline, increased at only 0.28% per annum
against a population increase of 2.6%. There was an average annual population shift from
rural to urban areas of 1.2%, mostly of the age group 20–29 (Table 6.1) (*ibid.*: 6). The
economy went into massive decline until about 1984, when the Economic Recovery
Programme of the present government began to show some positive results.

Table 6.1 Urban and Rural Population by Age Group, March 1960

| Age group | Percentage by age group | |
	Urban	Rural
0–9	31.4	35.3
10–19	19.7	17.7
20–29	21.1	16.4
30–39	13.1	12.8
40 and above	14.7	17.8

Source: Stoces (1966), p. 7

This chapter begins with a brief description of the nature of the economic decline that
took place. An attempt is made to distinguish the significant phases and the principal
economic sector whose collapse was most responsible. The chapter concentrates on the
political economy explanations associated with the different phases, with the object of
investigating the degree of recognition by the various political regimes of the delicate nature
of the economy, and how the conflicts in the political economy helped to induce the process
of decline.

94

Table 6.2 Indicators of Economic Decline: 1955–85

Year	Fiscal policy		Tax base		External sector		Growth indicators			Money &inflation	
	Govt. revenue ratio to GDP	Govt. expend. ratio to GDP	Cocoa export ratio to GDP	Total import ratio to GDP	Net reserves ratio to GDP	Measure of over- or under- valuation base 1960 (%)	Per- capita growth rate base 1975	Per capita savings ratio to GDP	Per- capita GDFCF ratio to GDP	Money supply change over previous year (%)	Rate of inflation (%)
1	2	3	4	5	6	7	8	9	10	11	12
1955	18.8	20.7	19.3	25.9	35.3	3.95				8.5	0.5
1956	14.0	16.7	14.4	25.2	32.4	2.15		13.8	16.0	4.4	4.1
1957	16.2	15.4	13.8	26.1	25.9	1.67	−1.0	12.4	15.3	−10.6	1.0
1958	17.1	19.4	16.0	21.7	25.4	0.21	−4.7	18.0	14.2	−7.3	0.0
1959	15.7	19.6	15.5	25.4	23.7	0.30	10.0	16.1	17.4	13.6	2.9
1960	17.5	23.4	13.9	31.0	21.2	0.00	3.4	15.2	20.5	11.4	0.9
1961	14.1	20.3	14.9	35.0	12.2	−0.09	1.1	12.7	20.8	15.4	6.2
1962	14.4	23.1	13.4	27.1	12.9	4.07	2.4	14.2	17.0	13.3	5.9
1963	14.1	22.3	12.4	26.3	12.1	7.41	1.0	13.6	18.3	0.0	5.6
1964	18.7	26.9	11.0	22.9	5.5	22.11	−0.2	14.6	17.2	41.2	15.8
1965	19.4	25..3	9.2	26.7	−0.5	45.39	−2.4	8.6	18.4	0.0	22.7
1966	15.2	18.3	7.7	19.6	−1.8	60.30	−2.1	8.0	13.1	4.2	14.8
1967	15.7	21.3	8.7	20.9	−3.5	19.84	−0.2	9.0	11.8	−4.0	−9.7
1968	17.5	23.5	10.6	21.7	−2.6	4.84	1.8	13.0	11.3	8.3	10.7
1969	16.6	19.8	11.1	21.4	−5.2	6.65	1.2	11.0	10.0	11.5	6.5
1970	19.3	20.7	13.3	23.9	−1.1	2.52	4.6	11.5	12.3	6.9	3.0
1971	18.0	21.0	8.1	27.5	−0.4	6.90	2.5	6.5	12.7	3.2	8.8
1972	14.9	19.3	9.8	15.2	4.5	−17.62	−5.3	14.3	8.8	43.8	10.8
1973	10.9	15.7	11.3	17.1	6.1	−8.95	2.5	12.1	7.7	28.3	17.1
1974	12.5	16.2	10.0	22.6	0.0	−5.82	3.7	8.0	12.0	18.6	18.8
1975	15.5	21.9	10.5	18.4	2.4	6.43	−15.0	12.7	11.7	44.3	29.8
1976	13.4	22.9	7.9	16.0	0.3	58.23	−6.5	9.6	9.9	41.6	55.4
1977	10.5	19.1	6.1	11.5	0.0	177.28	1.2	8.4	9.4	67.1	116.5
1978	6.6	15.1	4.7	9.7	0.1	220.37	4.8	4.1	5.4	72.8	73.1
1979	9.9	16.4	6.5	9.9	1.2	133.53	−6.7	5.9	4.2	13.3	54.5
1980	6.9	10.9	6.0	8.9	0.5	201.65	−3.3	5.0	5.8	30.1	50.2
1981	4.5	10.6	1.5	5.3	−0.3	563.57	−9.0	3.0	3.5	54.5	116.5
1982	5.6	11.0	1.2	3.0	0.0	693.88	−7.6	3.9	3.5	19.0	22.3
1983	5.6	8.0	3.4	9.3	−3.1	1278.70	−3.9	0.6	3.8	49.3	122.8
1984	8.4	9.9	4.7	7.7	−6.6	85.60	1.8	6.7	6.9	60.6	39.7
1985	11.7	13.3	5.3	11.6	−9.7	34.82	2.2	7.7	9.7	42.7	10.3

Source: Summarized from Tables in Annex I of Appendix

The Nature of the Economic Decline

The principal economic indicators, summarized in Table 6.2, show the nature of the economic decline in Ghana from about 1962. The detailed analyses, from which these summaries are derived, are given in Annex I of this book. By 1982, fiscal policy had completely collapsed. The government revenue base was a mere 5.6% of GDP (compared with 20–25% in other West African states). The cocoa sector tax base had shrunk to 1.2% and that of imports to 3%. The imbalance in the external sector had persistently worsened, particularly after 1975. By 1983, the degree of overvaluation of the currency was estimated at close to 1,300%. Inflation had been rampant in the two decades, and by 1982 was nearly 123%.

We have assumed, following Lewis, that the trends in the ratio of per capita savings to GDP (Table 6.2. col. 9), can also describe the path of decline.[2] Ghana's decline was a reversion from a 14% saver in 1962 to a 0.6% saver in 1983. Therefore, to determine the significant factors in the decline shown in Table 6.2, the ratio of domestic savings to GDP has been modelled using ratios of government expenditures, gross cocoa sector revenues, imports and net reserves to GDP, and the rate of inflation, as possible key factors. The savings function is usually modelled using independent variables such as GDP, rate of interest, prices, taxation, demographic factors, exports, etc. Since our purpose is to model economic decline, the variables used, apart from inflation, are ratios of GDP. Thus GDP itself is excluded, as a separate variable, from the model. Other less relevant variables, such as demography and interest rates, are also excluded. The model has been estimated as follows:

(Sample size = 29 [1957–85])

$$Sav = .39 \quad Exp + .99 \quad Cocoa -.34 \quad Imports + .07 \quad Reserves -.02 \quad Infl + .27$$

HC T-Values   (5.000)*   (6.352)*   (–5.326)*   (1.727)   (–2.209)**   (.195)

Adjusted R^2 = .9156 DW = 1.70

Notation:

Sav:	ratio of domestic savings to GDP
Exp :	ratio of government expenditures in GDP
Cocoa :	ratio of total value of cocoa exports in GDP
Imports:	ratio of total imports to GDP
Reserves:	ratio of total reserves to GDP
Infl:	annual rate of inflation

The cocoa, government expenditures, and import variables are very significant, at 0.0005 level (*). Inflation is only significant at .025 level (**). Net reserves are not significant. Detailed diagnostic testing has been performed, using Hendry's PC-Give Version 6.0, 1988. There are no autocorrelated errors, no ARCH errors and no heteroscedastic errors. The analysis of scaled residuals shows that there is no excess kurtosis. Test for normality gives $Chi^2(2)$ = 0.288. HC T-Values are heteroscedastic consistent T-Values and provide consistent estimates even if residuals are heteroscedastic in an unknown way. The estimate is derived through heteroscedastic consistent standard errors. In this case HC T-value is the Coefficient of the independent variable (Hendry, 1988) divided by HC Standard Error (White, 1980, MacKinnon and White, 1985).

The collapse of government expenditures is shown to have been a strong determining factor. Imports are also shown to have been significantly related to decline but in the opposite direction. As is indicated in Table 6.2, col. 5, the import ratio GDP remained high until 1975 when it also collapsed, but not to the same degree as other indicators; this is explained by the greater resilience of informal markets in the period of decline. What comes out clearly from the analysis is the importance of the collapse of cocoa incomes. Cocoa revenues are known to have had a great influence on government spending and on imports.[3] The primary export sector generally has been demonstrated in recent studies to be the principal factor in domestic savings and economic development.[4] This further emphasizes the role that the collapse of the cocoa sector played in Ghana's decline, and suggests a detailed study of that industry.

Four phases are identifiable in the period of economic decline under consideration. The first, 1961–5, was associated with the major attempt to accelerate economic development following the preparations made in the 1950s. The second, 1966–74, was a rather confused attempt to restructure the economy in the aftermath of failure of the first phase. This second phase was managed by three successive governments: the National Liberation Council (NLC) of military men, the Busia democratically elected government, and the first three years of the Acheampong military government. Ironically, this phase was the best period, relatively, in the long process of decline.

The third, 1975–83, was when the steepest rate of decline occurred. This phase was also shared by five successive governments: the second half of the Acheampong Government, the brief Akuffo period, the short Rawlings I Government of the Armed Forces Revolutionary Council (AFRC), the Limann democratically elected government, and the first part of the Rawlings II (Provisional National Defence Council [PNDC]) era. The fourth phase is the second and current part of the Rawlings II era of radical monetary and economic reform.

The analysis that follows investigates the critical factors of the political environment in which the various governments found themselves or which they created for themselves. It discusses the ambitions of the governments and the political and social pressures which dictated the trend towards inefficiency and self-destruction. The first three phases are discussed in the present chapter. The fourth phase is taken up in the concluding chapter.

The End of the Nkrumah Era

That Nkrumah's intentions to develop Ghana were genuine can be judged by the achievements of his period in power, which contrasted sharply with the immediately previous colonial era and almost all governments after him. In the area of social modernization, he raised the levels of medical and educational facilities. In economic infrastructure he improved the road and rail network, and constructed the Tema township with its new harbour and industrial facilities. The giant Akosombo Dam is to his credit; this has given Ghana strategic control over its energy resources, a critical factor after the oil price increases of 1973 and 1979. Nkrumah also raised African and Black consciousness, an achievement for which he is well remembered.

Yet this study postulates that he left behind a legacy of economic decline, with a fragile external sector, heavy debts, a delicate fiscal structure, an export sector in which the seeds of destruction had already been sown and state sector industries that were to become a long-term liability. He also left an impoverished urban class that was to haunt all successor governments. So where did the great African patriot go wrong?

The strategy of governance from 1960 onward is highly relevant to this question. It can be viewed in four aspects, with the object being to centralize state authority in a President, and in the Party in power. The first aspect was the creation of a highly state-centric system with power concentrated in the President. This was achieved through the Republican Constitution of 1960 and the declaration of a one party system in 1964 (Chazan, 1988). The strategy enabled government to become highly personalized and the Party supporters to become beneficiaries of state patronage and largesse. This implied the reduction of competition within and outside the Party.

The second aspect was the creation of a political doctrine and an ideology. This had the effect of focusing the mind of the nation, in particularly members of the Party, on the ideology of the President, and of developing a set of rules that had to be religiously observed. In the late Nkrumah period the doctrine promoted was Nkrumaism, an African version of socialism, developed at the Kwame Nkrumah Ideological Institute. Its components were particularly conducive to the sowing of the seeds of decline from the precarious economic situation in 1960. They were: a speedy and outright attack on underdevelopment, accelerated industrialization as the basic condition for economic growth, the rapid expansion of state initiative in production (Nkrumah, 1963:.119), and a realignment of foreign relations with emphasis on the Eastern bloc (see *Work and Happiness*, a booklet of ideological rules). It was within this framework that the Seven Year Development Plan was drafted, and the major unsuccessful attempt at industrialization launched (Killick, 1978).

The third aspect was the steady politicization of the public services, which brought in inefficiency and repression. With the 1960 Republican Constitution, the number of government departments was increased. The Party machine began to encroach on the process of administrative decision-making, and introduced a degree of overlapping in public service management (Amamoo, 1981). As part of this process, the personality cult of the President and of the Party was introduced into the public service. This led to excessive politicization of the bureaucratic system and the restriction of decision-making (Chazan, 1988). It had the effect of placing authority in the hands of new 'public servants' whose priorities were more political and less concerned with administrative efficiency.[5]

The fourth aspect was the induction into the Party of the so-called integral 'Wings of the Party': the Trade Union Congress, the UGFCC, the National Union of Ghana Students, the Young Pioneers and the Workers' Brigade. The intention, it is argued, was two-fold: to stifled the groups that were likely to oppose the government (after silencing the traditional opposition), and to use these integral wings of the Party to disintegrate the remnants of opposition. For example, as all workers became members of the Trade Union Congress they automatically became members of the Party. Also, as farmers became members of the UGFCC they became members of the Party, and the Secretary General of UGFCC became spokesman for the farmers as a whole. The UGFCC, for example, took the decisions to accept lower producer prices for cocoa and to donate farmers' funds for development.[6] Thus with the integration of these wings the full authority of the President over the Party in a much wider sense was assured.

When complete political power had been secured, of what benefit was it to the political purpose of a patriotic leader, in Ghana and in Africa, that the economy should decline? After all, a prosperous Ghana provided Nkrumah with a stronger foundation and a more credible platform for his African and international programme, if one were to assume that these were more important to him than Ghana. The answer is found in the fact that excessive centralization of political authority generates its own momentum towards destruction. It has the tendency to exclude liberal intellect from the core combination of state authority and leads to the withdrawal and distancing of the leadership from valuable alternative opinion.[7] The leadership is also more likely to make mistakes or to misunderstand the truth about conditions when an autocratic leader has become isolated.

Evidence of Nkrumah's intellectual isolation began in the early 1950s when he broke away from the UGCC and opted for a mass urban movement, youthful and populist, and rejected the more rural-based, entrepreneurial, and traditional interests (Chapter 4). The evidence of his isolation within the Party was also considerable. It ranged from fear of offending on the part of his advisers to a reluctance even to contribute new ideas.[8] The personal experience of the author at Cabinet meetings in 1965, when he was Deputy Governor of the Central Bank, indicated the President's absolute authority. He was observed to be unfamiliar with some relevant economic issues and, sadly, ministers and advisers were unable to point these out or disagree with him.[9] The President had been rendered powerless by his own ideology to tackle important issues in the economy.[10]

The general conclusion is that by the early 1960s Nkrumah had brought about sufficient disharmony in the core combination of state authority to generate considerable political and economic instability. He had created an ideology which was most conducive to political disintegration (Chazan, 1988); he had made promises to a youthful and populist constituency that could be fulfilled only by shifting resources from the productive sectors; he had created a state-centric system and absolute power for himself without the benefit of acceptable good advisers;[11] he had committed himself to irreversible economic doctrines which, in that period, could only sow the seeds of decline. Also significant were the subjection of cocoa producer prices to budgetary decision-making, and the introduction of exchange control in July 1961 and import licensing in December of the same year.[12] Combined with the socialist ideology, these latter factors pre-empted the key economic policy tool of nominal exchange-rate management as an effective alternative to trade policy in external sector management. By relying solely on trade policies and foreign exchange rationing, the government had opted to let demand pressures vent themselves on domestic prices. This policy suited socialist ideology. It enabled the government's investment programme, especially the distribution between state and private sectors, and within the private sector, to become subject to direct political control (Killick, 1978).[13] However, the resulting overvaluation of the currency introduced indirect distortions into the domestic pricing of export products.

1966–69 : The NLC Era

Major efforts were made in the period 1966 to 1974 to reverse the trend of decline, most seriously by the NLC and during the first three years of the Acheampong government. The objective apparently common to all three regimes in the period, apart from the early Acheampong years, was the reversal of the particular political characteristics of the Nkrumah state. The first radio broadcast by the leader of the coup that toppled Nkrumah on 24 February 1966 emphasized that the myth of Nkrumaism was broken. This demonstrated the extent of the charisma of Nkrumah and how important it was for the NLC to destroy that image.[14]

The moderate military and police leaders of the NLC coup had no ideology nor any desire to rule indefinitely. They planned economic recovery and political revival. They envisaged a return to barracks and implemented their intentions. However, they underestimated the extent to which the Nkrumah state was entrenched.[15] Uninhibited by political or economic ideology, they proceeded very quickly to dismantle uneconomic and irrelevant state commercial and industrial activities.[16] They introduced IMF-supported monetary reforms, devalued the currency and liberalized the external sector.[17]

Though the NLC membership underrepresented the Northern and Akan ethnic groups, this deficiency was more than repaired by the political infusion of the former leaders of the rural-based groups opposed to Nkrumah. Most notably, Busia ran a civic education campaign for the NLC government. The resistance that the NLC faced, including an attempted coup in which the leader of the coup that overthrew Nkrumah, General E.K. Kotoka, was killed, and a series of strikes, indicated the continued presence of the Nkrumah state. The NLC designed another Westminster-type constitution, quite oblivious of the failure of the first attempt, and handed power over to Busia's Progress Party (PP) in 1969.

1969–71: The Busia Era

Both the 1969 Constitution and the return of the PP to power were assumed to constitute a new order in which there was a revival of popular participation in the political process, an introduction of greater harmony in the core combination of state, and an end to dictatorial rule. The PP was a revised version of the UGCC and the NLM combined. The CPP had been proscribed, and that Party's dispersed elements refused to join the previously disaffected K.A. Gbedemah's opposition National Alliance of Liberals (NAL). Two major political handicaps soon became evident. Neither of the two principal parties was as broadly based nationally as the CPP. The elections resulted in a severe ethnic division in which the PP won no seats in the Ewe area and the NAL won no seats in the Akan areas. Thus the alliance between the Akans and the Ewes in the NLC disappeared to be replaced by ethnic hostilities which have coloured Ghana politics ever since. There was in fact no Ewe in Busia's Cabinet because there were none in his party in Parliament.[18]

The 1969 elections did not therefore resurrect adequate political competition, and did not give Busia enough political authority to continue with the economic reforms begun in 1966 with the same authority as the NLC had, despite the PP's significant parliamentary majority. In the words of Afrifa (1967: 124):[19]

> the irony of the present situation in Ghana is that it is quite possible that President Nkrumah and the CPP would command the support of a majority of the electorate .... in genuinely free elections.

Busia had, therefore, to pay as much attention to the urban masses as Nkrumah had done. But, ironically, Busia could not derive his power base from them, as Nkrumah could. For Busia, there was always the danger of his overthrow by the politically isolated groups, particularly the proscribed leaders of the CPP. Indeed the CPP possessed far more political resources than its proscribed status suggested. It was a rather difficult relationship; Busia as leader of the government was, in political economy terms, at the centre of an essentially Nkrumaist state that he did not identify with, and therefore could not control.[20]

Furthermore, in the designing of economic policy, Busia clearly favoured a shift of resources to the rural areas where his power base lay – a strategy which commended itself even to his most articulate political opponent, Kwesi Armah, who conceded that Busia 'achieved some success in rural areas by providing some water, electricity, feeder roads and health services' (Armah, 1974: 167). It was not possible, however, in the Busia period, when financial resources were so depleted and surplus production was non-existent, to achieve an immediate shift of the resource balance in favour of the rural areas without a significant reduction of welfare in the urban areas. The problems facing Busia in his attempt to maximize aggregate welfare were therefore greater than many, including members of the PP, imagined at the time.

The structure of authority in the Busia Cabinet differed significantly from that of Nkrumah and of the NLC. The 'verandah boys', having supported Nkrumah when the CPP was formed, with very few exceptions remained loyal to him throughout most of his reign. Their loyalty enabled him to build such an authority over them, and over the country, that for most of the time it was Nkrumah's personal decisions that mattered in national management.[21] The leadership of the PP never aspired to that level of personalized authority. For Busia, the situation was almost the opposite. An academic and intellectually inclined person, he reasserted the liberal intellectual aspects of state authority to the extent of running his Cabinet more like a college tutorial. Decisions were based on careful study and lengthy arguments. Individual members who were eloquent or persuasive tended to create and develop their own lines of thought and action, which were not necessarily those of the Cabinet, the Party or the Prime Minister.[22]

If as a leader Busia did not personally possess authoritarian characteristics, nevertheless he could not prevent other members of the Party leadership from developing this tendency, or indeed himself coming under the dictation of the wider authoritarian state that had been created by Nkrumah. The Busia effort foundered on three interrelated weaknesses in public policy pursued at the time, all of which illustrate weaknesses at the centre of authority, but more strongly, the fundamental fragility of the economy and the continued influence of the

Nkrumah legacy. There was a misunderstanding about how low the responsiveness of productive resources still was, even after the NLC economic reforms.[23] There was also a lack of understanding of the link between the rate at which administrative controls, especially those over imports, could be relaxed, and the strength of the balance of payments, given the weakness of the external sector that had developed in the preceding decade.[24] It was also not fully recognized that the government's ability to undertake economic expansion was severely limited by the increased sensitivity to external economic shocks.[25] These problems can be seen in relation to industrialization, fiscal policy and the external sector.

The wish to revert to a pace of industrialization similar to that adopted by Nkrumah was expressed in the very first Sessional Address to Parliament of the Busia Government. This rejected the 'mistaken notion that industrialization has been too fast'.[26] The pause in the rate of industrialization was explained as a strategy to raise the capacity utilization of existing installations. There are two possible explanations for this desire to follow the Nkrumah line. Both the NLC and Busia had failed to come to grips with the long-term implications of the imbalance created between agricultural and industrial policies in the Nkrumah period. It may be noted that J.H. Mensah, Minister of Finance and a key figure in the Busia Government, had been executive head of the Planning Commission in the Nkrumah Government, and had in fact drawn up Nkrumah's Seven Year Plan.[27] He was still wedded to the big push strategy and the idea of accelerated industrialization. The NLC and the initial Busia period might therefore have been regarded as a consolidation period for the resumption of the massive modernization process. The anxiety to produce a Two Year Plan in 1968 and a One Year Plan in 1970 would support such a view.[28] A second reason was the constraint imposed on Busia by the urban pressure groups, and his sensitivity to their demands. There was obviously the need to mobilize some kind of popular mass support at the urban level. The rural areas could not provide this since the rural programme could not be relied upon to produce, in the foreseeable future, the kind of increased productivity upon which to build both economic and political security (Chazan, 1988).

Whatever the reasons, the empirical evidence of the NLC and Busia periods would indicate that the policy regarding industrialization and project-based programmes, as opposed to price-based incentives, was not significantly different from that which Nkrumah pursued. The Busia Government (and also the NLC) would not appear to have been able to cope with the Nkrumah legacy or to respond adequately to its adverse effects.

The evidence on the attitude of Busia and the NLC to the private sector is in the NLC's policy document *Outline of Government's Economic Policy* published in 1967. It was emphasized that the government would assist private production in both agriculture and industry. In the document *Industrial Policy Statement*, published in 1968, as well as in the 'Two Year Development Plan, 1968', the NLC stated that its objective was to promote private enterprise. Similarly, in the PP Manifesto, the Busia Government promised its support and stated its confidence in the private sector.

The NLC's attempts at privatization took two forms: the sale of state enterprises to the private sector, to both Ghanaians and foreign companies, the latter in joint ventures, and the encouragement of completely new enterprises by both Ghanaians and non-Ghanaians. At the end of the Nkrumah regime 47 enterprises in the non-agricultural production and services sectors were fully state-owned, and there were four large joint state–private enterprises in textile, tobacco and cement production. Of the latter group, the NLC was able to sell off part of its interest in one textile mill.[29] The state also part-exchanged its interest in a soap-making factory with Lever Brothers.[30] Of the rest, the NLC was able to sell off only four, and these were fairly small establishments. It came up against the organized opposition of university staff.[31] Thereafter neither the NLC nor Busia had the courage to sell off any more state-owned enterprises. The sobering effect on both the NLC and Busia was an illustration of the potency of Nkrumah's ideology despite his demise. It would be correct to say that the effort at privatization failed.

Table 6.3 Value Added in Industrial Production Classified by Ownership, 1964–8   (Current prices million cedis)

	1964	1965	1966	1967	1968	
Amount						
State owned	18.4	18.4	24.7	33.2	40.6	
Joint state–private	4.6	7.0	11.5	14.2	17.9	
Co-operatives	0.2	0.1	0.1	–	–	
Private	74.7	83.7	99.1	106.5	118.2	
Total industry	97.9	109.2	135.4	154.0	176.7	
Index: 1962 = 100						Annual growth rate
State owned	110.8	111.2	149.1	199.8	244.7	30.0%
Joint state–private	136.2	208.0	339.0	420.8	530.4	36.7%
Co-operatives	303.3	128.8	226.7	160.0	20.0	–46.3%
Private	126.1	141.3	167.4	179.8	195.5	12.2%
Total industry	123.5	137.0	170.4	194.3	223.0	17.6%

Source: Economic Survey, OGS, 1968. p. 149

In terms of performance, during the NLC period the state-owned enterprises, after being reorganized and supplied with raw materials in a liberalized import regime, seem to have increased output faster than the private sector. Their share in total value added of the industrial sector rose from 16.8% in 1965 to 23.0% in 1968. Their share in total employment rose from 23.1% in 1965 to 27.1% in 1968, and then to 27.6% in 1971. It may also be observed from Table 6.3 that value added in industrial output in the state-owned enterprises was rising between 1965 and 1968 at an average annual rate of 30.0% compared to 12.2% in the private sector.

In so far as state industrialization was concerned, it can be concluded from the available evidence that the NLC and Busia came to fulfil, rather than to destroy, the ambitions of Nkrumah. The NLC did in fact create, between 1965 and 1969, four new state enterprises in produce and marketing, and an export company. Busia created one more state sector organization, perhaps the most important of all, the Ghana Industrial Holding Corporation, to coordinate the management of the state enterprises.[32] He also created the Special Task Force for Food Distribution in 1970 in an attempt to intervene in the marketing of local foodstuffs. It would seem that the concept of state ownership of commercial enterprises, and state operational intervention in the business sectors, had become accepted. When the NLC and Busia decided to retain socialized industries or to create new ones, they saw in such moves not a socialist political motive, but the desire to safeguard consumer interests or avoid public criticism.

Fiscal policy

In its first Sessional Address to Parliament, in October 1969, the Busia Government had given notice of its intention to expand economic activity. Nearly two years later, in July 1971, it still maintained this position despite deteriorating financial conditions. Its position was backed up by the substantial increases in capital spending. (Annex I, Table A6.1, col. 4). The Minister of Finance, introducing the 1971/2 budget, made the most significant statement yet.

> In the face of unfavourable trends which are forecast for tax revenues and the balance of payments, should the government cut back on development and even undertake measures of retrenchment in its operations? Or should government through its budget seek to support, maintain and perhaps increase momentum towards accelerated development which had begun to show in the economy? The decision of our government is that it is necessary and possible to maintain expansion. This decision is based in part on our general policy that after so many years of economic stagnation, the government should not, even in the face of considerable difficulties, take any action which would kill the trend towards economic expansion that has begun to emerge in Ghana in the past two years. We have many years of neglect to make up.

The budgetary results of the year (Annex I, Table A6.1, col. 4) indicate that the expansionary policy was indeed carried out. This trend in policy prompted an economic adviser in the Prime Minister's office to point out the similarity between Nkrumah and Busia:[33]

> In 1964–65 the then government [Nkrumah] opted for a very similar policy of unbalanced budgets as a means of stepping up the rate of growth of the economy. Quite apart from the political consequences, the economic ones were a full-scale balance of payments crisis, very rapid inflation and no acceleration in the real growth of the economy.

Significant sentences in the policy statement concern the wish to 'maintain and ... increase momentum towards accelerated development which had begun to show in the economy', and 'we have many years of neglect to make up'. Here another misconception of the economic trends in 1969 and 1970 is apparent. There had been some increases in food output in that period which are perhaps best explained by reductions in the fragmentation of urban–rural markets through an extension of the feeder road network. Industrial output had also increased, but this was explained by the import liberalization process. To say that a momentum towards accelerated growth had begun which should be nourished by fiscal expansion indicated unjustifiable optimism, which undermined the limited achievements of liberalization. Furthermore, the scope of further import liberalization as an instrument for increasing output was already very constrained by the structure of industry: the ratio of imports to value added was so high that further output was only possible through large foreign-exchange expenditures.[34] It would seem, then, that less than two years after being elected to power the Busia government had worked its way back to the fundamental problems that faced Nkrumah in his later years. In this context, the reference to 'many years of neglect' was mere political rhetoric.

The analysis of fiscal policy may be summarized as follows. The Busia government appears to have regarded most of the stabilization efforts of the NLC as having had an excessively contractionary effect on the economy, which it was necessary to reverse. The financial means to carry out this expansion were not available, and the expansion itself was not feasible, given the fragile state of the economy after Nkrumah. This does not appear to have been appreciated by the government. In the circumstances, two years were enough to completely undo the limited achievements of the NLC and to create far-reaching instability in the domestic economy. Furthermore, fiscal deficits were enough to foment resentments in sensitive areas in the urban sectors, and to destabilize the external sector. As we shall see in the following section, the effects of these factors on the external sector were crucial in the sequence of events that were to close the Busia era.

The external sector

The collapse of the external sector occurred very rapidly in 1971, particularly in the second half of the year after the 1971/2 Budget. Again this process was shrouded in considerable misunderstanding among the senior economic managers of the period. Public policy did recognize the important link between the balance of payments and the budget, as is evident in this note from the Prime Minister to the Minister of Finance:[35]

> As regards the budget, we must bring government revenues and expenditures closer to each other. We cannot redress our balance-of-payments if our budget remains in heavy deficit.... You do not appear to have dealt with this adequately in your proposal.

However, the basic philosophy that appears to have guided fiscal policy and external sector management was precisely the opposite:[36]

> Ghana, like every other developing country with a trade and production structure similar to ours, can expect to have a permanent balance of payments deficit. It is to fill this gap that aid is sought and private capital transfers occur. The only way to take Ghana out of this class of permanent deficit countries is to stop development. Therefore what we should be trying to do is not to remove the balance-of-payments deficit but to keep it down to manageable proportions.

This line of thinking would suggest that the new accumulation of trade debts, especially after the 1971/2 Budget, was not seen as short-term in character. This approach would have been reasonable in Ghana's circumstances at the time if the need to keep the balance-of-payments deficit 'down to manageable proportions' was in fact made an important condition for the management of development, trade and exchange liberation, and fiscal policies; if nominal exchange rate policy was made flexible enough to become a safety valve in the management of the external sector in the precarious reserve and credit conditions; and if the established export sectors were given the maximum incentives in the process of a more liberal approach to economic management. At this time approximately 76% of total imports had been liberalized (Table 6.4). The failure of the government to meet these conditions explains the rapid collapse of the external sector in the Busia period and the exchange rate devaluation in December 1971.

Table 6.4   State of Import Liberalization in July 1971

Type	Percentage
Open General Licence (liberalized)	76.1
Licensed (excluding fuels)	14.2
Fuels	6.0
Restricted	2.4
Banned	1.3
All imports	100.0

Source: Confidential Memo, dated 20 December 1971, to Prime Minister from Standing Development Committee

On incentives to cocoa producers, the evidence indicates that producer prices remained unchanged at C8 per load of 60lb throughout the Busia period. Relative to food prices, the real cocoa producer price fell from C3.84 in 1969 to C3.12 in 1971, at 1963 prices (Nyanteng, 1980: 16–19, Tables 3 and 5). Bateman (1971: 1–5) reported to the government from his study of the cocoa industry in 1971 that:

> The guaranteed producer price of C8.00 per load over the next five years will not stimulate the country's long run productive capacity, i.e. a producer price of C8 is not enough to induce new plantings...[and] is currently resulting in a 25,000–30,000 ton loss of production annually.

The high levels of public sector spending and the overvaluation of the exchange rate (Table 6.2) did not enable the appropriate policies regarding cocoa producer incentives to be implemented.

Table 6.5 Changes in Ghana's Short-Term Indebtedness in the Busia Period: 30 September 1969 to 30 June 1971 (US$ million current prices)

Nature of debt	30 Sept 1969	30 June 1971	Change
1. Pipeline of 180-Day Credit not yet matured	96.6	110.7	+ 14.1
2. Trade arrears and overdue accounts	40.0	63.9	+ 23.9
3. Arrears on invisible accounts	36.9	72.3	+ 35.4
4. Secured short-term banking loans	11.4	17.2	+ 5.8
Total short-term debts	184.9	264.1	+ 79.2

Source: Governor's statement to SDC, July 1971 on file 'Miscellaneous Debt Papers: Communications with Mr Heath, Prime Minister of Britain'. File No.1, p.9.

The problem of containing the country's external short-term debts was also a difficult issue (Table 6.5). In the Busia period these debts had increased by $65.1m by June 1971 (excluding trade debts not yet matured), and the expansionary effect of the 1971/2 Budget was beginning to impose a heavy strain on external management. Two issues were extensively debated at the time. The Minister of Finance argued that the accumulating debts were a temporary phenomenon which would be cured by a package of commercial bank loans. The Central Bank disagreed, arguing that it was the result of a long-term fiscal imbalance which required a moderation of policies relating to fiscal, development and monetary management.

A considerable effort was made in 1971, at the suggestion of the Minister of Finance, to explore ways to 'encourage American commercial banks to make available a line of credit of up to $45m to be utilized in support of the current balance of payments situation in Ghana'.[37] Letters to this effect were addressed by the Prime Minister to President Nixon and William Rogers, the US Secretary of State.[38] The response was negative because the Americans regarded this solution as undermining the ongoing multilateral negotiations on Ghana's debts and avoiding real measures to stabilize the Ghana economy. There was a general apprehension that Ghana was seeking to return to economic management strategies similar to those of Nkrumah.

The Prime Minister and other senior PP politicians were apprehensive about the new accumulation of debt, because of the belief 'which had grown up since 1966, and which Busia himself had helped propagate, that the medium-term debts incurred by the Nkrumah administration were the main cause of the problems of the economy' (Odling-Smee, 1972: 5). The senior politicians (apart from the Minister of Finance) therefore decided to explore the alternative of long-term concessional borrowing of $360m in order to retire the bulk of the short-term debts and leave $100 million for a 'cushion'. This decision was given priority in view of the growing repercussions of the 1971/2 Budget, notwithstanding the failure to collect the 15% import surcharges which had been imposed in July 1971.[39] There was an adverse effect on the urban pressure groups including the military, whose real incomes had already been reduced by the loss of allowances and fringe benefits in the 1971 budget.

Prime Minister Busia sought help from the British Prime Minister because of 'the long association between Ghana and the United Kingdom'.[40] Lengthy discussions were held between August and November 1971[41] with Mr Heath and British officials including the Governor of the Bank of England, Sir Leslie O'Brien. Approaches were also made to President Nixon, Chancellor Willy Brandt and President Pompidou. The Ghanaian leader had hoped that his personal good relations with the British authorities would elicit a sympathetic response from the British government. He also thought that his efforts at creating parliamentary democracy in Ghana, the threats to political stability caused by the severity of the 1971/2 Budget and the resulting strikes and public disturbances, would persuade the Western world to support him. He also believed that if the Finance Minister's assertion of the cyclical and short-term nature of the debt situation was correct, then it would not be difficult to obtain bilateral assistance. The impression gathered at meeting with Western leaders was that their response would be determined by the initiative of Britain.

The British response was negative. The British Government convinced Dr Busia that 'it would be impossible for any one country to undertake the major operation of providing a loan of $360m.[42] In a joint understanding the two prime ministers issued the following statement:[43]

> In a discussion of Ghana's foreign exchange problems, the two Prime Ministers agreed that the solution to Ghana's short-term indebtedness would be sought in an international framework. Mr Heath assured Dr Busia of the British Government's sympathetic support for action by Ghana to this end.
>
> Mr Heath took note of Dr Busia's view that an early reconvening of a conference between the Ghana government and its creditors was desirable with a view to reducing the burden in the short and medium term of the servicing of Ghana's medium-term debts as re-scheduled, and undertook to discuss with Ghana's other creditors the convening of a conference.....

In a Cabinet memorandum early in September 1971, on his discussions with the British authorities, Dr Busia invited and obtained the approval of his colleagues to:

(i) accept this report on my and the Governor's meetings with the British Authorities;
(ii) agree in principle that the IMF should be approached for short-term assistance, by means of a standby arrangement and by convening a meeting of Ghana's creditors;
(iii) agree that an attempt should be made to obtain from the Governments of the United States, West Germany and France a similar commitment to that made by the British Government.

It can be seen from the outcome of these initial discussions with the British government that the Busia government had been wrong in its assessment that the cyclical short-term debt problem could find an easy solution in a bilateral forum. It had also been wrong to expect that no conditionality would be demanded for such assistance. Indeed, it was clear from the discussions with Mr Heath (at which this author was present) and from this author's meetings with the Governor of the Bank of England and the British Treasury officials, that the purpose of shifting the discussions to an international forum was not merely to share the burden with others, but to ensure an enforceable conditionality through the IMF.[44] The rest of the world followed the British line and failed to agree with the Ghanaian government that Ghana was passing through a temporary cyclical phase in its balance of payments, and that help would be forthcoming outside an IMF framework.[45]

After nearly a month of negotiations in the Western capitals and a fruitless search for alternatives, Dr Busia received a letter from Mr Heath making it very clear that assistance was possible only through an international framework. The letter dated 30 September 1971 stated:

> On the short-term debt problem we are studying urgently the information which the Governor of the Bank of Ghana has provided for the Treasury and the Bank of England. We will let you know our advice as soon as possible. I can, however, confirm straightaway that in our view you would do well to make an early approach to the International Monetary Fund, and as I told you at Chequers, we would be glad to give this our sympathetic support.

What Mr Heath's letter also did was to shift the discussions to more fundamental issues concerning the general development problems facing Ghana. This again emphasized the disagreement of the creditor countries with the idea, then held by the Ghana government, that the balance of payments problem was of a short-term character. In the last paragraph of his letter, Mr Heath stated:

> Whatever your choice, it looks as if your soundest course will involve urgent action in curbing the rise of current expenditure, encouraging savings, increasing the proportion of expenditure on productive investment and creating a sustainable balance between current imports and exports to provide a margin to cover other external expenditure.

It was at this time, in the early part of October 1971, that a consensus appeared to be emerging at the top levels of economic management in the country that a policy of persistent balance-of-payments deficits was not likely to be supported by external donors or the international banks. Senior policy-makers began to recognize that the balance-of-payments problem resulting from the two PP budgets of 1970 and 1971 had to be settled in a broad international framework and should involve a review of basic economic management methods and development policy. But it was not until early December 1971 that policy changes actually began. In a statement to Cabinet on 8 December 1971, the Prime Minister announced that there was a major balance-of-payments problem, not a temporary short-term debt problem, and that the 1971/2 budget was to blame for the deteriorating economic situation. He accepted that corrective action must originate in the government. He also conceded that external support was necessary to support the government's efforts. This acknowledgement of failure formed the basis of the policy reformulation within the framework of economic liberalization that month. It culminated in the exchange-rate adjustment of about 42% on 27 December 1971.[46]

The analysis of policy in the Busia period has been undertaken in some detail for a number of reasons. First, it is necessary to demonstrate how fragile the economy still was after the NLC stabilization programme. It is noteworthy that the comparatively small attempt (compared with Nkrumah's) to expand fiscal spending in a more liberal economic environment seriously destabilized the external sector and required immediate and far-reaching modifications in management. The Busia experience showed clearly that, for many years after Nkrumah's fall, any attempt to reflate the economy was inappropriate for economic recovery and growth.

Secondly, it was clear that the exchange rate adjustment in December 1971 would not have been necessary if the economic managers had been more conscious of the Nkrumah legacy and had taken its effects more seriously. They would then have been less impatient about the need to 'end economic stagnation and resume economic expansion', as the 1971/2 budget statement put it. The decision to devalue became the highlight of the economic experience of the Busia period, and was reported to have brought down the government. A great deal of the discussion about this centred on secondary issues and missed the questions of primary importance that have been discussed in this section.[47] Thus another lesson of the Busia experience was the vulnerability of the external sector to any fiscal policy excesses. This factor was clearly perceived by Busia in his comment, when reporting on the Chequers meeting, on the critical link between the budget and the balance of payments, and also by the Minister of Finance in his note to the Prime Minister on the need to keep down the 'balance of payments deficit to manageable proportions'. These aspects were not, however, seriously pursued.

Thirdly, it would seem that it was in the Busia period that some appreciation became evident of the kind of long-term changes that were needed in the post-Nkrumah period for the reconstruction of the Ghana economy. Busia, despite his weak links with the Nkrumah state, had already accepted an economic reform programme which was politically unpopular but unavoidable. The lesson from this experience was that, in the post-Nkrumah period, Ghana needed a leader who was sufficiently courageous politically to take unpopular but appropriate measures and enforce them; who was able to recognize the important role of liberal intellect in the core combination of state authority and thereby gain a better understanding of the long-run analysis of trends in the Ghana economy; and, most importantly, who was capable of curbing the demands of the wider state of which the government was the nucleus. From what has been said, it is clear that the role of economic advisers, economic policy, research, and the dissemination of such research in any future programme of economic reconstruction were as important as political recognition of the phenomenon of decline and the authority to cope with it.

1972–74 : First Phase of the Acheampong Era

A principal reason offered by Acheampong for his takeover of power was that the two Busia budgets had reduced the real incomes of the military and the public servants. Acheampong also complained about the excessive rate of the devaluation, and opposed the implied redistribution of resources for the benefit of the declining export sector. The coup can therefore be interpreted as a rejection of the policies of the later Busia period that were beginning to recognize the inherent weaknesses of the economy and the legacy of Nkrumah. Instead, Acheampong accused Busia of permitting excessive international influence and of failure to take more radical action to suspend payment on the much publicized external debts.[48]

Consequently the first policy decisions of the Acheampong government were to restore allowances and benefits in the public services, to partially reverse the devaluation, and to repudiate the medium-term external debts. The new government immediately received political support from the Nkrumah elements and proclaimed a socialist-style policy of seizing the commanding heights of the economy. These actions were expected to have the immediate effect of worsening the economic situation in view of the above analysis of the precarious state of the economy in 1971.

That expectation was proved wrong. The economy prospered in the first three years of the Acheampong regime. Government revenues and expenditures as ratios of GDP shrank significantly between 1972 and 1974 (see Table 6.2), as did the ratio of imports to GDP. In 1972 in particular, the country recorded a trade surplus in every month of the year. Both gross and net external reserves rose to levels several times those in the Busia period as a result of the large trade surpluses in 1972 and 1973 (Annex I, Table A6.4). Do these trends therefore contradict our analysis? Some writers have praised the 'solid economic performance' of this half of the Acheampong era (Chazan, 1983 and Boahen, 1988: 8).[49]

It has been suggested that Acheampong's initial success derived from his ability to disentangle himself from the burdensome external debts and from commitment to doctrinaire ideas on economic development. It has been argued that this freed him to concentrate on practical and appropriate ideas such as Operation Feed Yourself (OFY) and Self Reliance,

(Chazan, 1983:163–4). The literature, however, has not yet found satisfactory explanations for the sudden failure of the Acheampong government after 1975. The following explanations support the view in the literature of the initial success and also offer some reasons as to why it did not last.

Immediately after the overthrow of the Busia regime, Acheampong was persuaded by the Bank of Ghana that the three principal arguments for the toppling the Busia government were not sustainable.[50] The Bank of Ghana argued for the retention of the December 1971 devaluation. Acheampong appreciated the argument, but would not reverse the major promise in his maiden speech to the nation. He insisted on at least a partial reversal of the devaluation and accepted the worse alternative of reimposing a restrictive trade policy regime similar to that of the Nkrumah era. [51]

In the context of the new trade and exchange regime, the Bank of Ghana negotiated for freedom to manage the external sector so that there would be no intolerable deficits. This strategy was designated as Self-Reliance in the external sector; it would work only if the Central Bank was able to enforce the pact. It was also agreed that if external debts were to be unilaterally repudiated, then the banking system would not be capable, for several years, of incurring further short-term debts. Imports would have to be paid for in advance, or the banking system would require larger balances to be able to negotiate trade credits for imports. The Bank of Ghana therefore negotiated with the government for a rapid accumulation of reserves to support the minimum level of desired imports.[52]

The reversal of some of the fiscal policies put in place by Busia implied a loss of government revenue. The Bank of Ghana negotiated for an understanding that these were equivalent to cuts in government spending and that fiscal self-sufficiency should be aimed at. This was incorporated in a wider definition of the philosophy of Self-Reliance. Based on the self-reliance pact, the Bank of Ghana agreed that the cedi might be revalued halfway to the pre-devaluation rate. The package of measures ensured, however, that the new nominal exchange rate remained effectively stronger than even the equilibrium rate in the period from 1972 to 1974 (Annex I, Table A6.6 and Figure A6.6), despite some weakening after 1973. As may be observed, the exchange rate then weakened at a phenomenal rate from 1975.

Finally, and perhaps most importantly, the Bank of Ghana suggested, and Acheampong agreed, that with unilateral debt repudiation, the possibility of both concessional and long-term bilateral capital flows and capital imports for industrialization and economic development was not to be considered for several years. Any chance of future economic growth therefore rested on the incentives for domestic agriculture. This explains what turned out to be the pragmatic policies towards self-sufficiency in agriculture.[53] This short period was perhaps the only one, outside the war emergency, when public policy focused on actively promoting the food sector.[54]

How long such a management system could have lasted depended on two factors. First, on how long the confrontation between Ghana and the creditor countries, and therefore the defiant attitude of the government and its supporters, continued. Second, for how long and under what conditions the pact between the Bank of Ghana and the government was respected. In both cases the period was not long. The self-imposed austerity programme was contrary to the original promise given by Acheampong to the urbanized constituents who supported his overthrow of Busia. The pressure within the government to settle the debt impasse was induced by the hope that better relations with the creditors would assist consumer imports that were drying up and capital flows for external sector-driven development.[55] The model of defiance was therefore not sustainable in the long term. The Acheampong government quietly reopened the debt issue with its creditors in Rome in 1973. Though the debts were renegotiated, capital flows did not increase in the Acheampong era. The pact with the central bank withered when the Governor was retired in February 1973, and a more accommodating relationship developed for a time between bank and government. In 1974 the international price of cocoa reached its historic peak and neutralized any adverse effect of the 1973 oil price increase. By 1975, the mood was no longer defiant towards the international community, but cocoa prices were on the decline and the Bank of Ghana was agreeable to print cedis to finance higher government spending.

While the defiant mood towards the international community lasted, Acheampong was able to subdue the demands of the state and thereby achieve a creditable economic performance in his first three years in power. We now investigate how, despite a more relaxed international environment and a more conciliatory relationship with the Bank of Ghana, the Acheampong government nevertheless took the economy into abysmal decline, and into political instability that would destroy four governments in the short space of five years. We also investigate the factors that forced the Rawlings II radical left-wing government to turn to the multilateral institutions for assistance and guidance.

1975–78: End of the Acheampong Era

A combination of factors was at work throughout this period to reverse the gains of Acheampong's first three years. The most important was the January 1972 decision to reverse the monetary stabilization and fiscal measures and the devaluation, and to unilaterally repudiate the external debts. These placed Acheampong in a policy straitjacket which reduced his ability to employ certain important policy tools. Once economic mistakes had been made, or exogenous factors had adversely affected the course of economic events, the government found itself unable to take decisions that contradicted the arguments for the coup. In effect, the Acheampong economic programme depended for its success on preventive strategies. The maintenance of a healthy external reserve 'cushion' was one such important condition. Unfortunately the cocoa export bonanza of 1974 and 1975 (Annex I, Table A6.5, ccl. 4) created a government expenditure structure that was not sustainable after 1975. The evidence is in the rapid rise in public sector spending in this period (Annex I, Table A6.1, ccl. 4, compared with lower revenues in col. 3).

Another factor was the collapse of Acheampong's military coalition with the bureaucracy, the business community and some of the traditional rulers. By appointing military men to all the top public positions including the boards of state financial institutions and of the Central Bank, the military became excessively exposed to, and tainted by, the changing economic circumstances.[56] As corruption also increased, the members of the coalition became the subject of public attack and resentment.[57] Acheampong's solution was to alter the character of the coalition by creating the Supreme Military Council (SMC) made up entirely of service commanders. The move enlarged the beneficiaries of state patronage and largesse and attracted even greater resentment from the lower ranks of the military (Jeffries, 1982; Chazan, 1988: 60). At this point the most senior bishops of the Catholic Church became so concerned as to send a memorandum warning the government of impending military insurrection.[58] They succeeded in creating some panic in the national leadership but no change in policies.

Acheampong's response was to attempt to accommodate the demands of his allies and supporters, particularly the members of the armed forces and businessmen. For this, the Head of State was given a special fiscal and foreign exchange allocation,[59] to be shared among friends and supporters. The process of placating possible forces of discontent led to the creation of a large mass of intermediaries between the formal resources and the informal markets. Inflation and the overvaluation of the cedi gave large profits to the beneficiaries of such state patronage at the expense of the ordinary people. The participation of the state at its highest level in the misuse of public funds also gave credibility to charges of pervasive corruption which came to be styled *karabule,*[60] or a licensed, beat-the-system approach to survival (Chazan, 1983: 194–7). There was virtual economic anarchy in which everyone broke the law.

Acheampong was thus able through state patronage to raise the barrier of entry to his throne for the orthodox contestants (the senior military officers) to such a height that the task of his removal fell on civilians and junior officers of the armed forces. The civilian revolts began in 1977, led by the Association of Recognized Professional Bodies (ARPB) and punctuated by student strikes. Other movements joining the pressure for Acheampong's removal were the People's Movement for Freedom and Justice (PMFJ) and the Front for the Prevention of Dictatorship (FPD), both of which were strongly supported by the *Catholic Standard.*[61] Acheampong's attempt to form another coalition under the guise of a Union Government was not successful (Oquaye, 1980: 67–110). The civilian pressure, joined by that of junior officers and other ranks in the military, forced his colleagues on the SMC to demand his resignation on 5 July 1978. He was arrested but not put on trial by the SMC.

Acheampong's demise shows a similarity with the Busia era in one important respect: the rapidity with which economic collapse occurred after a seemingly successful start. Acheampong was able to hold out a little longer because he was politically more cunning than Busia. He was prepared to use national resources to buy his security. The rapid collapse confirms the fundamental weakness of the economy – its inability to sustain fiscal acceleration given the underdeveloped food sector and low productivity. However, there were important political economy differences. Busia did not add to the numbers of the beneficiaries of state largesse. Rather, he underrated the potency of the forces in the urban sectors against his stabilization strategies in the latter part of his term. He therefore did not act with full awareness of the conflicts in the vampire state at whose centre he sat to manage the economy. The situation was different with Acheampong. He was bred in the Nkrumah state, his political authority derived from it, and he fully recognized its presence and power. The antagonized state got rid of Busia because he attempted to curb its adverse effects on economic growth, without adequate security safeguards.[62] Acheampong enlarged it, placated it, and was thrown out by it when no further benefits could be extracted from the devastated productive sectors.

Thus by the end of the Acheampong era the parasitic state was much larger and more demanding. Correspondingly, as the macroeconomic indicators in Table 6.2 show, the productive capacity of the economy had thoroughly shrunk. The remaining limited economic activity had withdrawn into havens of anarchy beyond the reach of state authority and state taxation. The rest of the period up to 1983 constitutes a classic example of a state that has lost control of its economy and therefore of its authority.

1978–81: The Akuffo, Rawlings I and Limann Interregnum

The pressures within the economy that led to Acheampong's removal could not be assumed to have evaporated with his departure. Governments were installed and removed depending upon what they could deliver from whatever resources that remained.

The remaining period of decline is therefore not difficult to summarize. Akuffo's Supreme Military Council (SMC II) was installed by other ranks and junior officers of the military, with the support of the ARPB. It quickly turned against its patrons when it introduced tough monetary measures and currency demonetization. Urban unrest returned. The military revolted ostensibly against the failure to punish Acheampong, and installed Rawlings I. The harsh cleaning-up measures and moral reforms were distasteful to the coup's promoters and also damaged the producers.[63] Substantial production and working capital were lost through confiscation of goods and arbitrary sales at below cost. The politicians persuaded Rawlings to hand over power as originally planned. Limann, who succeeded Rawlings I, was unable to undertake any measures of reform while the rate of inflation rose to the levels of the Acheampong era. Though he had been popularly elected, other claimants to power, obviously Rawlings and the military, remained threatening.[64] Limann, unlike Busia, may have had a better awareness of the conflicts in the vampire state, but the political and economic processes in the decayed state had evolved further in 1979 than in 1969. He was obviously impotent against it, in terms of appropriate economic measures and political measures to protect the government. Neither was he inclined to employ the extensive security apparatus required to sustain the needed radical economic reforms.

How then has Rawlings survived? The band with which Rawlings II took the stage in 1981 consisted of the discontented urban masses, disaffected other ranks in the military, students, the urban unemployed, lower-level trade unionists, a group of radical left-wing intellectuals and a sprinkling of disaffected politicians. All these were hard-core constituents of the urbanized vampire state. The declared enemies of the revolution included the entrepreneurs, the successful large farmers, the professional men and the business community.

The PNDC's approach to governance from 1982 to early 1983, focused on protecting the vampire elements in the state, was more destructive than that of any previous government. Its attempt at economic reform in 1982, within the framework of dependence on the socialist countries (the Four Year Economic Recovery Programme), failed to take off. The droughts of 1983 brought matters to a head, raising the inflation rate to 122.8% in 1983, the highest in the country's history. There can be little doubt that the PNDC would have been overthrown in 1983 if it had persisted in that strategy.

Conclusions

The essential features of the two decades of economic decline analysed in this chapter may be summarized as follows. The Nkrumah political and development strategies of the early 1960s had ignored the primary weakness of the economy, and public policy had also been oblivious of the precarious financial situation. Through a policy of aggressive modernization that brushed aside these impediments to growth, the government had sown the seeds of economic decline and created delicate problems of governance which have persisted ever since. Particularly important were the creation of virulent conflicts in the urbanized political economy, the excessive dependence of the state on the primary export sectors for revenue, the downgrading of the peasant food production sector, and the draining of the external sector.

The policies of the regimes that followed Nkrumah did not give the impression that the full implications of the Nkrumah legacy were known or appreciated. Post-Nkrumah governments, particularly in the latter halves of the Busia and Acheampong periods and in the brief Rawlings I interregnum, followed policies that could only worsen economic and political conditions. The decline of the economy and the disintegration of the political system were inevitable.

The unique political economy of the post-Nkrumah period helps to explain at least part of the process of economic decline. The Nkrumah coalition has remained to this day but without the central figure of its founder, more potent in his absence largely because he remains associated with the period before the major decline, whether or not he initiated it. Meanwhile the successor regimes have not been able to comprehend the nature of the decline or how to control it.

The Nkrumah coalition has indeed become increasingly potent and hostile to regimes that have tended to be liberal and less socialistic. This was the problem faced by the Busia and Limann regimes and the short-lived Akuffo government. It has been particularly hostile to economic reform measures under the influence of the IMF.

Post-Nkrumah regimes have therefore tended to accede to the escalating demands of the coalition at the expense of those sectors that more properly belong to their constituencies. It has been illustrated that the Busia regime was unable to raise the real producer price of cocoa. Neither was the Limann regime able to undertake economic reform measures at the time of Ghana's most massive economic decline.

Acheampong had promised benefits to the coalition on his first day in power in order to win its support. It has been documented that in the latter half of his regime, the demand for larger benefits contributed to the export price distortions and the exchange rate overvaluation.

In the first two years of the present Rawlings regime, it was again the influence of the Nkrumah coalition that dominated public policy until the unbearable conditions of 1982–83 forced a change in policy in which the influence of that coalition was reduced in favour of the hitherto marginalized rural economy, particularly the cocoa sector. But this was made possible through the massive exchange rate adjustments which provided the fiscal resources for higher real producer prices that had not been possible since the mid-1960s.

In 1983, the key economic indicators that required to be resuscitated if economic decline was to be halted were the share of cocoa sector incomes in GDP, the government's revenue base, and the level of imports. For this to be possible, a major economic rehabilitation was necessary which had to start with radical monetary and exchange rate measures. Also needed were measures to rehabilitate the export sectors and to promote domestic food production.

Since the early 1960s Ghana's development has been unable to benefit from external capital inflows of any magnitude. Nkrumah's dependence on expensive commercial credits, the so-called suppliers' credits, Busia's failure to obtain help from his British 'friends' or from other Western governments, the repercussions of Acheampong's unilateral debt repudiation on Ghana's external credit rating and the failure of Rawlings to obtain help from socialist governments, all illustrate the point. The implication for economic management in 1983 was that the large amounts of external capital required for rehabilitation would not be available if far-reaching monetary stabilization measures carrying the endorsement of multilateral institutions were not put in place.

The policy implications for economic recovery from such a situation are complex. In terms of macroeconomic management, orthodox techniques to reduce state expenditure in order to stabilize the economy are not applicable. Government expenditure as a ratio of GDP is already well shrunk. State authority, and therefore credibility, cannot be enhanced unless public policies employ measures to integrate sectors through liberalization. This is the more viable approach: to raise revenues through raising and formalizing production. Macroeconomic policy is therefore severely limited to nominal exchange-rate management and heavy dependence on external capital. In political economy terms, the policy options are also severely limited. The state has to gain firm control over the urban masses if adequate measures in the field of nominal exchange-rate management are to be implemented and sustained without adverse political repercussions, and if real resources are to be transferred to the rural food sectors and the export industries. All these imply a new policy perception which is diametrically opposed to that which has been pursued since independence.

These are the complex but crucial issues addressed in the final chapter of this book. The analysis that follows in Chapter 7 is undertaken to illustrate the particular problems of the cocoa industry, as an example of the decline and the requirements for recovery of a principal economic sector.

Notes

1. From *The Classification of Constitutions*, 1279.
2. Lewis (1955), Chapter 5, particularly pp. 225–7: 'the central problem in the theory of growth is to understand the process by which a community is converted from being a 5 per cent to a 12 per cent saver – with changes in attitudes, institutions and techniques which accompany this conversion.'
3. The use of expenditure variables (government expenditures and imports) means that the effect of cocoa revenues on them in the regression is indirect.
4. For example, in the Joint African Development Bank/Economic Commission for Africa document, *Domestic Resource Mobilization in Africa*, April 1988. The study concluded that the primary export sector of the African economy was the most significant source of savings. It also concluded that the massive decline of that sector does not make it possible for Africa to mobilize any significant domestic resources to support current economic recovery programmes.
5. A typical example was the creation, in 1961, of a large number of Agricultural Survey Officer posts, filled with political appointees with no knowledge of agricultural extension.
6. Farmers donated £25m. towards the Second Development Plan. They also agreed to deductions for the so-called 'compulsory savings' programme of the early 1960s.
7. The core combination of a well-functioning state authority is made up of the government (the nucleus), the party in power, the intellectuals and the armed forces. It is assumed that a harmonious relationship between them is necessary for the stability of the state and the economy.
8. This problem was brought home to the author rather forcefully when he began attending some Cabinet meetings in 1965.
9. 'Arthur Lewis, who worked with Nkrumah in drafting the Second Plan, says the man practically rejected the word impossible,' records Uphoff (1970: 293, note 5). Uphoff states further that 'the problem as they saw it [observers in the period] was that too few people around Nkrumah had a good grasp of economics and were will ng to risk his displeasure by standing their ground in disputation over policy.'
10. An important example in 1965 was the conflict between Nkrumah's forthcoming book, *Neo-Colonialism, the Last Stage of Imperialism* and the need for economic stabilization. The views expressed in the book sharply contradicted any proposed dialogue with the IMF and the World Bank, or any programme involving exchange-rate adjustments. The attempt to initiate economic stabilization in the middle of 1965 was therefore aborted.
11. The official economic advisers of the President at the time were Mr Ayeh-Kumi and Mr W.M.Q. Halm, who had built their respective reputations in private business and money-lending rather than in economic management.
12. These decisions were taken on the advice of Professor N. Kaldor, and against the protest of Mr Hubert Kessels, Governor of the Bank of Ghana (on loan from the Bundesbank, Frankfurt).
13. Killick (1978) refers to the Commissions of Enquiry into import licensing irregularities (Akainya and Abraham) during the Nkrumah period, and the Commission after Nkrumah (Ollennu), all of which reported not only that corruption was endemic in the system but also that the state and party supporters were the main beneficiaries of the rationing system.
14. This is from an interview with Afrifa shortly after the coup in February 1966.
15. An error which many NLC advisers committed, see note 23.
16. This effort, though, was limited.
17. An IMF Resident Representative arrived in Ghana three months after the coup and set up offices in the Bank of Ghana.
18. It is thus not correct that 'the urban-populist-autocratic construct of Nkrumah's was somewhat recreated in NAL' (Chazan, 1988). The NAL was not even close to the CPP in terms of ideology. K.A. Gbedemah had indeed organized the CPP in 1950 while Nkrumah was in prison, and had won the 1951 elections for Nkrumah. Nevertheless Gbedemah is a realist, not an ideologue. In 1969, he did not command national or urban support as Nkrumah did, as evidenced by the results of the elections in which he won no seats outside the Ewe ethnic areas.

19. Major Afrifa commanded the troops from Kumase in the Nkrumah overthrow.
20. The Nkrumah state is defined here as the interests involved in Nkrumah's mass mobilization for modernization, who benefited from previous economic decline. They included the enlarged bureaucracy, the military and police, the trade unions, students and other urban pressure groups. It would be synonymous with the vampire state.
21. As observed by the author at Cabinet and other meetings with Nkrumah.
22. This was particularly the case with J.H. Mensah, the Minister of Finance. Cabinet members, for example, were given little opportunity, no more than a brief period on the morning of the budgets, to discuss the two Busia budgets.
23. The author himself was in error in overestimating the degree of success of the NLC stabilization programme, and suggesting that new development strategies could begin. See Frimpong-Ansah, (1971: 8–10) (Valedictory Presidential Address to Fellows of the Economic Society of Ghana).
24. The Minister of Finance in particular had difficulty resolving this problem.
25. As is shown later, the Prime Minister was eventually persuaded of this fact, but not until considerable time had been wasted.
26. Sessional address, 2 October 1969, p. 6, quoted in Killick (1978: 324, note 44).
27. J. H. Mensah had disagreed, however, with Nkrumah on some policy issues and had resigned in 1964 to work for the United Nations. Nkrumah did not think these issues were important, and told the author that he was of the opinion that Mensah was attracted to the UN by monetary reward. This view is not to be taken seriously.
28. It is to be noted that Mensah was not alone in that period in believing that aggressive planning was still necessary to promote economic growth. Seers (1970), and many of the scholars who had supported or advised the Nkrumah Government on the Seven Year Plan, still had faith in strategies similar to those of Mensah.
29. The state sold off a minority interest in the Chinese-built Juapong Textiles to UAC, and gave the management to that company.
30. In this deal with UAC, the government gave up 49% of its shares in the Ghana Textile Printing Company (GTP) for 49% in the Lever Brothers soap factory, both at Tema.
31. Jones Ofori-Atta, then Lecturer in Economics at Legon, led a concerted attack on the return of state enterprises to the private sector. The most famous of the attacks was with respect to the part sale of the state pharmaceutical factory, with technical management, to Abbott Laboratories. Popular opinion at the time was that the attack might have been directed against a particular individual in the NLC Cabinet, rather than against the policy itself.
32. Before then state investments in commercial enterprises were coordinated by the State Enterprises Secretariat, a civil service organization in the President's Office.
33. This quotation comes from a paper, prepared in response to a request from the Prime Minister, entitled 'The Economic Consequences of the 1971/72 Budget', dated 25 September 1971. On file 'Post-Budget 1971/72 Papers, Office of the Prime Minister', Accra.
34. W.F. Steel, 'Import Substitution Policy in Ghana in the 1960s', Ph.D thesis, MIT, 1970, p. 142. Also 'Import Substitution and Excess Capacity in Ghana' *Oxford Economic Papers*, July 1972, pp. 226–7. Steel suggests that with liberalization real marketable capacity would not exceed 33% in most factories.
35. Note dated 15 December 1971 from the Prime Minister to the Minister of Finance. Miscellaneous File No. 1, Office of the Prime Minister, Accra.
36. J.H. Mensah, Minister of Finance, note to the Prime Minister on the subject of 'US Contribution to the Solution of the Debt Problem', dated from Washington, 5 November 1971, p. 2. Office of the Prime Minister, Accra.
37. Minister of Finance's note dated 5 November 1971, p. 3.
38. Prime Minister's letter to Mr William Rogers, US Secretary of State, dated 13 November 1971. Office of the Prime Minister, Accra.
39. The import surcharge of 15% was a tariff which was designed to have the effect of a nominal exchange-rate devaluation. The effective collection was assessed at the time at 8%.
40. Minutes of the meeting held at Chequers on Tuesday, 24 August 1971 between Mr Heath and Dr Busia, p. 2. Office of the Prime Minister, Accra.
41. Most of them attended by the author.
42. Minutes of the Chequers meeting Heath/Busia, 24 August 1971, p. 2.
43. 'Understanding between Mr Edward Heath and Dr K.A. Busia following their meeting at Chequers 24 August 1971'. Office of the Prime Minister, Accra.
44. There was a distinct impression that the British authorities had no intention of shouldering any bilateral burden at all, above their normal aid to Ghana. This was not because the meetings were not well prepared. There was no feeling of sympathy. Dr Busia thought at first that there was some distrust of J.H. Mensah, because of his uncompromising stance at the July 1970 debt meeting at Lancaster House in London. Later it became clear, especially after the meetings in the Treasury and the Bank of England, that there was no sympathy for Ghana's case.

45. The reaction in the PP was one of surprise and disappointment, because there was a general belief in the power of Busia's British ties and trust in J.H. Mensah's argument. The Central Bank was not surprised because its position on the fundamental economic problem was similar to that of the British. The Central Bank would however have preferred a bilateral arrangement to an IMF standby if management in the Ministry of Finance had been more moderate.

46. Characteristically, the failure of the negotiations with Britain was not a major disappointment for Busia. He considered the episode unfortunate, but one that furthered his education in the economic problem. He became more aware of the need for self-reliance. He was rather more resolved to follow a pragmatic approach to economic management, and he had already removed the portfolio of Economic Planning from Mensah. The fact that the Prime Minister ignored the advice of his Finance Minister and initiated the monetary reforms without first signing an IMF Letter of Intent testifies to his resolve.

47. See, for example, Libby (1976). Libby blames external pressures, particularly from the IMF, for the fall of the Busia Government. This involved an attack on the policies of the Bank of Ghana at the time the author was the Governor. The arguments gave credit to the Minister of Finance for opposing the monetary reforms, particularly the devaluation. External management techniques in Ghana (and in Africa generally) have changed significantly in the two decades since then and present-day economic managers in Ghana would perhaps appreciate better the position taken by the Bank of Ghana in those days, which perhaps could have spared them some of the present difficulties.

48. First radio and television statement by Acheampong, 13 January 1972.

49. Chazan moderates her opinion considerably in her 1988 paper, however.

50. These discussions took place at the Teshie Brigade Commander's Office on 14 January 1972 between the Governor of the Bank of Ghana and the new NRC Government. Interrogation shifted to negotiation after the policy implications of the new government's maiden statement had been analysed by the Governor.

51. It was immediately agreed that Brigadier Ashley-Larsen, who was at the meeting, was to take over the job of Commissioner of Trade and Acheampong himself that of Finance.

52. It should be noted that countries with inconvertible currencies often have to maintain higher levels of reserves to be able to negotiate letters of credit for imports. Despite its apparent poverty, Ghana, for example, has always maintained higher reserve levels than Côte d'Ivoire for this purpose.

53. The Attorney General, Mr Moore, who before the Acheampong coup was a director of the Bank of Ghana, played a key role in the negotiations between the Bank of Ghana and the new Acheampong government.

54. This is also an area which is wholly unresearched.

55. Interview with Rev. Col. K.A. Quashie, Commissioner (Minister) for Trade in the Acheampong Government. He recounts the anxiety of the National Redemption Council during the period of confrontation, and how the members thought the solution would improve economic conditions. Table A6.4 and Figure A6.4 in Annex I illustrate how imports were constrained by export earnings in the Acheampong period.

56. Soldiers in uniform were jeered at in urban centres.

57. Businessmen and women who had become successful in the Acheampong period, particularly those who had exploited their good relations with Acheampong, were rightly or wrongly associated with the destruction of the economy. Examples were Kowus Motors and Tata Brewery which were expropriated in the Rawlings I revolution.

58. This author was asked by the Catholic bishops to assist in drafting the Memorandum in early 1977.

59. This was confirmed to this author by Dr Donkor Fordwor, then Special Assistant to the Head of State and responsible for finance. The object, apparently, was to reduce his direct interference in the rationing system. See also Ocquaye (1980: 35) for an account of the system of state patronage and the distribution of largesse.

60. The word is assumed to derive from the Hausa '*kara bude*' meaning 'keep it quiet' or 'hide it'.

61. The *Catholic Standard* turned itself into a people's watchdog in these difficult days.

62. That J.H. Mensah would disagree with this opinion was indicated recently in a speech at a Memorial Service for Busia. He is of the opinion that Busia's political philosophy, which emphasized public liberty and the rule of law, is what should be cultivated, because it is the way in which the best cooperation between government and producer can be assured.

63. This affected several businesses and small traders, particularly food distributors and sellers of the so-called essential commodities.

64. Discussions on this issue took place between the author and Mr Kofi Batsa, President Limann's Party Information Spokesman, in June 1981, following the author's criticism of lack of action by the government to deal with the rapid decline of the economy. The message conveyed to the author was that the Rawlings problem came first.

PART III
The Failure of Cocoa

Part II has demonstrated the key role of the cocoa industry in the long-run decline of the Ghana economy. In particular, the compressive effects of the industry's failure on fiscal policy, on the external sector and on economic development were highlighted. A principal object of Part III is to highlight the cocoa industry as a case study of the destructive impact of the ruling alliance on a vital economic sector in the intitial stages of modernization. This Part therefore contains a chapter which considers in detail the long-run growth and decline of the cocoa industry, assessing the effects of price distortions on producer incentives and suggesting the degree to which the key productive and export sector of the economy may be decayed. The final chapter then proceeds to review the current Economic Recovery Programme in the light of the limitations imposed by the destructive impact of the vampire state.

7 An Economic Analysis of the Cocoa Industry

> It is better to keep the wolf out of the fold than to trust to drawing his teeth and claws after he shall have entered.
>
> Thomas Jefferson[1]

This study has emphasized the important role of the cocoa industry in the growth and decline of the Ghana economy. In this chapter we ask the question: what would have been the long-run trends in production in that industry if adverse public policies had, instead, been optimal? The methodology adopted is the following. An attempt is made to establish a long-run capacity base of the industry in order to estimate short-term, long-term and very long-term producer responses over the history of the industry from the turn of the century to 1985.[2] Optimal equilibrium producer prices are estimated for the period from 1954, as well as optimal production capacity based on these prices. Supply functions are generated from the analysis and different simulations are performed, using optimal equilibrium prices, long-run predictions of output from existing capacity, and optimal production capacity to determine production shortfalls since the mid-1950s due to direct and indirect effects, in the short run, long run and very long run.

A brief survey of the various attempts recorded in the literature to construct Ghana's cocoa supply functions and to estimate short- and long-run elasticities is appropriate in this introduction, to show the variations in the results and to illustrate some computational problems that should be noted in the interpretation and use of the results. The earliest recorded attempts were by Merrill Bateman in 1965 (Bateman, 1965a, 1965b). In these attempts Bateman contributed the idea of a farmers' effort coefficient and the vintage capacity matrix, which have become important props of most subsequent analyses, including the present study.

Important statistical limitations pose conceptual problems in the estimation of supply functions for cocoa in Ghana. These are long-run factors, such as the absence of data on tree population, new planting, or acreage, and short-term factors, such as rainfall data and smuggling across borders. Bateman attempted to overcome some of these limitations by using a two-equation structure in his econometric model to enable an iterative approach in the estimation of the coefficients. The first equation, the 'average capacity' equation, was expected to be distorted because of the absence of short-run variables. The second equation, a 'short-run fluctuations' equation, with short-term variables, uses the results of the capacity equation iteratively until the final results are statistically acceptable.

The Bateman average capacity equation is expressed as

$$X_t = A_o + A_1 C_t \dot{P}_t + \mu_t \quad \ldots\ldots\ldots 1$$

where X_t = acreage planted in year t

C_t = farmers' effort coefficient in year t computed as a function of Price (P_t)

μ is the stochastic error term

$C_t = e^{-B/\dot{P}_t}$ where $\dot{P}_t > 0$

or $\quad = 0$ where $\dot{P}_t \le 0$

$$\dot{P} = (P_t - \hat{P}_t), \text{ if } (P_t - \hat{P}_t) < \dot{Q} \text{ where } \dot{Q} \text{ is a constant}$$

or

$$= \dot{Q} \text{ if } (P_t - \hat{P}_t) > \dot{Q}$$

P_t = real producer price in year t

$\hat{P}_t$ = estimated real producer price in year t at which new planting will not occur.

As the Bateman model has been relied upon extensively in this study, certain assumptions in the model must be listed. First, it is assumed that farmers will ultimately respond rationally to changes in real producer prices in making their short- and long-term decisions. Second, it is assumed that the difference between the real producer price (P_t) and the cost of new planting $(\hat{P}_t)$, denoted by $\dot{P}_t$ is a key factor in farmers' decision to plant. Third, it is assumed that the wider the differential the more planting will occur, but that there is a ceiling after which no more new planting will occur. The limit of the ceiling is determined by such natural barriers as the reducing relative command over complementary resources in the short run, lack of certain comforts in the rural environment, and the relative attractiveness of urban investments. The farmers' effort coefficient is therefore assumed as a non-linear relationship $(C_t = e^{-B/\dot{P}_t})$ with the characteristics of a rapid increase to a point, then a slower pace up to a maximum that approximates, but would not exceed, unity. The ceiling is denoted by the constant $\dot{Q}$ placed on the differential $(P_t - \hat{P}_t)$ so that whenever $(P_t - \hat{P}_t)$ is greater than $\dot{Q}$, the price incentive coefficient is assigned the value $\dot{Q}$. Fourth, and implicit in the last assumption, is that the development of the cocoa industry is the result of autonomous local capital formation and not of the import of non-local capital, since capital for new planting is assumed *ex post* from the savings from existing investment. Finally, the Bateman model does not allow for any modification in the constant $\dot{Q}$ at the maximum between the nascent period of the industry and its mature state nearly ninety years later, and therefore does not account for the changes in populations engaged in the industry.

The Bateman 'vintage matrix' was developed from the estimates of the capacity equation as iterated with the short-run fluctuations equation. From the matrix was estimated the 'normal production' series as a variable, along with the short-term variables of 'swollen shoot' and insecticide for the generation of Bateman's supply function. For the period 1946–62, Bateman's estimate of supply response to capacity (not elasticity) was 0.392 for Asante and Brong Ahafo and 0.232 for the remaining producing areas grouped together. For the longer period 1932/3–1969/70, Bateman estimated, in 1971, supply responses of 0.2925 for Asante and Brong Ahafo and 0.2211 for other producing areas of Eastern, Central and Western regions of the southern forest areas of the country (Bateman, 1971).[3]

Other early estimates, using different methods, were by Behrman (1968) who obtained a national long-run price elasticity of supply of 0.71 for the period 1946/7–1963/4 and Ady (1968) who had two long-run price elasticities for Asante at 0.49 over the 1951–64 period, and 0.56 over the longer 1947–64 period. Ady's national long-run elasticity for the period 1947–64 was 0.18 which suggests a very low price elasticity for the areas outside Asante as a group.

In more recent times there have been renewed efforts to study the subject, largely in the search for more knowledge of the industry in connection with the Economic Recovery Programme (ERP). The first was by Akoto (1985). Using a linear programming model he estimated the long-run supply elasticity as 0.3040 for Asante and 0.2964 for the Eastern Region based on Agricultural Census data for the year 1970/71. This result was the smallest, so far, of the long-run elasticities estimated for Asante and Brong Ahafo. In a World Bank draft paper, Akiyama, in July 1985, employed a Bateman-type vintage matrix to produce data on 'normal' production classified by average age and yield for the period

1968/9–1983/4. The variables in his supply function were 'normal' production (capacity), real producer prices and insecticide use. Akiyama's results were a short-term supply elasticity of 0.24 with respect to producer price and 0.29 with respect to insecticide. He also estimated an elasticity of new planting with respect to producer prices – short-term 0.50, and long-term 1.50. His planting data, however, related only to hybrid trees, a small ratio of the total crop (see Table 7.3), and the results on planting response were therefore neither national nor regional. But his was the first effort since Bateman to interpret the long-term elasticity of supply in terms of planting rather than as an interval of years reflecting the average optimum yield from initial planting.

Stryker and his colleagues made a major attempt in 1988, covering the period 1945/6–1985/6, the longest sequence so far constructed. Their attempt is also significant because it picks up the analysis from the tail-end of the post-war boom, thereby covering the last major upsurge in planting in the Brong Ahafo and Western Region phase, and also incorporates the period of long-run decline since the mid-1960s. Stryker *et al.* based their analysis on Bateman's model and developed a vintage matrix of normal production capacity from 1945/6–1985/6 for traditional planting. For capacity before 1945/6 their calculation was based on an assessment of the rate of decline of trees between 1968/9 and 1985/6, with extrapolation back to 1945/6 based on the level of production in the mid-1940s.[4] This approach may be acceptable for the period of the Stryker *et al.* study, but it leaves some problems to be solved in the long-term analysis envisaged in this study. Production capacity in the starting and decline periods of the industry cannot be estimated in this way, because there is considerable asymmetry between the rate of growth to the peak and the rate of decline from the peak in the yield profile of cocoa trees (Bateman, 1971: Annex, p. 1.9). Moreover, the production pattern in the mid-1940s was influenced by the collapse of prices in the 1930s and was therefore not representative of the development phase of the industry.

Stryker *et al.* also adopted all of Bateman's assumptions and parameters, except the cost of planting which was re-estimated at a new higher figure of cedi 130 (at 1963 prices) from cedi 100 and kept constant for the estimation period since constant 1963 prices have been employed in the analysis. They introduced new variables, however, in the form of maize and cassava to reflect possible shifts of investment from cocoa in periods of decline. The coefficient of the cassava variable was found to be very insignificant and was excluded from the final analysis. It is common knowledge that cassava has never been an alternative crop in the forest regions of Ghana. It is not a staple food and is considered by farmers to be destructive of soil nutrients.

Several periods were experimented with for the best econometric results and Stryker *et al.* selected 1953/4–1985/6 for their estimation of elasticities. Their results were as follows:

1. Short-run elasticities with respect to:
Real Cocoa Producer Price	.22
Real Maize Producer Price	−.14

2. Long-run elasticities with respect to:
'Normal' Cocoa Production	.62
Real Maize Producer Price	.40

The long-run elasticity in their calculation is not a long-run steady state elasticity which must assume optimum levels of tree stock. Optimum levels have not been consistently achieved and therefore the empirical evidence does not exist for an estimation to be made. Normally such an analysis should focus not on a single parameter such as the long-run elasticity of supply but on all those assumptions underlying the Bateman capacity equation.

As will be explained later, these factors in combination have played a greater role in the rise and decline of the Ghana cocoa industry than any single parameter. Therefore, in the analysis that follows, elasticities are estimated as a guide and as a comparison with other results by other researchers, but in the determination of producer responses to producer pricing and other policy the simulations employ all the variables and their coefficients in the supply functions.

The Ghana Long-Run Cocoa Supply Function

The model that is estimated for the cocoa supply function is

$$\ln QC_t = A_o + A_1 \ln NC_t + A_2 \ln QC_{t-1} + A_3 \ln PPC_t + A_4 \ln PM_t + \mu_t \ \text{...... 2}$$

Where: QC_t is actual annual production of cocoa in year t
NC_t is 'normal' production capacity of cocoa in year t
PPC_t is the cocoa producer price at constant 1963 prices in year t
PM_t is the producer price of maize at constant 1963 prices in year t
μ_t is the stochastic error term

The lagged dependent variable Q_{t-1} is introduced into the equation to provide for the effect of the previous year's prices on current production. The effect assumed here, as argued by Stryker *et al.*, is not that of Nerlovian expectations (Nerlove, 1956, 1958); as cocoa producer prices are announced well in advance of the season, it is an indication of the resources that become available (or not) to the farmer in the previous season for tending (or neglecting) his farm.

The data on real cocoa producer price from the beginning of the industry to 1969 are taken from Bateman (1971). For the period 1970–85 nominal prices are those supplied by the Ghana Cocoa Board (COCOBOD), adjusted to constant 1963 prices by the consumer price index. Constant 1963 maize producer prices are introduced in the supply function to capture the effect of possible shifts from cocoa in the period of decline as in Stryker *et al.* (1988: 161). In our case the introduction of the maize price variable in the very long-run series allows for the effect of a short-term alternative activity to cocoa to be captured throughout the industry's history. But, as will be noted later, the alternatives to cocoa in the introductory period were rubber and palm nut collection, not maize.[5] However, the resurgence of the oil palm industry since the 1960s, coinciding with the collapse of cocoa, has involved new large-scale plantations and not shifts from peasant production of cocoa. Therefore a palm oil variable has not been introduced into the long-run supply function.

The short-run price elasticity is taken to be the coefficient A_3 in the supply function. The long-run elasticity is estimated as $A_3/(1-A_2)$, A_2 being, in this case, the coefficient of adjustment (Nerlove and Addison, 1958; Koutsoyiannis, 1977: 313). It is also possible to estimate from the supply function a short-term elasticity (A_1) and a long-run normal capacity-base elasticity, $A_1/(1-A_2)$. The short-run capacity base elasticity, assuming that the estimated normal capacity in terms of tree population has remained intact and not been destroyed in the period of protracted decline, would provide an indication of the limit of the industry's capacity to respond, in the immediate term, to price incentives. The long-run capacity base elasticity would suggest the long-run response or the expected rate at which farmers would return to the industry.

The long-run values of the normal capacity are therefore important not only for the estimation of the supply function but also for the determination of capacity-base elasticities that are useful for policy guidance in the period of reconstruction of the industry. This task is taken up below.

Estimating 'Normal Production'

Evidence from Ghana official sources[6] indicates that Basel missionaries were the first to introduce *Theobroma cacao*[7] into the Gold Coast from Mexico in 1868 in an attempt to produce small quantities of chocolate. In 1878 or 1879 a Gold Coast blacksmith called Tetteh Quarshie, returning from the 'Bights' (presumed to be Fernando Po) brought in a single cocoa pod. Only one tree survived from what he planted at Mampong Akwapim. The records show that due to the demand generated by the work of the Basel missionaries, Tetteh Quarshie was able to sell his harvested pods in the mid 1880s for the high price of £1 each. Following this domestic demand for seeds, Governor Sir William B. Griffith is recorded as having procured in 1886 'a large box of pods from San Thome and sent them to Aburi where a botanical garden was being established'. Local chiefs and Basel missionaries acted as agents for the distribution of seeds from the Aburi botanical garden.

Table 7.1 Commencement of Ghana Cocoa Exports 1892–1926

Five-year period	Average annual shipment (tons)
1892–6	12
1897–1901	418
1902–6	4,771
1907–11	20,934
1912–16	58,306
1917–21	118,290
1922–6	205,858

Source: Golden Harvest. GIS, Accra 1953, p.1

Available evidence suggests that exports began in 1892, from the product of seeds distributed earlier by Tetteh Quarshie and the missionaries, and picked up as seeds became available from the Aburi botanical garden (Table 7.1). The acceptance of the industry in the nineteenth century and its initial rapid growth have been attributed to very high initial prices paid by the government to farmers, 30 shillings per 60lb load (equivalent to £56 per ton) and the direct involvement of the government in promoting and purchasing all available production until 1902. Producer prices were almost halved after 1902 when the government handed over purchasing to local trading firms (17.5 shillings per 60lb load). Based on this early history, the starting date for the commercial development of the cocoa industry in the Gold Coast is fixed at 1895 for the construction of the long-run capacity vintage matrix.

Some important modifications, based on the available evidence, are also made to some of Bateman's assumptions. First, in the initial period of the industry's development, not all of the population in the climatically suitable areas of the Gold Coast participated, and therefore the optimum farmers' planting effort coefficient has had to be modified. In the best rain forest belt of the Western District of Asante, cocoa had not been accepted as late as 1904.[8] In the equally fertile Ahafo district of Asante it was introduced within 'a few years of the suppression of the Yaa Asantewa rising' (Dunn and Robertson, 1973: 42) and did not become accepted until about 1906 (*ibid.*: 46). Based on later regional production ratios, the farmers' optimum planting response factor has been graduated from a low of 9.315 in

1895 to the maximum of 74.516 in 1910,[9] instead of the maximum from the beginning of the industry as assumed by Bateman.

The second modification relates to the introduction of non-local capital from Asante into cocoa production in the post-war boom of the 1940s.[10] This means that instead of farm development being financed from savings, as Bateman suggests, capital imports for farm development are estimated to have begun with the 1940s boom.[11] In this study, therefore, optimum producer investment is assumed to start from 1944/5, when the new price increases began, and not from 1947/8 as assumed by Bateman.

With these modifications to the Bateman assumptions, a vintage matrix for normal capacity, starting from the beginning of the industry, can be constructed 1) to overcome the difficulties of Stryker *et al.* in estimating capacity for the period before 1945/6, 2) to provide a long-run normal production capacity as a key variable in the construction of a long-run cocoa supply function for Ghana covering the entire life of the industry, and 3) to estimate short- and long-run supply elasticities with respect to the capacity base of the industry. The availability of a reliable normal capacity base also enables a fair estimate to be made of the extent of tree destruction in recent years of protracted adverse producer incentives.

The following are the specifications of the long-run vintage matrix. First, the yield profile over the observed tree life of approximately 55 years adopted here is based on the results of cocoa variety trials at the West African Cocoa Research Institute (WACRI) at Tafo.[12] The yield coefficients shown in Table A7.1 and plotted in Figure A7.5 in Annex II are actual experimental results. As may be observed from both the table and the figure, the yield of the average cocoa tree begins three years after planting and rises rapidly to a peak from about the twelfth to the twentieth year. It then declines more gradually until the 55th year when it dies or becomes sterile. In constructing the long-run matrix, the yield coefficient is the multiplier of the assumed planting in any one year to determine the yield profile over the productive life of that particular year's vintage.

The second specification is the farmers' planting effort coefficient described above. The coefficients as developed by Bateman are accepted for this study with the modifications listed above for the initial development phase of the industry up to 1910, and the heavy investment phase in the post-World War II boom. The effort coefficients and the estimated vintages in the respective years $(C_t.\dot{P}_t)$ are shown in Annex Table A7.2.$(C_t.\dot{P}_t)$ is the factor from Bateman's capacity equation (Equation 1 above). The coefficient, A_1, of the factor in that equation has been computed as a weighted average from the Bateman results for the Asante and Brong Ahafo regions and for the rest of the country. For the period before 1947 when the greater proportion of cocoa was produced in the Southern regions of the country, the coefficient has been computed as .24577 and for the period after 1947 as .26440.[13]

The farmers' long-run response factors for each year are estimated separately for Asante and Brong Ahafo, and for the Eastern, Central and Western regions, and totalled as in Table 7.2. These totals[14] are carried into the vintage matrix as the vintage planting factors for each year from 1895 to 1985 (Annex Table A7.2). Each such vintage factor is multiplied by the respective coefficients of the yield profile spread over the 55-year life of the trees to form the columns in the vintage matrix. Estimated normal capacity in tonnes in each year is obtained by summing the factors across all vintages in that year and multiplying by the appropriate Bateman-derived coefficient. A summary of the vintage matrix is provided in Table 7.2 with the 'normal' capacity in tonnes, and the equivalent hectarage (converted at 150 kg per hectare) and tree population (converted at 1,700 trees per hectare[15]).

The normal production capacity derived from the long-run vintage matrix represents the traditional varieties only and requires to be adjusted for the incidence of swollen shoot from the early 1930s, the effect of cutting out from 1945, the application of insecticides

Table 7.2 Estimated Ghana Cocoa Capacity Base, Traditional Stock, 1895–2000

Year	Farmers' long-run planting response variable (c)	Estimated normal capacity tonne '000 (d)	Estimated yielding capacity hectares '000 (e)	Estimated tree population million (f)	Year	Farmers' long-run planting response variable (c)	Estimated normal capacity tonne '000 (d)	Estimated yielding capacity hectares '000 (e)	Estimated tree population million (f)
1	2	3	4	5	1	2	3	4	5
1895					1948	792.0	209.4	1396.1	2373.4
1896					1949	785.1	207.6	1383.8	2352.5
1897					1950	786.3	207.9	1385.9	2356.0
1898	0.3	0.1	0.5	0.8	1951	789.8	208.8	1392.2	2366.8
1899	1.2	0.3	2.0	3.5	1952	794.0	209.9	1399.6	2379.3
1900	4.6	1.1	7.5	12.7	1953	800.0	211.5	1410.1	2397.2
1901	9.5	2.3	15.6	26.5	1954	807.4	213.5	1423.2	2419.5
1902	15.4	3.8	25.3	43.0	1955	843.4	223.0	1486.6	2527.2
1903	24.5	6.0	40.1	68.2	1956	882.4	233.3	1555.4	2644.2
1904	36.3	8.9	59.4	101.0	1957	921.4	243.6	1624.2	2761.1
1905	53.3	13.1	87.3	148.5	1958	962.3	254.4	1696.2	2883.5
1906	76.5	18.8	125.4	213.2	1959	1004.1	265.5	1770.0	3008.9
1907	100.8	24.8	165.2	280.9	1960	1047.2	276.9	1845.8	3137.9
1908	125.7	30.9	205.9	350.1	1961	1091.1	288.5	1923.2	3269.5
1909	154.4	37.9	253.0	430.1	1962	1136.2	300.4	2002.8	3404.7
1910	183.6	45.1	300.9	511.5	1963	1182.3	312.6	2084.0	3542.9
1911	219.8	54.0	360.2	612.3	1964	1226.7	324.4	2162.3	3676.0
1912	256.6	63.1	420.5	714.8	1965	1269.1	335.6	2237.0	3802.9
1913	294.9	72.5	483.2	821.5	1966	1304.1	344.8	2298.7	3907.8
1914	335.9	82.6	550.4	935.7	1967	1327.4	351.0	2339.8	3977.7
1915	386.2	94.9	632.8	1075.7	1968	1340.1	354.3	2362.2	4015.7
1916	441.6	108.5	723.5	1229.9	1969	1347.2	356.2	2374.6	4036.8
1917	497.9	122.4	815.8	1386.8	1970	1351.6	357.4	2382.4	4050.2
1918	554.2	136.2	908.1	1543.7	1971	1354.7	358.2	2387.9	4059.5
1919	610.7	150.1	1000.7	1701.2	1972	1350.5	357.1	2380.5	4046.9
1920	666.7	163.9	1092.4	1857.1	1973	1333.7	352.6	2350.8	3996.4
1921	734.6	180.5	1203.7	2046.2	1974	1306.4	345.4	2302.7	3914.6
1922	799.3	196.4	1309.7	2226.4	1975	1273.2	336.6	2244.3	3815.3
1923	854.7	210.1	1400.4	2380.6	1976	1237.4	327.2	2181.1	3707.8
1924	892.7	219.4	1462.6	2486.5	1977	1198.9	317.0	2113.3	3592.7
1925	922.0	226.6	1510.6	2568.1	1978	1158.3	306.3	2041.7	3470.9
1926	947.7	232.9	1552.8	2639.7	1979	1115.7	295.0	1966.6	3343.2
1927	970.7	238.6	1590.5	2703.8	1980	1070.9	283.1	1887.6	3209.0
1928	991.4	243.7	1624.4	2761.5	1981	1024.7	270.9	1806.1	3070.4
1929	1002.8	246.5	1643.1	2793.2	1982	979.1	258.9	1725.8	2933.8
1930	994.3	244.4	1629.1	2769.5	1983	935.6	247.4	1649.1	2803.5
1931	987.1	242.6	1617.3	2749.5	1984	893.0	236.1	1574.1	2676.0
1932	989.5	243.2	1621.2	2756.0	1985	851.8	225.2	1501.4	2552.4
1933	999.7	245.7	1638.0	2784.6	1986	810.7	214.3	1428.9	2429.2
1934	1001.9	246.2	1641.6	2790.7	1987	769.5	203.5	1356.4	2305.8
1935	997.5	245.2	1634.4	2778.5	1988	728.6	192.7	1284.3	2183.4
1936	981.9	241.3	1608.9	2735.1	1989	687.7	181.8	1212.1	2060.6
1937	957.8	235.4	1569.4	2667.9	1990	646.8	171.0	1140.1	1938.3
1938	951.6	233.9	1559.1	2650.5	1991	605.9	160.2	1068.0	1815.5
1939	951.8	233.9	1559.5	2651.1	1992	567.0	149.9	999.5	1699.2
1940	940.6	231.2	1541.1	2619.9	1993	528.3	139.7	931.2	1583.0
1941	934.5	229.7	1531.1	2602.9	1994	489.5	129.4	862.8	1466.7
1942	925.3	227.4	1516.0	2577.2	1995	450.7	119.2	794.5	1350.6
1943	907.0	222.9	1486.1	2526.4	1996	412.0	108.9	726.2	1234.5
1944	881.2	216.6	1443.8	2454.5	1997	373.2	98.7	657.9	1118.4
1945	851.3	209.2	1394.8	2371.1	1998	334.5	88.4	589.6	1002.3
1946	821.5	201.9	1346.1	2288.3	1999	297.9	78.8	525.1	892.6
1947	792.2	209.5	1396.4	2374.0	2000	263.3	69.6	464.1	789.0

Notes c) Summation of rows in Vintage Matrix
d) Col c multiplied by Bateman coefficient (see para 7.3.07, Chapter 7)
e) Estimated at 150 kg. per hectare
f) estimated at 1,700 trees per hectare (COCOBOD Memo, July 1988)

Table 7.3 Long-Run Normal Cocoa Yield Capacity, 1955–85. Estimated at Actual Producer Prices

Year	Estimated traditional yielding capacity hect. '000	Estimated tree population million	Estimated normal traditional capacity tonne '000	Insecticide yield factor tonne '000	Swollen shoot cutout tonne '000	Hybrid yield tonne '000	Estimated total capacity tonne '000	Actual production tonne '000	Variation from normal capacity loss(-) tonne '000	Percentage variation loss (-)
1	2	3	4	5	6	7	8	9	10	11
1955	1486.6	2379.3	223.0	9.6	-9.6		223.0	229	6.0	2.7
1956	1555.4	2644.2	233.3	4.2	-11.8		225.7	264	38.3	17.0
1957	1624.2	2761.1	243.6	12.3	-5.8		250.1	206	-44.1	-17.6
1958	1696.1	2883.5	254.4	37.6	-8.1		283.9	256	-27.9	-9.8
1959	1770.0	3009.0	265.5	67.0	-11.4		321.1	317	-4.1	-1.3
1960	1845.8	3137.9	276.9	96.7	-20.4		353.2	430	76.8	21.7
1961	1923.2	3269.4	288.5	116.3	-24.7		380.1	409	28.9	7.6
1962	2002.8	3404.8	300.4	117.9	-24.7		393.6	413	19.4	4.9
1963	2084.0	3542.8	312.6	116.4	-20.6		408.4	428	19.6	4.8
1964	2162.3	3675.9	324.4	121.2	-24.8		420.8	538	117.2	27.9
1965	2237.0	3802.9	335.6	104.8	-24.8		415.6	401	-14.6	-3.5
1966	2298.7	3907.8	344.8	79.3	-24.8		399.3	368	-31.3	-7.8
1967	2339.8	3977.7	351.0	54.5	-24.8		380.6	315	-65.6	-17.2
1968	2362.2	4015.7	354.3	51.3	-24.8		380.8	323	-57.8	-15.2
1969	2374.6	4036.8	356.2	61.4	-24.8		392.8	403	10.2	2.6
1970	2382.4	4050.1	357.4	75.0	-24.8		407.6	413	5.4	1.3
1971	2387.9	4059.4	358.2	78.6	-24.8	0.1	412.1	462	49.9	12.1
1972	2380.5	4046.8	357.1	74.3	-24.8	0.2	406.8	415	8.2	2.0
1973	2350.8	3996.4	352.6	73.2	-24.8	0.5	401.5	349	-52.5	-13.1
1974	2302.7	3914.6	345.4	71.8	-24.8	0.8	393.2	376	-17.2	-4.4
1975	2244.3	3815.3	336.6	53.3	-24.8	1.3	366.4	394	27.6	7.5
1976	2181.1	3707.9	327.2	33.1	-24.8	2.0	337.5	319	-18.5	-5.5
1977	2113.3	3592.6	317.0	14.8	-24.8	3.1	310.1	271	-39.1	-12.6
1978	2041.7	3470.9	306.3	20.2	-24.8	5.3	307.0	265	-42.0	-13.7
1979	1966.6	3343.2	295.0	23.7	-24.8	9.2	303.1	296	-7.1	-2.3
1980	1887.8	3209.3	283.1	21.1	-24.8	15.2	294.6	258	-36.6	-12.4
1981	1806.1	3070.4	270.9	35.7	-24.8	23.4	305.2	225	-80.2	-26.3
1982	1725.8	2933.9	258.9	42.1	-24.8	29.7	305.9	179	-126.9	-41.5
1983	1649.1	2803.5	247.4	53.9	-24.8	38.9	315.4	159	-156.4	-49.6
1984	1574.1	2676.0	236.1	50.4	-24.8	48.4	310.1	175	-135.1	-43.6
1985	1501.4	2552.4	225.2	55.0	-24.8	57.4	312.8	219	-93.8	-30.0

Notes   Col. 2 hectarage calculated at 150kg. yield per hectare
Col. 3 tree population estimated at an average of 1,700 trees per hectare
Col.4 normal traditional yield from Table 7.2
Col. 5 insecticide yield factor from Bateman (1971)

Col 6 swollen shoot effect is assumed to be stabilized from 1964 (Bateman 1971)
Col 7 hybrid yield capacity from Stryker et al. (1988), World Bank
Col. 8 normal yield capacity is sum of Cols. 4–7
Col 10 is Col. 9 less Col. 8; Col. 11 is Col. 10 as percentage of Col. 8

Table 7.4 Long-Run Optimum Cocoa Yield Capacity, 1955–85 Estimated at Producer Prices Equal Border Prices

Year	Estimated traditional yielding capacity hect. '000	Estimated tree population million	Estimated optimum traditional capacity tonne '000	Insecticide yield factor tonne '000	Swollen shoot cutout tonne '000	Hybrid yield tonne '000	Estimated total capacity tonne '000	Actual production tonne '000	Variation from normal capacity loss(–) tonne000	Percentage variation loss (–)
1	2	3	4	5	6	7	8	9	10	11
1955	1486.7	2379.3	223.0	9.6	–9.6		223.0	229	6.0	2.7
1956	1555.3	2644.1	233.3	4.2	–11.8		225.7	264	38.3	17.0
1957	1624.0	2760.8	243.6	12.3	–5.8		250.1	206	–44.1	–17.6
1958	1696.0	2883.2	254.4	37.6	–8.1		283.9	256	–27.9	–9.8
1959	1770.0	3009.0	265.5	67.0	–11.4		321.1	317	–4.1	–1.3
1960	1846.0	3138.2	276.9	96.7	–20.4		353.2	430	76.8	21.7
1961	1923.3	3269.7	288.5	116.3	–24.7		380.1	409	28.9	7.6
1962	2002.7	3404.6	300.4	117.9	–24.7		393.6	413	19.4	4.9
1963	2084.0	3542.8	312.6	116.4	–20.6		408.4	428	19.6	4.8
1964	2163.3	3677.7	324.5	121.2	–24.8		420.9	538	117.1	27.8
1965	2243.3	3813.7	336.5	104.8	–24.8		416.5	401	–15.5	–3.7
1966	2322.7	3948.6	348.4	79.3	–24.8		402.9	368	–34.9	–8.7
1967	2402.0	4083.4	360.3	54.4	–24.8		389.9	315	–74.9	–19.2
1968	2481.3	4218.3	372.2	51.3	–24.8		398.7	323	–75.7	–19.0
1969	2561.3	4354.3	384.2	61.4	–24.8		420.8	403	–17.8	–4.2
1970	2640.7	4489.2	396.1	75.0	–24.8		446.3	413	–33.3	–7.5
1971	2720.0	4624.0	408.0	78.6	–24.8	0.1	461.9	462	0.1	0.0
1972	2799.3	4758.9	419.9	74.3	–24.8	0.2	469.6	415	–54.6	–11.6
1973	2877.3	4891.5	431.6	73.2	–24.8	0.5	480.5	349	–131.5	–27.4
1974	2952.7	5019.2	442.9	71.8	–24.8	0.8	490.7	376	–114.7	–23.4
1975	3023.3	5139.7	453.5	53.3	–24.8	1.3	483.3	394	–89.3	–18.5
1976	3090.7	5254.2	463.6	33.1	–24.8	2.0	473.9	319	–154.9	–32.7
1977	3154.0	5361.8	473.1	14.8	–24.8	3.1	466.2	271	–195.2	–41.9
1978	3214.0	5463.8	482.1	20.2	–24.8	5.3	482.8	265	–217.8	–45.1
1979	3270.0	5559.0	490.5	23.7	–24.8	9.2	498.6	296	–202.6	–40.6
1980	3322.7	5648.6	498.4	21.1	–24.8	15.2	509.9	258	–251.9	–49.4
1981	3371.4	5731.3	505.7	35.7	–24.8	23.4	540.0	225	–315.0	–58.3
1982	3419.4	5812.9	512.9	42.1	–24.8	29.7	559.9	179	–380.9	–68.0
1983	3467.4	5894.5	520.1	53.9	–24.8	38.9	588.1	159	–429.1	–73.0
1984	3512.7	5971.6	526.9	50.4	–24.8	48.4	600.9	175	–425.9	–70.9
1985	3557.4	6047.5	533.6	55.0	–24.8	57.4	621.2	219	–402.2	–64.2

Notes

Col. 2: hectarage calculated at 150kg. yield per hectare
Col. 3: tree population estimated at an average of 1,700 trees per hectare
Col. 4: optimum traditional yield from Table A7.5 Annex II
Col. 5: insecticide yield factor from Bateman (1971)

Col. 6: swollen shoot effect is assumed to be stabilized from 1964 (Bateman 1971)
Col. 7: hybrid yield capacity from Stryker et al. (1988), World Bank
Col. 8: normal yield capacity is sum of Cols. 4–7
Col. 10 is Col. 9 less Col. 8
Col. 11 is Col. 10 as percentage of Col. 8

from 1956, and the additional capacity from the introduction of hybrids in 1971. These modifications are incorporated into Table 7.3 to derive the long-run normal production variable that enters the equation for the supply function.

Table 7.5 Age Classification of Cocoa Trees, 1970–79 (COCOBOD Survey)

Age class	Area ('000 ha)	
Class A (0–7 years)	181.1	
Class B (8–15 years)	351.6	1677.5
Class C (16–30 years)	1,144.8	
Class D (Above 30 years)	313.4	
Total	1,990.9	

Source: COCOBOD Memo. 1988, p.1

The accuracy of the econometric result has been tested by the results of the most recent field surveys conducted by the Cocoa Marketing Board. The Board's memorandum of July 1988 contains the following information from the 1970–79 survey: 'the total area of cocoa in Ghana was estimated [in the period] at about 2,052,000 hectares ... of this, about 60,000 hectares were under sparse or abandoned cocoa, giving a total producing cocoa area of about 1,990,000 hectares'. Table 7.5 shows the age distribution of trees.

Compared with the above survey results, our long-run 1895–1985 vintage matrix yields, in Table 7.6, the hectarage estimations and age classes for the period of the COCOBOD survey. In the median year (1975) the vintage matrix yields a total hectarage of approximately 2,089,000 hectares which compares with 2,052,000 hectares from the COCOBOB Survey.[16] In terms of age distribution of trees, hectarage of land with trees aged below 30 years is slightly smaller from the matrix than from the COCOBOD Survey, and vice versa for trees older than 30 years. The reason, it can be argued from the COCOBOD Survey (Table 7.5), is that, despite the non-economic producer prices elsewhere, farmers near the border were expected to continue planting for markets across the border. The COCOBOD Survey indicates the abandonment of old farms in other areas or their destruction to make room for other products (*ibid.*: 1). The data generated in the vintage matrix are therefore acceptable as representative of a general long-run production capacity of the industry. The plot of the normal or capacity base variable against actual production is in Figure A7.1 of Annex II.

Table 7.6 Age Classification of Cocoa Trees (Based on Vintage Matrix)[a]

Year	Area in thousands of hectares		
	0–30 years	Above 30 years	Total
1970	1463	753	2216
1971	1515	709	2224
1972	1547	668	2215
1973	1558	631	2189
1974	1549	592	2141
1975	1533	556	2089
1976	1512	519	2031
1977	1489	480	1969
1978	1470	441	1911
1979	1459	404	1863

a   After adjustments for hybrids and swollen shoot
Source: Vintage Matrix

Parameters of the Cocoa Supply Function

Four cocoa supply functions have been generated based on Equation 2 above. They are 1) one using the series covering the long-run life of the cocoa industry from 1905 to 1985;[17] 2) one for the first period of the industry from 1905 to 1955, the latter date being when the industry became seriously disturbed by the confrontation between the government and farmers in the upheavals of the National Liberation Movement (discussed in Chapter 5); 3) that for the latter half of the period, 1944–85, the overlap enabling the effect of the post-war production boom to be captured; and 4) one using the series for the whole life of the industry but reserving 30 observations from 1955 to 1985 to enable a forecast to be computed for the purpose of measuring the long-run effect of pricing policy.

The estimated parameters of the four equations are presented below. A summary of the results of diagnostic testing is given in Annex II.

1. 1906–85 sample less zero forecasts (80 observations)

$$InQC_t = -.640 + .405InNC_t + .704InQC_{t-1} + .068InPPC_t - .081InPM_t ...(3)$$

T-values	(−2.124)	(4.162)	(10.526)	(2.561)	(−1.983)
HCSE	(.297)	(.095)	(.075)	(.031)	(.047)
Std Error	(.301)	(.097)	(.067)	(.026)	(.041)

$R^2 = .99957$

$DW = 2.02$

LM test for Autocorrelated Error (lagged dependent variable):

.04 $F[1, 74]$ Crit. Value = 3.97

The coefficients of all the independent variables have the expected signs, the negative sign of the maize price variable indicating that over the long-term history of the cocoa industry maize could be considered as a short-term crop into which cocoa farmers might transfer their interest. The coefficients of all the variables except maize are significant at the .01 level, and that for maize at the 0.05 level. The estimated supply elasticities are the following:

Real Cocoa Producer Price:	Short-Run	.068
	Long-Run	.230
Real Maize Producer Price:	Short-Run	−.081
	Long-Run	−.274
Normal Cocoa Base Capacity:	Short-Run	.405
	Long-Run	1.368

2. 1906–55 sample less zero forecasts (50 observations)

$$InQC_t = -1.056 + .714InNC_t + .450InQ_{t-1} + .033InPPC_t + .003InPM_t ...(4)$$

T-values	(−2.629)	(4.581)	(4.162)	(1.356)	(−.084)
HCSE	(.440)	(.173)	(.124)	(.028)	(.440)
Std.Error	(.402)	(.156)	(.108)	(.025)	(.402)

$R^2 = .99975$

$DW = 2.27$

LM Test for Autocorrelated Error (lagged dependent variable) :

2.04 F [1,44] Crit. Value = 4.06

The coefficients of all the variables, except the maize price, have the expected signs. The positive sign for the maize price, if the coefficient were statistically significant, would suggest that in the initial half of the history of the cocoa industry, maize farming did not offer any serious competition. The very low producer price of maize for most of the period under study, and the evidence of the more predominant interest in rubber and oil palm in the cocoa-growing forest belts, would make such an explanation plausible for this period, if not for the totality of the industry's history, as indicated above. The coefficients for normal production capacity ($InNC_t$) and for the autoregressive term ($InQC_{t-1}$) are significant at the 0.01 level; that for the real cocoa producer price at the 0.05 level; but that for the real producer price for maize is not significant. If suitable long-term statistical data were available the introduction of other variables such as new feeder road mileage and the real producer prices for collected rubber and peasant wild palm oil could have improved the general results of the supply function for this period. The estimated supply elasticities from this function are the following:

Real Cocoa Producer Price:	Short-Run	.033
	Long-Run	.060
Real Maize Producer Price:	Short-Run	.003
(Not significant)	Long-Run	.005
Normal Cocoa Base Capacity:	Short-Run	.714
	Long-Run	1.298

3. 1944–85 sample less zero forecasts (42 observations)

$InQC_t =$ −1.498   + .591InNC$_t$ + .565InQC$_{t-1}$ + .183InPPC$_t$ − .088InPM$_t$....(5)

T-Values	(−1.837)	(4.058)	(5.224)	(3.951)	(−.877)
HCSE	(.883)	(.136)	(.108)	(.047)	(.146)
Std.Error	(.816)	(.146)	(.108)	(.046)	(.100)

$R^2 = .99956$

$DW = 2.01$

LM Test for Autocorrelated Error (lagged dependent variable):

.05 F [1, 36] Crit. Value = 4.12

In this sample, the coefficients of all the variables have the expected signs. The coefficients of all the variables except that of the price of maize are significant at the 0.01 level. That for the price of maize is not significant and casts doubts on the general assumption that farmers departing from cocoa may have shifted to maize in a major way for price reasons, though the current sign does indicate maize as an option. The following are the estimated supply elasticities:

Real Cocoa Producer Price :	Short-Run	.183
	Long-Run	.421
Real Maize Producer Price:	Short-Run	−.088
	Long-Run	−.202
Normal Cocoa Base Capacity:	Short-Run	.591
	Long-Run	1.359

4. 1906–85 sample less 30 forecasts (80 observations)

The parameters and test results are the same as those in equation (4), but this analysis provides a one-step forecast over the period 1956–85 which is intended for measuring any abnormalities which might have occurred in the process of accelerated decline, particularly from the mid-1970s onwards. The forecast results are in Table A7.4 of Annex II. From the test of parameter constancy over the forecast period, 1956–85, the forecast Chi² (30)/30 is 5.97 which is higher than the acceptable 2.0 in this case. The Chow Test (30,45) is 3.1 against an F[30, 45] critical value of 1.72. These results indicate that the forecast values are poor *ex ante*, an observation which is quite clear from the plot of the forecast against the actual values (Figure A7.6 in Annex II). This result confirms an abnormality in the relationship between actual and expected performance. The plot suggests that the abnormality is concentrated in the later 1970s and the first half of the 1980s, when the forecast values were consistently higher than the actual values.

An important explanation is found in the Ghana Cocoa Board Memorandum (July 1988). In the 1970s the hectarage and production trends were close to the capacity trends established in our long-run vintage matrix (Tables 7.4 and 7.5), thus validating the computed 'normal' capacity base. A decade later a rapid deterioration had taken place which was out of trend with that predictable from normal capacity established by the vintage matrix. The projection of normal production for 1988 is 263,700 tonnes from approximately 1,758,000 hectares, 30% of which are hybrids. The Cocoa Marketing Board states, however, that 'the general consensus in COCOBOD is that the present area of viable cocoa is about one million hectares,[18] of which about 20–30% consists of hybrids'. This implies that approximately 34% of the expected hectarage as estimated from the authenticated long-run capacity matrix may no longer exist.[19] We therefore have theoretical argument to support the COCOBOD prognosis of a probable hectarage of cocoa that has been destroyed or abandoned to make way for other crops in the period of absolute decline from the mid-1970s. We can conclude that for purposes of estimating the long-run effect of price distortions on output, the use of the forecast values is appropriate, and that the test values themselves are an approximate measure of the magnitude of the long-run damage to the industry.

Price Distortion and Cocoa Output, 1955–85

The period 1955–85 is taken for the detailed measurement of the effect of price distortions on cocoa output as the year 1955 marked the victory of the state over the farmers in the agitations of the National Liberation Movement (see Chapter 5). Producers' frustrations therefore began about this date and increased as real producer prices dropped until producer investments in traditional planting ceased from 1963 (Annex II, Table A7.2). Planting effort coefficient has been zero to 1985, the end-date of our analysis.

An appropriate method of measuring the effect of the state's policies on the cocoa industry, suggest Krueger, Schiff and Valdes (1987), is by estimating the direct and indirect effects of price distortions on production. The direct effects are defined by them as those that normally result from policies relating to taxes and subsidies, from restrictions on trade, and from domestic price restrictions. The indirect effects are those that result from distortions in the economy as a result of deviations of the official exchange rate from the equilibrium exchange rate. The major issue in the analysis that follows is to show that the decline in production is largely the result of direct and indirect effects emanating from public policy, measured, as noted earlier, for the short run, long run and very long run, following the estimation methods of Stryker *et al*. To simplify the present analysis, the direct and indirect effects of pricing policy have been combined to produce a series from 1954 to 1985 of an optimum equilibrium producer price for cocoa. This is justified because cocoa is a wholly tradeable product, for which there is relatively no local market; the producer price is fixed by the government and reflects all the direct effects; and the fixing of the domestic producer price takes account of the relationships between the equilibrium and the official exchange rate.

The method of estimation and the resulting series are shown in Table 7.7. The steps in the calculation are as follows. The price in US dollars is multiplied by the estimated equilibrium exchange rate to obtain a series for annual optimum border values per tonne. From this series is subtracted marketing board costs in order to arrive at optimum border producer prices per tonne. A net tax rate of 10% (including subsidies) is applied to the gross optimum producer price series to obtain fair nominal prices per tonne to the producer. This series is then adjusted by the non-agricultural price index (base 1963) to obtain a series of real optimum equilibrium producer prices. Some of the estimation methods provided in the notes to the table require detailed explanation.

The *equilibrium exchange rate* is estimated by the purchasing power parity (PPP) approach. Trading partners' inflation is based on the import-weighted average of Ghana's seven largest trading partners and those of Togo and Côte d'Ivoire (Annex I, Table A6.6). In that table the results of the PPP approach are compared with those of other methods, namely, the ratio of the non-agricultural, non-tradeable consumer price index to the manufacturing unit value index of industrial countries, and the elasticities approach which 'estimates the change in the exchange rate that would be necessary to equate the demand for and the supply of foreign exchange if unsustainable balances in the current account and all distortions in the prices of tradeable goods were to be removed' (Stryker *et al.*, 1988: Annex 2, 2–12). The PPP approach, despite its known conventional defects, in this case gives a steadier trend while not being significantly different in magnitude.

The nominal producer border price usually has two components: the official producer farmgate price and the published COCOBOD costs for collection and transportation to the port of shipment, in this case the port of Tema. For the period studied (1954–85) a number of factors have affected COCOBOD's costs, the most important relating to those aspects that can be justified as marketing costs. Employment in the Board has not always been related to real marketing needs, especially in the late 1950s and early 1960s when the Board was heavily politicized following the NLM rebellion. Some activities, such as the management of extension, the supply of inputs and research have been undertaken at above real costs (Dadson, 1971: 212, 280). And some of these activities such as extension and the supply of inputs have shifted between the Board and government ministries. Thus the values that are estimated from the Board's accounts may be unstable and may inflate border prices in certain years. These are limitations that are not possible to resolve. The non-agricultural price index includes all items except local and imported foods, beverages and tobacco.

All the supply functions, equations 3 to 5, can be used in estimating the optimum levels of output in the related periods and from there the measurement of the effects of price distortions. Three different measurements are also possible, namely, the short-run effects, the long-run effects and the very long-run effects. For our purposes, the supply function for the period 1944–85 has been selected for analysis as interest is focused on the period from the post-war boom of the 1940s to the collapse of the industry since the 1960s. For this period the short-run, long-run and very long-run effects have been estimated.

The short-run effect

Under normal conditions, the short-run price elasticity would provide a satisfactory basis for measuring the short-run effect. In the case of the Ghana cocoa industry, this approach could give misleading results because, as was observed in the supply function, the significance of the coefficient of the price variable was not the most important. The price factor also works through the 'normal' capacity variable, and, in the short term, the effect of the autoregressive term was important, in that farmers' decisions to tend cocoa trees depended very much on the previous year's returns. For these reasons, the method used in estimating the level of equilibrium output in the short run is to substitute the real optimum equilibrium price from Table 7.7, col. 11 for the real actual producer price in the supply function and estimate new predicted values for Q_t as the short-run equilibrium output. It is assumed, as in Krueger, Schiff and Valdes (1986), that stochastic variations will be the same in equilibrium conditions as in the distorted situation. The reason given is that the factors involved, chiefly fluctuations in weather, are exogenous to both situations (Stryker *et al.*, 1988: 168).

The results of the short-run analysis are shown in Table 7.8 and may be interpreted as follows. As, by definition, the determination of the short-run effect assumes existing capacity and only takes into account the effect of the gap between the optimum equilibrium price and the real actual producer price, the estimated values of distortion are expected to be less than those of the long run and very long run. They involve only the resources for short-run maintenance of trees. The results show that it was only in 1956 that the real actual producer price was higher than the equilibrium price equivalent. Up to 1962, there was a rapid widening of the gap to a peak of 9.2% in 1959 before it fell to 2.6% in 1961. In this period, the percentage of distortion remained in single figures though there were wide fluctuations. The double-digit threshold was broken in 1964 after a rapid resumption of price distortion from 1962.

Though the worsening of the producer price short-run distortion appears to have been halted by the NLC in 1967, the effort was short-lived and by 1969 a new peak of 16.6% had been established. A 25% increase in nominal producer prices in the transition from the NLC to the Busia regime, and the generally satisfactory external sector performance in 1972 by the Acheampong government, significantly reduced price distortions facing cocoa producers between 1970 and 1972. The upward trend was resumed, however, from 1973 and short-run distortions worsened steadily to a peak of over 40% in 1977. Policies in the Limann administration stabilized the short-run distortions but did not reduce them, and so did the first phase of the Rawlings II era. A significant reduction was observed only in 1985, coinciding with the more effective exchange-rate adjustments to the greater benefit of cocoa producers.

The analysis of the short-run price distortions on output gives rise, however, to a much more general and important observation. The adverse producer incentive starting from the

Table 7.7 Equilibrium Border Cocoa Producer Prices, 1954–85

Year	Export price London US$/tonne (a)	Cocoa export fob price cedi/tonne official exch.rate	Export fob price US$/tonne (b)	Equilibrium rate cedi=US$ base 1963 (c)	Optimum export value cedi/ton (d)	Less CMB costs cedi/ton (e)	Optimum producer price cedi/ton (f)	Net of tax optimum prod.price cedi/ton (g)	Non-agric. index base 1963 (h)	Adj.optimum producer price c/ton base 1963 (i)
1	2	3	4	5	6	7	8	9	10	11
1954	1274	637	892	0.68	608.5	33	575.5	518.0	72.2	717.2
1955	825	436	610	0.68	416.5	36	380.5	342.4	74.1	462.3
1956	600	391	547	0.67	368.5	37	331.5	298.3	75.9	392.9
1957	677	632	885	0.67	595.6	37	558.6	502.7	79.6	631.3
1958	977	550	770	0.66	511.2	38	473.2	425.9	79.6	534.8
1959	805	439	615	0.66	408.0	36	372.0	334.8	79.6	420.5
1960	622	342	479	0.65	313.5	35	278.5	250.6	81.5	307.6
1961	496	318	445	0.65	291.5	35	256.5	230.8	83.3	277.0
1962	469	337	472	0.68	321.9	39	282.9	254.6	87.0	292.6
1963	573	357	500	0.71	354.9	43	311.9	280.7	100.0	280.7
1964	591	278	389	0.80	312.2	42	270.2	243.2	109.3	222.6
1965	400	262	367	0.96	351.7	43	308.7	277.9	124.1	224.0
1966	541	396	554	1.05	582.8	47	535.8	482.2	137.0	351.9
1967	658	562	551	0.93	512.9	46	466.9	420.2	138.9	302.6
1968	767	761	746	0.99	735.8	49	686.8	618.1	150.0	412.1
1969	997	818	802	1.01	805.7	45	760.7	684.6	159.3	429.9
1970	733	643	630	0.97	610.1	45	565.1	508.6	163.0	312.1
1971	565	688	669	1.01	678.4	88	590.4	531.4	170.4	311.9
1972	672	824	625	1.09	679.9	146	533.9	480.5	185.2	259.5
1973	1341	1294	1111	1.16	1290.7	211	1079.7	971.7	211.1	460.3
1974	2113	1688	1468	1.20	1759.6	314	1445.6	1301.0	259.3	501.8
1975	1520	1526	1327	1.37	1823.2	397	1426.2	1283.6	329.6	389.4
1976	2446	2596	2257	1.94	4371.3	336	4035.3	3631.8	446.3	813.8
1977	4709	3942	3428	3.43	11758.4	1071	10687.4	9618.6	648.1	1484.0
1978	3720	10396	6862	5.61	38472.2	1492	36980.2	33282.2	1161.1	2866.4
1979	3491	9120	3316	7.65	25378.4	2120	23258.4	20932.6	1757.4	1191.1
1980	2796	6300	2291	9.96	22811.6	3573	19238.6	17314.7	2564.8	675.1
1981	2234	5000	1818	19.84	36074.8	5200	30874.8	27787.3	5644.4	492.3
1982	1885	30558	1018	22.22	22612.8	11000	11612.8	10451.5	6448.1	162.1
1983	2240	60666	2020	46.88	94702.8	27000	67702.8	60932.5	12651.9	481.6
1984	2558	83323	2358	62.01	146221.5	44024	102197.5	91977.8	22661.1	405.9
1985	2378	120983	2238	63.75	142689.8	55416	87273.8	78546.5	29287.0	268.2

Notes: a) Export Price London Source IMF, IFS Yearbook, 1988;
b)FOB price, CMB,Accra; c) Source Frimpong-Ansah et al. ECOWAS Lagos 1987; d) Optimum value is col.4 times col.5 at full decimals;
e) CMB cost source Stryker et al., World Bank, 1988; f) Col.6 less Col.7; g) Fair tax assumed at 10% of gross farmers' income, still higher than average; h) Non-Agricultural Index Source Stryker et al.,
World Bank, 1988; i) Net of Tax Optimum Producer Price adjusted by Non-Agric. Index base 1963

Table 7.8 Short-Run Effect of Price Distortion on Cocoa Output, 1955–85

Year	$\ln Q_{t-1}$ (a)	$\ln N_t$	$\ln$Pcocoa	$\ln$Pmaize (b)	Constant	Q_t(total)	Add residuals	Adjusted Q_t(total)	Short-run optimum production tonne'000 (c)	Actual production tonne'000	Direct & indirect loss (−) tonne'000 (d)	Loss(−) percent (e)
1	2	3	4	5	6	7	8	9	10	11	12	13
1955	3.046	3.197	1.151	−0.367	−1.498	5.528	−0.043	5.485	241	229	−12	−5.0
1956	3.068	3.204	1.079	−0.383	−1.498	5.470	0.086	5.556	259	264	5	1.9
1957	3.148	3.265	1.095	−0.347	−1.498	5.664	−0.319	5.345	210	206	−4	−1.9
1958	3.008	3.340	1.165	−0.374	−1.498	5.642	−0.002	5.640	281	256	−25	−8.9
1959	3.131	3.413	1.128	−0.351	−1.498	5.822	0.033	5.854	349	317	−32	−9.2
1960	3.252	3.469	1.069	−0.343	−1.498	5.949	0.166	6.115	453	430	−23	−5.1
1961	3.424	3.512	1.019	−0.374	−1.498	6.083	−0.042	6.041	420	409	−11	−2.6
1962	3.396	3.533	1.004	−0.362	−1.498	6.072	−0.017	6.055	426	413	−13	−3.1
1963	3.401	3.555	1.027	−0.368	−1.498	6.116	0.042	6.159	473	428	−45	−9.5
1964	3.421	3.572	1.043	−0.378	−1.498	6.160	0.296	6.456	637	538	−99	−15.5
1965	3.550	3.565	0.975	−0.379	−1.498	6.213	−0.082	6.131	460	401	−59	−12.8
1966	3.384	3.542	1.036	−0.370	−1.498	6.094	−0.024	6.070	433	368	−65	−15.0
1967	3.336	3.513	1.049	−0.326	−1.498	6.074	−0.196	5.879	357	315	−42	−11.8
1968	3.248	3.513	1.076	−0.361	−1.498	5.979	−0.047	5.932	377	323	−54	−14.3
1969	3.262	3.532	1.121	−0.389	−1.498	6.028	0.153	6.181	483	403	−80	−16.6
1970	3.387	3.554	1.049	−0.366	−1.498	6.126	0.010	6.136	462	423	−39	−8.4
1971	3.401	3.560	0.980	−0.360	−1.498	6.082	0.110	6.192	489	462	−27	−5.5
1972	3.464	3.552	0.997	−0.384	−1.498	6.132	−0.054	6.078	436	415	−21	−4.8
1973	3.403	3.545	1.183	−0.376	−1.498	6.203	−0.169	6.034	417	349	−68	−16.3
1974	3.306	3.532	1.086	−0.368	−1.498	6.155	0.020	6.174	480	376	−104	−21.7
1975	3.348	3.491	1.086	−0.364	−1.498	6.063	0.076	6.138	463	394	−69	−14.9
1976	3.374	3.442	1.211	−0.398	−1.498	6.132	−0.038	6.093	443	319	−124	−28.0
1977	3.255	3.392	1.368	−0.395	−1.498	6.123	−0.003	6.120	455	271	−184	−40.4
1978	3.163	3.386	1.307	−0.348	−1.498	6.010	−0.001	6.009	407	265	−142	−34.9
1979	3.151	3.379	1.275	−0.340	−1.498	5.965	0.127	6.093	443	296	−147	−33.2
1980	3.213	3.362	1.201	−0.382	−1.498	5.895	0.061	5.956	386	258	−128	−33.2
1981	3.135	3.383	1.145	−0.369	−1.498	5.795	−0.092	5.703	300	225	−75	−25.0
1982	3.058	3.384	1.069	−0.354	−1.498	5.659	−0.225	5.435	229	179	−50	−21.8
1983	2.929	3.402	1.116	−0.418	−1.498	5.530	−0.113	5.417	225	159	−66	−29.3
1984	2.862	3.392	1.078	−0.349	−1.498	5.486	−0.023	5.463	236	175	−61	−25.8
1985	2.916	3.397	0.992	−0.325	−1.498	5.483	0.019	5.502	245	219	−26	−10.6

Notes:
a) Cocoa supply function is for period 1944–85, see Annex I
b) All variables are unchanged except cocoa producer price which is replaced by equilibrium border price from Table 7.7.
c) Short-run optimum production is antilog of $\ln Q_t$ of the supply function
d) Col.11 less Col.10
e) Col.12 as percentage of Col.10

mid-1950s remained in force in the 30-year period of this analysis, and was significantly worsened in the period after 1961. The measurements of the short-run price distortions in Table 7.8 provide indications of the transfers of the proportion of border prices (after adjustment for fair net taxation) to non-cocoa activity, and the denial to this important industry of short-run incentives continuously for three decades. Such a protracted disincentive could not fail to destroy the cocoa industry.

Short-run producer incentive is assumed to be maximized when the nominal exchange rate is allowed to remain in equilibrium, and farmers are paid a producer price which is the border price net of a fair net tax of 10%. Production estimations based on these optimum assumptions have been consistently higher than was the case for production under the protracted conditions of distorted or sub-optimal producer pricing. It can also be observed from Table 7.8 that the short-term optimum incentive output levels were considerable, with the expected peak of 637,000 tons in 1964.

The long-run effect

The method of estimating the long-run distortions substitutes the forecast values of the dependent variable for the lagged dependent variable. By this method, the notion of the long run is two-fold. The producer's revenue considerations in the current year are based on an optimum price and on production free from fluctuations. The influence of the previous year's revenues is similarly based and therefore producers are able to take an optimum long-run view of investment under existing general conditions. Since the major variables remain the lagged forecast dependent variable and unlagged 'normal production' (the capacity base), the long-run horizon projected in the analysis is not that of a steady-state situation of optimum investment in new planting. The long-run equilibrium production is therefore that in which farmers are assumed to take maximum advantage of stable optimum prices to maintain production at its optimum through tree improvement. An aspect of the constraint imposed by declining normal capacity and the forecast dependent variable is that, notwithstanding the optimum efforts at tree maintenance in this scenario, reversals in production are unavoidable in the long run and the equilibrium production must begin to decline.

The results of the estimation of the long-run equilibrium production are shown in Table 7.9. The following observation and interpretations are possible. First, the years 1957 and 1961 are those in which there appeared to be no distortions in real actual producer incentives as compared to the optimum. However, as in the short-run analysis, distortion rose in the intervening years and reached an estimated high of 22% in 1958. Secondly, the picture presented for the remainder of the period is very similar to the short-run scenario except that, in this long-run analysis, the magnitudes of distortion are significantly higher. The highest degrees of long-run distortions were in 1977 and 1978 when the levels of optimum production were estimated to be over 51% higher than actual production.

Within the constraints imposed by limited and reducing production capacity in this period, the analysis indicates that in the long run the maximum output could have been 657,000 tons in 1964, when output of 22% above attained high levels of 538,000 tons was possible. A steady decline would then have taken place and output in 1985 would have been approximately 25% above the already low actual level of production of 219,000 tons. The analysis therefore suggests the need to investigate further the options of greater optimization in a very long-run steady state of estimated production. Maximum levels of farmers' incentives would aim to maximize investment in tree stock and new planting, with limitations imposed only by land availability, vis-à-vis other staple and export crop needs, and international market conditions.

Table 7.9 The Long-Run Effect of Price Distribution on Cocoa Output, 1955–85

Year	lnF$_{t-1}$ (a)	lnN$_t$	lnPcocoa	lnPrmaize (b)	Constant	Q$_t$(Total)	Add residuals	Adjusted Q$_t$(total)	Long-run optimum production tonne'000 (c)	Actual production tonne '000	Direct and indirect loss tonne'000 (d)	Loss (–) percent (e)
1	2	3	4	5	6	7	8	9	10	11	12	13
1955	3.046	3.197	1.151	–0.367	–1.498	5.528	–0.043	5.485	241	229	–12	–5.0
1956	3.121	3.204	1.079	–0.383	–1.498	5.523	0.086	5.609	273	264	–9	–3.3
1957	3.088	3.265	1.095	–0.347	–1.498	5.604	–0.319	5.285	197	206	9	4.6
1958	3.198	3.340	1.165	–0.374	–1.498	5.832	–0.002	5.830	340	256	–84	–24.7
1959	3.186	3.413	1.128	–0.351	–1.498	5.876	0.033	5.909	368	317	–51	–13.9
1960	3.287	3.469	1.069	–0.343	–1.498	5.985	0.166	6.151	469	430	–39	–8.3
1961	3.359	3.512	1.019	–0.374	–1.498	6.018	–0.042	5.976	394	409	15	3.8
1962	3.435	3.533	1.004	–0.362	–1.498	6.111	–0.017	6.094	443	413	–30	–6.8
1963	3.428	3.555	1.027	–0.368	–1.498	6.144	0.042	6.186	486	428	–58	–11.9
1964	3.453	3.572	1.043	–0.378	–1.498	6.192	0.296	6.488	657	538	–119	–18.1
1965	3.478	3.565	0.975	–0.379	–1.498	6.141	–0.082	6.059	428	401	–27	–6.3
1966	3.508	3.542	1.036	–0.370	–1.498	6.218	–0.024	6.194	490	368	–122	–24.9
1967	3.441	3.513	1.049	–0.326	–1.498	6.179	–0.196	5.983	397	315	–82	–20.7
1968	3.429	3.513	1.076	–0.361	–1.498	6.160	–0.047	6.113	452	323	–129	–28.5
1969	3.376	3.532	1.121	–0.389	–1.498	6.141	0.153	6.294	541	403	–138	–25.5
1970	3.403	3.554	1.049	–0.366	–1.498	6.143	0.010	6.153	470	423	–47	–10.0
1971	3.459	3.560	0.980	–0.360	–1.498	6.140	0.110	6.250	518	462	–56	–10.8
1972	3.434	3.552	0.997	–0.384	–1.498	6.101	–0.054	6.047	423	415	–8	–1.9
1973	3.462	3.545	1.128	–0.376	–1.498	6.262	–0.169	6.093	443	349	–94	–21.2
1974	3.502	3.532	1.183	–0.368	–1.498	6.351	0.020	6.371	585	376	–209	–35.7
1975	3.475	3.491	1.086	–0.364	–1.498	6.190	0.076	6.266	526	394	–132	–25.1
1976	3.423	3.442	1.211	–0.398	–1.498	6.181	–0.038	6.143	465	319	–146	–31.4
1977	3.462	3.392	1.368	–0.395	–1.498	6.330	–0.003	6.327	559	271	–288	–51.5
1978	3.457	3.386	1.307	–0.348	–1.498	6.304	–0.001	6.303	546	265	–281	–51.5
1979	3.393	3.379	1.275	–0.340	–1.498	6.208	0.127	6.335	564	296	–268	–47.5
1980	3.368	3.362	1.201	–0.382	–1.498	6.051	0.061	6.112	451	258	–193	–42.8
1981	3.328	3.383	1.145	–0.369	–1.498	5.988	–0.092	5.896	364	225	–139	–38.2
1982	3.272	3.384	1.069	–0.354	–1.498	5.873	–0.225	5.648	284	179	–105	–37.0
1983	3.195	3.402	1.116	–0.418	–1.498	5.797	–0.113	5.684	294	159	–135	–45.9
1984	3.122	3.392	1.078	–0.349	–1.498	5.746	–0.023	5.723	306	175	–131	–42.8
1985	3.097	3.397	0.992	–0.325	–1.498	5.664	0.019	5.683	294	219	–75	–25.5

Notes: a) Cocoa supply function is for period 1944–85, see Annex II

b) In this estimation the equilibrium border price replaces the real producer price, and the forecast values replace the lagged values of Qt

c) Long-run optimum production is antilog of lnQ$_t$ of the supply function

d) Col.11 less Col.10

e) Col.12 as percentage of Col.10

The very long-run effect

The very long-run effect is measured by retaining the variables and parameters of the long-run equation, except the variable for 'normal' production capacity (lnN_t). This variable is replaced by that derived from the long-run vintage matrix which is estimated on the assumption that from 1944 producers' incentives had been maintained constantly at the optimum, so that new plantings were limited only by factors other than the producer price (Annex II, Table A7.5). In the period studied the land constraint was assumed at zero since the limits on land had not been reached in either the Western Region or the Brong Ahafo areas. The notion of the very long run therefore differs from that of the long run in the following way: while the long run limits itself to possibilities within the limited capacity as constrained by adverse policies on investment in new planting, the notion of the very long run incorporates a steady expansion in normal capacity (Table 7.10, col. 3). The very long-run optimum production series (Table 7.10, col. 10) reflects the steady expansion in 'normal' capacity. Nevertheless, estimated output rises to a peak of over 757,000 tons in 1979 and declines to 444,000 tons in 1985. The determining factor in this decline is the collapse of the forecast values of the dependent variable [lnF_{t-1}]. Thus the notion of the very long run retains the influence of the forecast values of actual production and therefore those of all other variables incorporated in the original supply function.

Highest production expectations under the very long-run scenario are concentrated in the period 1974–80, with a peak of 757,000 tons in 1979. This period coincides with that of the highest international prices achieved in recent years (Table 7.7, col. 2) when actual production was only between 37% and 56% of the very long-run production possibilities, if there had been no producer price distortions. In that period Ghana remained a significant world producer, with over 10% of the total world market. In that scenario, Ghana would have remained a leading producer and a principal influence on international prices. The loss of production and of foreign exchange earnings are both significant. It is arguable whether new producers in the Far East would have invested in the industry if Ghana had remained a leading producer.

The estimated very long-run effects of price distortions on cocoa output, as shown in Table 7.10, are significantly greater than those of the long run (Table 7.9) and of the short run (Table 7.8). The greater distortions and differences in the effects of the different scenarios have taken place in more recent years, especially after 1973.

Comparisons with Other Studies

A summarized statement of the supply functions and supply elasticities derived from this study is given in Table 7.11. The elasticities are compared with results from other studies and explanations are offered where possible. First, we may observe that the construction of the long-run vintage matrix has enabled this study to estimate supply functions for the entire history of the industry which show very significant differences between the parameters in the early and later periods.

The results that can be compared with other studies are those for the period 1944–85. In terms of methodology, the Stryker and Akiyama studies are those closest to this one. Equation (4) in Table 7.11 covers the same period as that of Stryker *et al.* for purposes of comparison of the parameters.[20] From this supply function, the short-term price elasticity is the same as that obtained by Stryker *et al.* The long-run elasticity is smaller, most probably because the 'normal' capacity data estimated by Stryker *et al.* are generally somewhat higher than those in this study. The resulting fit of 'normal' production to actual production

Table 7.10 The Very Long-Run Effect of Producer Price Distortion on Cocoa Output, 1955–85

Year	InF_{t-1} (a)	$InOPN_t$ (f)	InPcocoa	InPmaize (b)	Constant	Q_t(Total)	Add residuals	Adjusted Q_t(total)	Very long-run optimum production tonne'000	Actual production tonne'000	Direct & indirect loss (–) tonne'000	Loss (–) percent (e)
1	2	3	4	5	6	7	8	9	10	11	12	13
1955	3.046	3.170	1.151	-0.367	-1.498	5.501	-0.043	5.458	235	229	-6	-2.6
1956	3.121	3.200	1.079	-0.383	-1.498	5.519	0.086	5.605	272	264	-8	-2.9
1957	3.088	3.279	1.095	-0.347	-1.498	5.617	-0.319	5.298	200	206	6	3.0
1958	3.198	3.336	1.165	-0.374	-1.498	5.827	-0.002	5.825	339	256	-83	-24.5
1959	3.186	3.407	1.128	-0.351	-1.498	5.871	0.033	5.904	367	317	-50	-13.6
1960	3.287	3.454	1.069	-0.343	-1.498	5.969	0.166	6.135	462	430	-32	-6.9
1961	3.359	3.506	1.019	-0.374	-1.498	6.012	-0.042	5.970	392	409	17	4.3
1962	3.435	3.533	1.004	-0.362	-1.498	6.112	-0.017	6.095	444	413	-31	-7.0
1963	3.428	3.561	1.027	-0.368	-1.498	6.150	0.042	6.192	489	428	-61	-12.5
1964	3.453	3.639	1.043	-0.378	-1.498	6.259	0.296	6.555	703	538	-165	-23.5
1965	3.478	3.639	0.975	-0.379	-1.498	6.215	-0.082	6.133	461	401	-60	-13.0
1966	3.508	3.547	1.036	-0.370	-1.498	6.223	-0.024	6.199	492	368	-124	-25.2
1967	3.441	3.528	1.049	-0.326	-1.498	6.194	-0.196	5.998	403	315	-88	-21.8
1968	3.429	3.541	1.076	-0.361	-1.498	6.188	-0.047	6.141	465	323	-142	-30.5
1969	3.376	3.573	1.121	-0.389	-1.498	6.183	0.153	6.336	565	403	-162	-28.7
1970	3.403	3.607	1.049	-0.366	-1.498	6.196	0.010	6.206	494	423	-71	-14.4
1971	3.459	3.628	0.980	-0.360	-1.498	6.208	0.110	6.318	554	462	-92	-16.6
1972	3.434	3.638	0.997	-0.384	-1.498	6.187	-0.054	6.133	461	415	-46	-10.0
1973	3.462	3.652	1.128	-0.376	-1.498	6.369	-0.169	6.200	493	349	-144	-29.2
1974	3.502	3.664	1.183	-0.368	-1.498	6.482	0.020	6.502	666	376	-290	-43.5
1975	3.475	3.654	1.086	-0.364	-1.498	6.353	0.076	6.429	620	394	-226	-36.5
1976	3.423	3.643	1.211	-0.398	-1.498	6.381	-0.038	6.343	568	319	-249	-43.8
1977	3.462	3.633	1.368	-0.395	-1.498	6.571	-0.003	6.568	712	271	-441	-61.9
1978	3.457	3.654	1.307	-0.348	-1.498	6.572	-0.001	6.571	714	265	-449	-62.9
1979	3.393	3.674	1.275	-0.340	-1.498	6.503	0.127	6.630	757	296	-461	-60.9
1980	3.368	3.686	1.201	-0.382	-1.498	6.375	0.061	6.436	624	258	-366	-58.7
1981	3.328	3.720	1.145	-0.369	-1.498	6.326	-0.092	6.234	510	225	-285	-55.9
1982	3.272	3.742	1.069	-0.354	-1.498	6.231	-0.225	6.006	406	179	-227	-55.9
1983	3.195	3.771	1.116	-0.418	-1.498	6.165	-0.113	6.052	425	159	-266	-62.6
1984	3.122	3.784	1.078	-0.349	-1.498	6.137	-0.023	6.114	452	175	-277	-61.3
1985	3.097	3.802	0.992	-0.325	-1.498	6.069	0.019	6.088	441	219	-222	-50.3

Notes: a) Cocoa supply function is for period 1944–85, see Annex I; b) In this estimation the equilibrium border price replaces the real producer price, and the forecast values replace the lagged values of Q_t; c) Long-run optimum production is antilog of InQ_t of the supply function; d) Col.11 less Col.10; e) Col.12 as percentage of Col.10; f) Estimated production capacity based on optimum producer prices from 1944 to 1985 replaces capacity based on actual price in the supply function

(Stryker *et al.*, 1988: Annex 4, p. 4.9, Fig. 11) is therefore not as good as the fit obtained in this study (Annex II, Figure A7.2). Consequently also the estimated production data in Stryker *et al.*, based on the very long-run scenario, exceed one million tons in some years, which the authors themselves admit 'would have encountered severe constraints in terms of both the effect they would have had on world market prices and the availability of land' (Stryker *et al.*, 1988: 168, note 12). This problem is overcome in the present study largely because the long-run vintage matrix is fully derived from the beginning of the industry.

The smaller price elasticities obtained in this study compared with other studies, except Akoto's linear programme approach (1985), follow from the above argument and this emphasizes the effect of what may be a more correct productive base variable. It is also in line with the negative correlation observed in the results between the real producer price and output. This was particularly pronounced in the period before 1955 where both the short- and long-run elasticities approach zero.

The elasticities which appear to be more relevant in the Ghana cocoa industry are those of the capacity base. In Akiyama (1985) this elasticity, determined with respect to price in both the short and long run, is high and compares well with the results in this study, which have been derived differently, as supply elasticity with respect to the capacity base. Here it is hypothesized that the levels of production have been determined more by the tree stock than by producer prices. This would thus be further evidence in the 'vent for surplus' debate (Myint, 1958; Caves, 1965; and Ingham, 1987). Though considerable analytical sophistication has gone into other analyses such as Ady (1968) and Behrman (1968), the periods covered by these studies (15 to 18 years by Ady and 18 by Behrman) are rather short to capture the long-run significance of some of the important variables.

Conclusions

A number of findings can be drawn from the analysis in this chapter. The first is that the real producer price played a key role in the establishment of the industry, even though the optimum price took a considerable time to entice farmers away from other pursuits. The analysis indicates that the very high producer prices that enabled the industry to take off have scarcely been equalled since the first two decades. Real producer prices have subsequently followed a consistent downward trend, but for most of the history of the industry they have been competitive with other farming products such as maize, oil palm or rubber.

The second finding is that throughout the history of the industry a sustained optimum incentive has been available only for two periods: from the initial phase to about 1917, and from 1947 to 1960. The development of the entire tree stock has been the result of these two maximum incentive phases alone (Figure 7.1). The present major decline of the industry is the result of nearly thirty years of sub-optimal incentives and distorted prices since about 1961. The present phase of price distortion has been so prolonged and the decline of the industry so massive that it would require sustained maximum incentives for an equally extended period for full confidence to return to the industry. The present evidence is that the higher prices resulting from the removal of distortions from exchange-rate overvaluation are benefiting short-term restoration of farms and are therefore advantageous to the industry. Sustained higher prices are required for the very long-run rebuilding of the tree stock (Seini, Howell and Commander, 1987: 28). This would indicate that producer price enhancement has yet to attain the optimum Bateman incentive coefficient (Annex II, Table A7.5, col. 7).

The third finding is that all governments from the mid-1950s to 1983 have contributed

Table 7.11 Parameters of the Cocoa Supply Functions

Equation	Period	lnNC(t)	lnQ(t−1)	lnPPC(t)	lnPPM(t)	Constant	R^2	LM test for autocorrelation lagged dependent variable
1	2	3	4	5	6	7	8	9
(1)	1906–85	0.405 (4.162)*	0.704 (10.526)*	0.068 (2.561)*	−0.081 (−1.983)**	−0.64 (−2.124)**	0.99957	0.04 F(1, 74)Crit.Val.=3.97
(2)	1906–55	0.714 (4.581)*	0.45 (4.162)*	0.033 (1.356)	0.003 (.084)	−1.056 (−2.629)**	0.99975	2.04 F(1, 44)Crit.Val.=4.06
(3)	1944–85	0.591 (4.058)*	0.565 (5.224)*	0.183 (3.951)*	−0.088 (−.877)	−1.498 (−1.837)**	0.99956	0.05 F(1, 36)Crit.Val.=4.12
(4)	1953–85	0.880 (4.256)*	0.478 (3.899)*	0.223 (4.064)*	−0.022 (−.212)	−3.171 (−2.863)*	0.99961	0.26 F(1, 27)Crit.Val.=4.21

T–Values in Parentheses

Comparisons of Known Estimates of Ghana Cocoa Supply Elasticities

		Price		Capacity base	
		short–run	long–run	short–run	long–run
Frimpong–Ansah (1989)					
	1906–85	0.07	0.23	0.405	1.368
	1906–55	0.03	0.06	0.714	1.298
	1944–85	0.18	0.42	0.591	1.359
	1953–85	0.22	0.43	0.880	1.685
Stryker et al. (1988)					
	1953–85	0.22	0.62		
Akiyama (1985)					
	1968–83	0.24		0.50	1.50
Akoto (1985) LP Model					
	1970–71		Ashanti .304 Eastern .296		
Bateman					
(1969)	1933–64			.71–1.0 Elasticity	
(1971)	1933–69			Ashanti .293 Marginal response Rest .221	
Berhman (1968)					
	1946–63		0.71		
Ady (1968)					
	1951–64		Ashanti .49		
	1947–64		Ashanti .56 National .18		

Sources: As per respective authors

to the decline of the industry by means of excessive taxation. Real producer prices began to fall in 1955. Prices fell below the maximum incentive level in 1959 and below the minimum incentive level in 1964. Accelerated decline began in 1974.

The fourth finding is that a major shift has taken place since the 1980s which may have wiped out approximately 34% of the tree stock. This finding would suggest that average normal production (exclusive of weather factors) may not be more that 250,000 tons until a major sustained optimum producer price policy has been enforced for at least the ten years it takes to reach the optimum production cycle of trees. Significant financial resource mobilization for cocoa-based economic recovery cannot be expected, therefore, for at least the next decade and a half.

These findings place a severe limitation on the short- to medium-term contribution to economic recovery of the cocoa sector, which, until its decline, had provided most of the external and domestic revenues and savings of the Ghana economy.

Figure 7.1
Ghana Cocoa
Production Performance,
1905–83

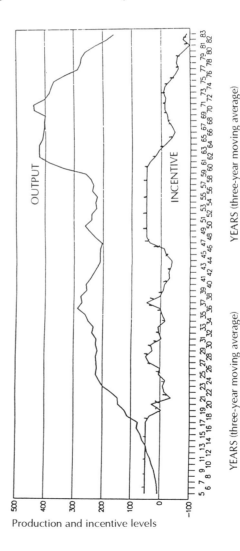

Notes

1. Thomas Jefferson, *Notes on Virginia: The Writings of Thomas Jefferson*, p. 165.
2. In some cases the analysis is brought up to 1988 with projections to 2000.
3. An abridged version was published as 'Economic Analysis of Ghanaian Cocoa Supply' in R.A. Kotey, C. Okali and B.E. Rourke (eds), *Economics of Cocoa Production and Marketing* (ISSER, Legon, 1974), pp. 286–326.
4. Stryker *et al.* (1988), Annex, p. 4.4. The assessment of the rate of decline of cocoa trees was that provided in an analysis by the World Bank's Commodity Studies and Projections Division.
5. Ormsby-Gore (1926) states that 'formerly the oil palm industry in the Gold Coast was considerable. The exports ... some forty years ago [i.e., 1886] were worth about £1,000,000, but they are now worth only about one tenth of that sum. The decline ... is entirely due to the success of cocoa, in which the labour is less arduous and the returns greater.'
6. *Golden Harvest: The Story of the Gold Coast Cocoa Industry* (Ghana Information Services Department, Accra, 1953), p. 1.
7. Literally 'cocoa, food of the gods'.
8. The Commissioner for the Western District of Asante was reported to be still making efforts to persuade farmers, against local scepticism, and against lower returns compared to the collection of rubber from wild trees. An adult person took 25 man-days to collect 60lb of rubber with a value of £4.15.0, while it took several years to produce 60lb of cocoa which was worth only 16 shillings. Administrative Records, Ghana National Archives No. 54/1/1, 284/04, Accra.
9. Ghana National Archives, Acc 574, Remarks in October 1912 Diary. It is stated that 'when Martinson visited Mim (Ahafo) in October 1912 he was to report that the farms were kept well cleaned'.
10. Dunn and Robertson (1973: 50) state, concerning the period of the 1940s, that 'many of the largest cocoa farms in Ahafo represent the product not of autonomous local class formation but the import of external rural capitalists and rural proletarians.'
11. This was confirmed in interviews with Bafour Osei Akoto, one of the largest investors in cocoa in Ahafo (December 1985) and with Opanyin Takyi, a leading Kwahu cocoa farmer at Kukuom, Ahafo (1981).
12. As reported in World Bank (1970: Annex 2, Table 1) and in Bateman (1971: Annex 1, Table II–6).
13. These would be the equivalent of the coefficient of the variable $[b_1 C_{t-1} P_{t-1}]$ in the Bateman average capacity equation, estimated on a national basis for the two periods.
14. The regional factors as revised by Stryker *et al.* are adopted for this study, with the modifications described earlier.
15. Estimate of 1,700 trees per hectare is based on Ghana Cocoa Board Survey, 1970–9. COCOBOD memorandum, CE/47/RD/52, 5 July 1988 to author.
16. Capacity base reported in hectares (Table 7.2) excludes effect from insecticide application since 1955. The normal capacity variable, however, includes yield effect from insecticide application.
17. Analysis starts from 1905, not 1895, as suitable price index data are not available before 1905.
18. The actual figure given by the Ghana Cocoa Board is 1,034 million hectares made up of:

0–7 years old	64.5 million
8–15 years old	98.6 million
16–30 years old	457.7 million
Above 30 years old	413.0 million

    Compared with distribution in 1979 (our Table 7.6), the loss would appear to affect all age classifications of trees, particularly the older cohort. There is an indication of generalized destruction.
19. Calculated as follows for 1988: traditional yield from matrix = 192,700 tons. Plus hybrid yield (66,400 tons, increasing from 1985 level at 5% annually based), less cutting-out factors (24,800 tons) equals 234,300 tons. Converted into hectares at 150 kg per hectare is 1,562,000 hectares. Estimated hectarage of 1,034,000 by COCOBOD (p. 2 of memorandum, July 1988) represents 66.2% of the expected hectarage (1,034,000/1,758,000). Hectarage not accounted for equals 33.8%.
20. The supply function over the period 1953–85 could not be the best for the present analysis because the sample was too small for some of the required diagnostic tests.

8 Conclusions: Managing the Economic Recovery in Ghana

> The Governor of She asked about government. The Master said, 'Ensure that those who are near are pleased and those who are far are attracted'.
>
> Confucius (*Analects*, XIII.16)

The central thesis of this study has been that public policy in Ghana, dominated over the years by a predatory coalition of revenue-hungry governments, profit-seeking businesses, price-conscious consumers and defected farmers, has failed to recognize the structural impediments to accelerated development inherent in unproductive and fragmented peasant agriculture and instead has excessively taxed the cocoa industry, in particular, to finance the interests of the coalition under the guise of development. This policy has not only failed to achieve development but has also destroyed the cocoa industry which would otherwise have provided the savings for a more moderate pace of development. The lack of recognition of this structural impediment by successive governments has been a contributory factor in the major decline of the economy that has occurred.

In this concluding chapter, the principal findings of the study are brought together. An attempt is made to discuss their implications for the economic recovery and development programmes that were introduced in 1983. The conflicts within the political economy over programmes of economic stabilization and restructuring are also discussed.

Chapter 1 discussed the relevance of orthodox development theory and concluded that the excessive focus on capital constraint approaches has induced external indebtedness, given the slow productive responses and low domestic saving. In Chapter 2, the evolution of development thinking in Ghana, from the colonial period to the start of aggressive modernization in the 1960s, was reviewed. The focus of the analysis was on the quality and relevance of the contribution of professional economists; the identified economic characteristics of the underdeveloped state; and the clarity of development ideas.

The Ghana economy on the eve of decolonization was found to have the following characteristics:

- A weak and primitive productive base for food crop agriculture. This phenomenon was observed by Cardinall, Dudley Seers and C.R. Ross, and Arthur Lewis, as well as by African political leaders. Lewis was able to place this problem in his development model as the greatest hindrance to modernization.
- The characteristic of monetary fragility identified by Seers and Ross suggested that the pace of economic development could not exceed that of monetary modernization, and supply side response.
- The problems of a single dominant crop were observed by Guggisberg, Cardinall, the War Council and Nkrumah. Various attempts at diversification and deconcentration failed, however. The reason given in the literature was the relative ease with which cocoa could be produced.
- Arthur Lewis drew attention to the weakness of the public services: productivity was low and they lacked the correct orientation for the promotion and management of development.

- The combination of weak productive capacity and monetary fragility implied a weak economic structure for accelerated economic development. This structural weakness was masked by the relatively advanced primary agricultural and mineral export sectors.
- The country's large external financial reserves on the eve of decolonization also concealed structural weaknesses. They gave the incoming indigenous politicians the means to conceive aggressive modernization at a rate incompatible with the weak structural base.
- These findings suggested a study from a long-run perspective employing a political economy model to investigate the nature of the incentives (or lack of incentives) for the capital-producing primary export sectors in the process of economic modernization.

Chapter 3 introduced and discussed such a model for the study of economic decline. The model assumes a distinction between the producer and the state. It also assumes that the state, if it is enlightened, will protect its self-interest by fostering the primary export sectors in an initial period of moderate development. If it is unenlightened, the state will neglect and destroy the primary sectors to satisfy the interests of the coalition in the spirit of aggressive modernization, and ultimately set the economy on a path of decline. The model also assumes that the state will employ taxation and other methods of producer price distortion to achieve the political and economic objectives of the coalition.

Chapters 4, 5 and 6 examined the trends in the Ghana economy in the long-run period from the turn of the century to 1983, in the context of the analysis employed in the study. The following are the conclusions.

- With the possible exception of the Guggisberg era, the colonial predatory coalition generally ignored the development of the indigenous economy, except where it benefited imperial trade. It carried out policies that were often contrary to economic conditions in the country. While some development resources could be mobilized from the incomes of the primary agricultural and mineral sectors, the real development potential of the Ghana economy on the eve of independence cannot be assessed unless account is taken of structural weaknesses and the fragmentation of the peasant sector.
- The findings in Chapter 5 are particularly relevant to the central proposition of this study. They show how, contrary to the identified structural weaknesses of the economy, the immediate post-independence state proceeded aggressively to modernize the economy. Nkrumah's development strategies were influenced by his Pan-African vision, his belief in the 'big push', and the pressures from the urban alliance he had mobilized with the political rhetoric associated with the drive to independence.
- Unlike Guggisberg's, the Nkrumah development programme of the 1950s was not targeted towards immediate production but involved infrastructural preparations of a general kind for accelerated economic modernization. In these preparations, industrialization, not agriculture, was the principal objective. Agriculture in this period remained as fragmented and as underdeveloped as previously. By the end of the 1950s, the government had pushed the financial resources of the country to their limits. The economy was primed for stagnation and decline. Future development needed to concentrate on productive investment if economic stability was to be preserved.

The analysis in Chapter 6 showed that the warning signs visible by 1961 were not heeded. The coalition expanded. Policies of successive governments led to a steady decline of the economy from the early 1960s. The trend was halted briefly between 1967 and 1974 in all the indicators except the relative size of the cocoa sector in the economy. The long-term situation was not helped by this brief recovery. Productivity in the food sector remained stagnant, as it has been for generations. Public policy failed to reduce fragmentation. The steepest overall economic decline took place from 1975 to 1983.

The later Nkrumah era (1961–5) was the period in which Party ideology had become conducive to political disintegration. The evolved Nkrumah state integrated dependent farmers, the trade union and youth wings of the Party, the new politicized bureaucracy, and state industries, with the whole web benefiting from state largesse. Resources were shifted from the productive sectors to the large unproductive populist constituency. Socialist economic doctrine pre-empted the use of important policy tools such as the exchange rate and, instead, through trade and exchange controls, brought the management of the external sector directly under inefficient government control.

Post-Nkrumah governments failed to perceive the full extent of the legacy of the Nkrumah policies or the structural weakness of the economy. Attempts to halt the decline in 1966 to 1974 extended through the terms of three governments, and therefore policies were not always consistent. The NLC's attempt at economic stabilization was the most serious but it was short-lived and largely incomplete. The Busia regime took a considerable time to get to grips with the Nkrumah legacy. Meanwhile it accumulated short-term debts. It attempted unsuccessfully to obtain external assistance from assumed 'friendly' Western governments. When it seriously began to address itself to correcting the economy it offended the urbanized predatory coalition, which had remained intact, and was therefore removed. Principal observations on the Busia era were the apparent lack of recognition of the potential dangers still posed by the Nkrumah state, and the continued fragility in the domestic economy plus the very delicate external sector.

The early success of the Acheampong government derived from a defiant attitude towards the international community on external debts. Buttressing this philosophy was the self-imposed fiscal and external sector discipline within the coalition, and the drive for food self-sufficiency in which food farmers were, to a limited extent, admitted into the alliance. The strategy disintegrated when the self-imposed discipline evaporated.

The findings on the final stages of decline from 1975 to 1983 are important to the central arguments of this study. They illustrate the characteristics of a decaying state when the productive sectors have been virtually destroyed. The political instability from the end of the Acheampong era to the beginning of the Rawlings II era was simply a manifestation of such a state. Between 1978 and 1981 Ghana experienced the rule of four different governments, three of which had come to power through violent *coups d'état*. At this stage the primary weaknesses and fragmentation had been worsened by the decay of basic infrastructure; furthermore, the financial state of the government and the economy had become so fragile that the scope for economic reforms was severely limited. Finally, the predatory alliance was faced with disharmony and severe internal conflicts. The urban wage-earner elements, including the armed forces, had become destitute and militant; the dependent farmers had fallen prey to the state, like other farmers; the industrialists faced losses and disintegration at a time of economic distortions when only the informal markets survived. Briefly, the state had become wholly illegitimate.

The State and the Cocoa Industry

An economic analysis of the cocoa industry (Chapter 7) has shown that the industry was at the core of this political and economic decline. Tax policy had squeezed farmers' incomes excessively to fund failed development and other uneconomic state expenditures. The result is that the high producer prices that persuaded farmers into cocoa at the turn of the century have not been equalled since about 1917.

Prices, in real terms, remained on the decline until about 1985. The cocoa farmer has benefited from sustained maximum incentive prices in only two periods in the industry's history, 1895–1917 and 1947–60. The bulk of the industry's tree stock is attributed to the positive policies of these two periods alone.

The present major decline of the industry is accounted for by nearly 30 years of price distortion. Short-run producer price distortion reached its peak in the period from 1977 to 1980 and cost the industry between 33% and 40% of output per year. Long-run direct and indirect distortions were at their peak around the same period and cost the industry up to 51.5% of output. The very long-run adverse effects were even higher and at their peak in 1978 and 1983 cost the industry 62.6% in output. If very long-run incentives had been provided the industry would have reached a peak production of about 757,000 tons in 1983, compared with the actual output of 296,000 tons.

This study has produced, for the first time, a reliable annual profile of hectarage, tree stock and normal production expectation for the entire history of the cocoa industry. It has therefore been possible to estimate supply responses to producer price and to the industry's capacity base. Both the short-run and long-run price elasticities of supply are extremely small, approaching zero for the period before 1955. The supply elasticities have increased for data sets relating to more recent periods, but they are generally smaller than those of most previous studies, particularly the long-run elasticities. The elasticities with respect to tree stock are the largest and the most relevant for the long-run rehabilitation of the industry. The long-run responses to price improvements have been less than other studies have predicted, and therefore the long-run recovery of the industry would require maximum price incentives that work through tree stock building.

Based on the analysis of the forecast for the period 1956–85, and confirmed by the Ghana Cocoa Board, there is the possibility that some 34% of the estimated tree stock may have been destroyed or abandoned since the late 1970s.

The revenues that could be mobilized by the state with the maximum and minimum incentive producer prices have been compared to determine the benefits to the state and the economy at different levels of taxation, (Annex II, Tables A7.7, A7.8 and A7.9). If producer prices had been fixed at the optimum incentive level in the period 1955–85, C3,582.7m could have been mobilized in constant 1963 prices. The estimate over the same period, on the basis of the distorted producer prices paid, is C3,529.4m in constant 1963 prices. There was thus no benefit in total mobilization through higher taxation. This result argues against state predatoriness towards the cocoa industry as a method of mobilizing long-run resources for economic development.

The Economic Recovery Programme 1983–88

Given the abysmal economic decline in 1983, it was not to be expected that an Economic Recovery Programme (ERP) targeted at quick remedies would succeed. There were large institutional, managerial and political constraints. Rather, the programme of recovery had to be designed with short-, medium- and long-term goals (World Bank, 1984: 34–68). Within the general programme, recovery was planned in two phases, ERP I (1984–6), and ERP II (1987–9).

The principal goals of ERP I were to control inflation, restore overseas confidence, arrest and reverse the decline in production, particularly in agriculture, rehabilitate the decayed productive and social infrastructure, stimulate exports, curb the consumption of luxury imports, and mobilize domestic and external resources to restore living standards (Government of Ghana, 1984, 1985, 1987a, 1987b). The goals for ERP II are to ensure economic growth at around 5% per annum in real terms, stimulate significant increases in savings and investment, improve public sector management and place the external sector on a sound footing.

The short-term strategy was aimed at monetary stabilization. This was largely an effort to restore macroeconomic balance. The principal component was a strategy of progressive exchange-rate adjustments and other methods to reduce price distortion in both the productive sectors and the market for consumer goods. The specific targets, apart from the exchange rate, were wage rates, energy, public utilities, infrastructural prices, fiscal policies and subsidies.

The medium-term strategy took the form of an economic rehabilitation programme with macro as well as sectoral aspects. The macro programme was designed to provide some basic rehabilitation of the productive infrastructure that would enable producers, mostly exporters, to take advantage of the reduction of price distortion in the stabilization phase. The rehabilitation programme was therefore targeted at the supply of critical imports, such as spare parts for machinery and transport, the road network, the fishing fleet, the railways and the ports. Also important in the medium-term programme are the reorganization and streamlining of the decision-making process and the institutional support for management. For the implementation of the medium-term rehabilitation programme the government formulated an initial three-year investment programme (1984–6). The programme was not ambitious and aimed at restoring productive capacity to the levels attained five years before, in 1979. The anticipated costs of rehabilitation of the different economic sectors are summarized in Table 8.1.

Table 8.1 ERP I: Three-Year Investment Programme, 1984–6

	Amount US$m.	Percentage
1. Export-oriented sector	494	12.6
2. Other productive sectors	791	20.2
3. Physical infrastructure	1,200	30.6
4. Fuel and power	1,250	31.9
5. Social sector	185	4.7
Total	3,920	100.0

Source: World Bank (1984:50)

The long-term programme is aimed at liberalization and growth. Initial steps in this direction were contained in the short-term stabilization programme, but the programme of liberalization which in 1983 was considered to be a condition for the resumption of economic growth was more far-reaching and suggested a fundamental change in the philosophy of economic management. The essential features were the following: a strategy for the relaxation and eventual abolition of quantitative trade and exchange restrictions; the phasing out of official and quasi-official management of price fixing and control, monitoring and enforcement; the phasing out of public monopolies in production and distribution by permitting competitive private organizations; a conscious policy to remove factors leading to price distortion in the production and marketing of domestic and tradeable goods.

The success of the adjustment programme in Ghana has been acclaimed as the most remarkable in recent years. This claim has considerable justification, whether Ghana's performance is evaluated by comparing it with that of other countries, with performance before the programme was introduced, or against specific targets set for the programme.[2] The trends in the macro-economic indicators, summarized in Table 8.3, would support such a claim, especially as the programme has been undertaken 'without a reduction in GDP, in total or per capita, [and has been] based on increasing rather that reducing real imports, [and] involved raising, rather than cutting, government spending' (Loxley, 1988: 26).[3] From our analysis in Table 6.1, all these aggregates were too depressed to have any scope for further reduction.

Table 8.2 Phase II: Public Investment Programme, 1986–8 (current cedis, millions)

	Total projects	Local costs	Foreign costs	Total	%
Productive sectors	78	11,852	62,340	74,192	30.2
Agriculture	50	6,251	19,096	25,346	10.3
Industry	14	1,846	7,334	9,180	3.7
Mining & forestry	14	3,755	35,910	39,666	16.2
Economic infrastructure	96	43,414	115,545	158,959	64.7
Roads & highways	28	24,039	30,573	54,612	22.2
Transport & communications	38	7,675	45,732	53,407	21.7
Energy	21	8,789	28,228	37,017	15.1
Water supply	9	2,911	11,102	13,923	5.7
Social infrastructure	27	6,440	5,934	12,374	5.0
Education	10	2,546	1,014	3,560	1.5
Health	17	3,894	4,920	8,814	3.6
Total	201	61,706	183,819	245,525	100.0

Source: Government of Ghana (1987a: 41)

Table 8.3 Selected Indicators of Economic Performance in Real Output Ghana: 1983–6

	1983	1984	1985	1986
Real GDP (1975=100)	89.0	97.6	102.6	108.0
Real GDP per capita (1975=100)		73.0	78.0	79.7
Inflation (% per annum)	122.0	40.2	10.4	24.6
Cereal production (1970=100)	36.0	112.0	91.0	105.0
Cassava production (1970=100)	72.0	170.0	129.0	127.0
Cocoyam production (1970=100)	63.0	63.0	53.0	51.0
Cocoa production (000s tonnes)	159.0	174.0	219.0	230.0
Minerals production (1977=100)	50.2	57.9	65.3	60.3
Forestry: logs (000s M^3)	560.0	578.0	620.0	890.0
Forestry: sawn timber (000s M^3)	189.0	180.0	223.0	232.0
Manufactures: value added (%)	−11.2	12.8	22.2	6.8
Electricity (million kwh)	2575.0	1819.0	3020.0	3599.0
Crude oil refining (1983=100)	100.0	155.0	199.0	205.0
Per capita consumption (1982=100)	98.4	110.0	112.6	113.6
Investment rate (% GDP)	4.1	7.6	7.3	10.3
Savings rate (% GDP)	0.3	4.7	3.1	6.6

Source: Loxley (1988: 23)

This Study and the ERP

There has been no evaluation, however, of the ERP within the framework used in this book, namely, the weakness of the peasant agricultural sector, the long-term decline of the cocoa sector, the fragility of the economy as a whole, the financing problem, and the conflicts in the political economy. In this concluding section the attempt is made to assess the future of the programme in the context of these issues.

The food production sector

This study has concluded that the peasant agricultural sector has remained fragmented and underdeveloped, and that the failure to address this weakness in past development attempts has been a principal factor in their lack of success. The data in Table 8.3 suggest that the food sector has responded to ERP I and II. This impression is misleading, however. Loxley (1988: 28) states that 'Ghana's food situation is quite precarious and policy towards this [peasant agricultural] sector is both ambiguous and inadequate.' As in previous economic strategies in Ghana, the peasant sector has been neglected in the current programmes. Richard Pearce (1989) confirms this by concluding from his assessment of the present programme that the rural sector, outside the cocoa industry, has not benefited from the economic improvement that has taken place. Loxley states further that 'both the World Bank and the IMF do not explicitly deal with food production and the Bank acknowledges that this is a great weakness in its programme.' Serious discussions with the World Bank on an agricultural programme only began in March 1989, six years after the start of the ERP, and government policy remains very underdeveloped in so far as the food sector is concerned. The process of admission of the food sector into the alliance is therefore slow and will be one of the principal handicaps of the programme.

Table 8.4 Food Production Per Capita, and Relative Prices of Food: Ghana 1977–87

.	1977	1980	1981	1982	1983	1984	1985	1986	1987
Per capita production									
Cereal (1970=100)					26	78	62	70	
Cassava (1970=100)					52	119	88	84	
Cocoyam (1970=100)					45	45	36	34	
Relative prices of food									
Terms of trade food/ non-food consumer		96	91	112	138	86	60	57	55
Relative prices of food/ cocoa production	100	138	92	125	184	136	64	51	42

Source: Loxley (1988: 29, Tables 9 and 10)

Table 8.4 shows that per capita food production has not been sustained at its 1984 level. The programme has also turned the terms of trade against the food farmer in favour of the cocoa farmer. It is reasonable that the cocoa farmer should be able to benefit from the improvements in exchange-rate policy, but it is ironical that policies aimed at economic rehabilitation do not adequately benefit the food farmer whose rising productivity, this study has established, must play a crucial role in long-term economic development. It is not reasonable that food prices should be deteriorating relative to non-food prices. With value-added manufacturing volume falling (Table 8.3), the larger supply of food and non-food consumer items must be the result of increased imports due to liberalization.[4]

The cocoa sector

Present doubts about the short-term response to cocoa producer price increases support the findings of this study. The over four-fold nominal increase (real two-fold) in the producer price between 1984 and 1987 yielded a one-third increase in output. This suggests a short-term supply elasticity with respect to price of 0.165 (according to Loxley, 1988: 31). This compares with our result of 0.18.

From the analysis in this study, the cocoa producer price did not exceed the minimum incentive price threshold (approximately C120 per kilo) until 1987 (Annex II, Table A7.7). It was a long way from the maximum incentive price (approximately C200 per kilo). If the improving trend since 1985 continues at that rate the optimum incentive is expected to be reached in 1994. This means that, in so far as traditional planting is concerned, output expectations should not average more than 120,000 tons in the second half of the 1990s (Table 7.2). Adjusted for hybrids and swollen shoot effects, and short-term responses, total output in the second half of the 1990s should average only approximately 250,000 tons. This level is a little over half of the industry's capacity in the peak 'development' period of the 1950s and 1960s.

Meeraus, Okyere and O'Mara (1989) confirm in their 30-year analysis (1959–88) that C120 per kilo was the critical producer price in 1987 in Asante. They have estimated, in that cocoa area, the arc elasticity of supply (long-term) of raising the price from this level to C140 as between 1.2 to 1.6.[5] They have also observed that 'the rate of planting over the past four years accounts for an area under cocoa trees eight times that of any comparable older surviving cohort', where there had been major neglect. This implies that farmers, in areas with old neglected trees, may have responded quicker, and before the maximum incentive producer prices were reached. Newbery (1989) considers this finding remarkable and argues that

> it seems reasonable that near the point at which the returns to producing cocoa begin to exceed those from growing alternative crops (allowing for risk) there would be a substantial switch back into the traditionally favoured cash crop, cocoa. The evidence suggests that after a long period in which cocoa was relatively unattractive, recent money price increases have persuaded farmers that cocoa will once more become the most profitable crop.

This would be particularly so if the switch from cocoa, in the period of decline, had been to short-term crops, or to less familiar non-agricultural pursuits, or had been merely a withdrawal into subsistence. Combining these observations with the findings in this study, the policy implication is that the expectations of farmers that public policy now favours cocoa must be sustained if the long-term recovery of the industry is to be attained. However, the diminishing long-term arc elasticity, as the producer price increases, suggests that, while the policy to raise producer prices to the optimum should be maintained, a strategy of raising the producer price too rapidly should be resisted if financial resources are limited and if the greater priority is to promote the food sector.[6] Public policy should also note the trends in the world producer market, particularly the major investments in cocoa in the Far East (Malaysia and Indonesia), and their effect on the world market price. Given these factors, the contribution of cocoa to economic recovery in the next decade is best set conservatively at an annual production of 250,000 tons.[7]

Inflation

The inflation figures in Table 8.3 give the impression that policies have not succeeded in holding inflation down after the rapid falls in 1984 and 1985. Inflation was rising again in

1986. Official estimates are 25% in 1987, 32% in 1988 and 22% in 1989 (to March). Some analysts disagree with the official estimates and suggest rates for 1987 and 1988 of 49% and 70% respectively (Loxley, 1988: 32). Whichever estimates are used, it would seem that the relatively low level (10.4%) achieved in 1985 is unlikely to be attained again in the near future. The factors in the return of inflationary pressures are the unification of the foreign exchange auction since 1987, the scarcity of food due to lower production and increases in urban demand, and the increases in wages since 1985. There are strong indications that the urban pressures have been difficult to contain since 1985.

Financing Adjustment

An adjustment programme, given the condition of Ghana's massive infrastructural decay, will require large amounts of external finance and will need to anticipate long delays in supply response. It has been shown in this study that the financial situation has been precarious since the early 1960s. A significant factor in the adjustment programme has been the country's over-dependence on the IMF and the World Bank for finance, and therefore on their conditionality. The other significant factor has been the rapidly growing debt burden, most of which is sacrosanct IMF and World Bank loans. Most people argue that the two institutions will not let the programme fail because of the indebtedness to themselves. What cannot be disputed is that Ghana's external debt problem will worsen until productivity has increased sufficiently to allow for savings to exceed debt repayments.

Ghana's debt-service ratio was 53% in 1987 (Table 8.5) and has been increasing. The World Bank (1987b: 69) has estimated Ghana's debt service in 1988 as approaching 60% of export earnings. The present study argues that real increases in productivity can start only from the neglected food agricultural sector. The problems of economic rehabilitation and development are obviously far from resolved with the present programme. Indeed, they are still not well understood.

Table 8.5 Ghana's External Debt and Debt Service, 1983–7

	1983	1984	1985	1986	1987
External debt, including IMF, World Bank, oil credits	1552	1860	2051	2163	
Debt service, as % of exports excluding arrears (%)	26.0	36.3	53.4	46.5	53.0

Source: World Bank, (1987b)

The Political Economy Perspective

A principal conclusion of this study is that there had been a major disintegration of the political economy in the early 1980s. This was manifested both in political instability, where conflicts in the urbanized political economy predominated, and in the destruction of the producing sectors of the economy, where the few principal productive industries were the victims of the vampire coalition. Under these circumstances, the success of the Economic Recovery Programme depends on a new political conviction in favour of radical economic reforms that will have the effect of admitting the demobilized rural sectors into the inner circle of the core combination, curbing the demands of urban interest groups, and redistributing substantial real resources in favour of the productive sectors, such as the food agricultural sector, and viable domestic and export industries.

The political conviction in favour of radical economic reform in these conditions includes the will to change, fundamentally, the political and social ideology of domestic politics. It can be argued that this requires a rare political stimulus, perhaps inspired by a violent social and moral shock, associated with decline, that leaves no room for less radical alternatives.[8] There is some evidence that such a situation existed early in 1983. The primary cause of the Rawlings II Revolution of December 1981 has been summarized as the 'continuing crisis in the economy, society and politics of Ghana' (Ray, 1986: 20). But, as the present analysis indicates, supported by other observers (Chazan, 1983: 173–9; Ocquaye, 1980: 28), the economic crisis had persisted for some time, and was indeed worsened in the first 15 months of the Rawlings II regime. The stimulus igniting political conviction did not occur therefore with the birth of Rawlings II, but later, presumably late in 1982 to early 1983. Before then an urgent desire for improvement may have existed, but the larger body of opinion favoured reform of a corrupt capitalist system, suggesting methods to root out corruption, seize assets, stamp out smuggling, collect taxes, and generally to 'investigate persons whose life styles and expenditures substantially exceeded their known or declared incomes' (PNDC Law 1, Section 4).

The authority of the government remained fragile. The approach to economic reform and reconstruction remained eclectic and there was an urgent need to decide on a single and consistent approach (Ray, 1986: 61–2). It had also become clear that capital to repair and rebuild the decayed infrastructure was the first priority. Early in 1983 it was recognized that this capital requirement was too substantial to be supplied by Libya or the communist world on a continuing basis. An Acheampong self-reliant model was not viable because it could not supply the capital, and could not benefit the cocoa sector, which in 1983 was in absolute decline.[9] The only alternative left was the IMF/World Bank, which had been thoroughly discredited in Ghana throughout 1982.[10] The fact that Ghana selected the IMF/World Bank channel for economic reconstruction suggests that the economy was perceived, even by the radical politicians, to be *in extremis*. The need for state security left it no choice if total economic and political disintegration was to be avoided.

Evidence that the government had a better understanding of the economic process at the time is supported by the fact that the original programme of reform was designed and initiated by the Ghana authorities themselves and not by the IMF.[11] Opposition from extremist elements within the new alliance was avoided by likening the programme to Lenin's New Economic Policy and Chairman Mao's National Democratic Phase (Ray, 1986: 63) which recognized the role of capitalist reconstruction under socialist direction in the building of the socialist state.

By designing and initiating the 1983 Economic Reconstruction Programme themselves, the authorities acknowledged the true market conditions and were therefore neither propagating incorrect notions of the state of the economy nor depriving themselves of vital economic management tools. Later, moreover, when the IMF participated in the programme, the government was able to retain the initiative in negotiations and therefore maximum faith in the prescriptions that were agreed. This explains Ghana's exceptional ability to remain on course in the early difficult phases of stabilization which involved massive devaluations (Annex I, Table A6.6, col. 5), compared with other African countries in a lesser state of economic decline.

The participation of the Marxist groups, particularly the New Democratic Movement (NDM), in the economic reform process was an important factor in its acceptance. Another reason is that the radical groups now in power were those who, in the past, had publicly denigrated IMF/World Bank economic reforms.[12] Effective opposition to the programme outside the government itself was therefore small.

A further important reason is that the government had the ability to enforce action within its own coalition and outside it against opposition to its authority: summary trials and imprisonment or execution were a powerful deterrent especially against the planning or execution of coup attempts. Ray (1986: 103–12) records that in barely three years from coming to power (December 1981–January 1985) the Rawlings II regime endured nine coup attempts.

The above analysis explains the special stimulus existing in Ghana in 1983 and also illustrates important aspects of the government's philosophy. The government appears to be fully aware that its survival depends on economic recovery. It understands the methods necessary to tackle the short- to medium-term recovery problems. It has demonstrated a greater political will to persevere with its programme than any previous government, and has been able to back up that will with whatever action is necessary. This is a rare combination in contemporary Africa, and can hardly be described as a model for the rest of the continent.

Even so, in order to sustain recovery over the long term, the above conditions, though necessary, are not sufficient. Political pluralism is lacking and therefore alternative approaches have had to come from multilateral institutions or the donor community by virtue of their financial support. Such views are inferior to informed domestic alternatives; moreover, the present coalition remains essentially urban and cannot fully guarantee the membership of the rural economy in the long term. It is important to acknowledge that public policy is still underdeveloped with regard to the fundamental problems of development identified in this study and that the peasant food sector thus remains the primary concern. These are important political and economic issues in the relationship between the state and the proven productive sectors of the economy, that have yet to be fully resolved if satisfactory production responses are to be expected from the bold macroeconomic reforms that have been introduced.

The Political Economy of Development

The study has tackled fundamental questions on what an appropriate theory of *ab initio* development should emphasize. The analysis supports Arthur Lewis's original idea that 'the secret of industrialization is a rapidly progressing agriculture, and more particularly ... measures to increase food production per head'. It emphasizes, in this regard, the importance of eliminating fragmentation in peasant food producer pricing and marketing. It is argued that, despite the colonial stigma on primary production, savings from this sector are crucial for nascent development. Public policy must therefore ensure optimum incentives for the primary export industries throughout the period of development. It is also argued that in the primary state, the underdeveloped economy is structurally too weak and fragile to carry the burden of accelerated modernization. An important condition for successful economic development and for avoidance of nascent economic decline is a moderate pace of modernization, in tandem with increasing productivity in the peasant food sector.

It is in these respects that economic factors in the political process become important determinants in the efforts of a country to make the transition from the underdeveloped stage to the industrialized. A ruling coalition that excludes or oppresses a mobilized and influential rural component stands no chance of successfully making the transition. Indeed the evidence shows clearly that such an economy will stagnate and decline.

Notes

1. See also *A Programme of Structural Adjustment*, Fourth Meeting of Consultative Group, Paris, Accra, May 1987.
2. This has been a World Bank/IMF view. See also Loxley (1988).
3. Loxley (1988) argues that the fact that per capita consumption was able to rise enabled the government 'to implement its policies with little political opposition'.
4. Dr Kwesi Botchwey, PNDC Secretary for Finance (Ghana) is reported to have told the Ghana Manufacturers' Association that 'certain industries have been reeling under the pressure on the liberalization programme'. While the government would be protective of industries potentially viable in the adjustment framework, it would not use protectionist strategies to support 'infant industries that had a tendency to stay babies with big teeth'. *West Africa*, 6–12 March 1989. There are obvious problems of supply response to policy changes in both the manufacturing and domestic food sectors.
5. Between C140 to C160 per kg the arc elasticity is estimated at 0.5–0.6, and from C160 to C180 per kg it is 0.45–0.5. The reducing arc elasticity confirms the behaviour of Bateman's farmers' planting effort coefficient.
6. It has already been noted that the terms of trade have already moved against the food sector.
7. With favourable rains, production in 1987–8 was 250,000 tons. Official estimate for 1988–9 is 300,000 tons (Ministry of Agriculture).
8. In this sense the stimulus in Ghana occurred long before that in the Eastern bloc of Europe. However in the case of the latter, political pluralism and economic reforms are expected to go in tandem.
9. It should be noted that world cocoa prices were rising in the early Acheampong period, and so the external sector was less difficult to manage.
10. *The Workers' Banner,* a mouthpiece of the Marxist leadership, had accused the IMF of being 'this monster, the mercenary headquarters of the imperialist monopolist companies (which aimed) to squeeze our finances, sabotage the economy, destroy the revolution and thus ensure the continued exploitation and oppression of our people.' *Banner,* 16–23 September 1982.
11. It is significant that, despite criticism by the state press of this author for his IMF initiatives in the Busia period, he was the one approached by the government for the financial package in support of Ghana's initial independent effort in 1983. It suggests a new and different understanding of the economic problem, and also a new political conviction and will.
12. As in the case of the support that Acheampong received from radicals in 1972 when he overthrew Busia after the 1971 devaluation.

ANNEX I
The Long-Run Decline
of the Ghana Economy

The long-run trends in the Ghana economy from the middle of the 1950s are described here in tables and supporting diagrams. The analyses are based on data drawn from IMF, World Bank and Ghana official sources. The tables describe trends in fiscal policy, external sector management, growth indicators, and money and price trends. The results may be summarized as the failure of fiscal policy due mainly to the erosion of the tax base of the principal sources of public revenue; the failure of the external sector due principally to the destruction of the major contributors to export performance, namely cocoa and the minerals sectors; and the failure of production arising from the failure of savings and consequently of investment, due to the destruction of the export sector which had been the main direct and indirect source of savings. The analyses show that economic decline on a major scale has taken place in Ghana.

Fiscal Performance

The trends in Table A6.1 (fiscal performance 1955–85) show that until 1970 the state succeeded in maintaining its ability to collect revenues at a satisfactory level. The total tax base from the import sector (Table A6.2, col. 11) remained high but that of the cocoa sector had begun a steady decline. Two peaks of revenue mobilization (1965 and 1970) do not correspond to similar peaks in the tax base of the principal sources, and suggest that the peaks had no sustainable base. Revenue reached its lowest level at 4.5% of GDP in 1981. This level, the lowest recorded in West Africa (ECOWAS, 1987) was an indication of the massive withdrawal of the tax-paying community into occupations beyond the tax range (such as into staple foodstuffs) or the failure of production where withdrawal was not possible, as in the mining sector. The other principal reason was the low volumes of import duties and excise duties resulting from the rapid erosion of the import tax base (Table A6.2, col. 11). The trends in Figure A6.1 show this picture most vividly.

Expenditure trends followed a similar pattern. Expenditures, however, remained above revenues throughout the period 1955–85. The gap widened to a peak in 1964. For the remainder of the period, expenditures were drastically cut following the failure of revenues, except in the short period 1973–5, which was helped by high international cocoa prices.

Total collapse of fiscal policy was quite unmistakable. By 1982 the cocoa sector tax base had shrunk to a mere 1.2% of GDP compared to its highest level of 19.3% in 1955 (Table A6.2, col. 5). Also in 1982, the import tax base was as low as 3% compared with a peak of 35% in 1961. It should be noted that the rate of decline of the import base was faster than that of the cocoa tax base. This indicates that the failure of the ability to import was due to factors other than cocoa, including the oil price increase in 1973. The collapse of the fiscal base has been mitigated since 1983, a period which coincides with the present government's reform policies and particular efforts in revenue collection and economic recovery in general.

External Sector Performance

External reserve trends in the period 1955–85 show four distinct phases: 1) the long phase of decline in the period to 1965; 2) the further period of decline in net reserves, but with the gross reserves stabilized indicating larger short-term credits, from 1966 to 1970; 3) a failure of external reserve management from 1971 to 1981; and 4) rising gross reserves accompanied by a sharp decline in net reserves from 1982 to 1985. The fact that the gross reserves ratio to GDP was static from 1965 to 1981 shows that the manoeuvrability of external management was limited in that period to the short-term credits that were available, and depended on the monetary stabilization measures the state was prepared to undertake.

At the beginning of the 1960s, the external reserve position became critical (Chapter 5) with considerable losses in 1961, and the consequent imposition of restrictive trade and exchange policies. The trends from that date in both gross and net reserves were steadily downward. Net reserves were mostly negative (Table A6.3, col. 3) and remained so to the latest date of our analysis.

Net reserves declined steeply in tandem with gross reserves for the period 1955–65, with a small, though steadily increasing, gap between them. This shows the poor credit rating of the period. The moderate increases from 1961 to 1965 are usually accounted for in the literature by suppliers' credits (Killick, 1978). The period 1966–70 was one of improved credit status which would normally enable greater investment and rehabilitation, with some increases in productivity. Associated with this period were monetary stabilization and economic rehabilitation. It is worth noting that this pattern is similar to the rehabilitation and monetary stabilization period since 1983, even though the scale is clearly larger in the latter instance. The other distinguishable phase is 1972–81 with a pattern similar to 1955–65, but with important differences. External borrowing capability was smaller and static, obviously the result of debt repudiation in 1972 and the government's inability to undertake monetary and economic stabilization. The external gross reserve ratio to GDP was generally stable though at a slightly lower level than in the previous period. Net reserves were at a stable higher level, indicating a larger need for reserves to finance imports. Both factors indicate a greater inflexibility in external sector management than in any other phase in the long-run period.

The decline in gross and net external reserves in the period 1955–85 was reflected in trends in import compression, as shown in Table A6.4 and in Figure A6.4. By 1982, imports and exports were at their lowest ratios to GDP in the country's history, 3.2% and 3% respectively. Recovery began in 1983, but again the constraint imposed by exports on the ability to import was unmistakable. The high levels of imports between 1960 and 1965 could not be sustained by exports. This was the period in which little in the way of external credits, except expensive suppliers' credits, were available to finance the higher volumes of imports. Higher import levels in relation to GDP, when little credit was forthcoming, had the effect of depleting the reserves and creating external debts. This process is illustrated by the rapid decline of external reserves shown in columns 2 and 3 of Table A6.3. The rest of the period to 1981 may be described as one in which a failed export sector dragged down with it the import content in GDP.

A major contributor to the collapse of the external sector from 1960 was the failure of the cocoa industry. Cocoa exports, which accounted for 23% of GNP in 1955, were 10% in 1965 and 5% in 1985. Cocoa sector incomes ratio to GNP also declined rapidly (Table A6.5, col. 7). The lowest ratio (1.3%) was reached in 1984. Cocoa's decline was not mitigated by policy changes in the late 1960s or from 1983 to 1985 (Figure A6.5). It is therefore clear that the decline in the role of cocoa in total economic activity has been induced by factors that are deeper and of longer-term consequence than those affecting the other economic variables.

The final aspect in the decline of the external sector is the trends in the exchange rate in the period 1955–85. Figure A6.6 illustrates the comparative trends in the nominal and the equilibrium exchange rates. Columns 10 and 11 in Table A6.6 are World Bank estimates (Stryker *et al.*, 1988). These can be compared with new estimates provided for the purpose in this study, which has used the weighted average of the inflation rates of Ghana's seven largest trading partners plus Côte d'Ivoire and Togo. The World Bank's method relies only on the inflation rates of the United Kingdom and the United States. In the period of the steepest economic decline, 1971–83, the World Bank estimates show a lesser rate of overvaluation than do the estimates in this study, when using either 1950 or 1960 as base years. But both sets of estimates illustrate the dramatic decline of the value of the cedi in this period.

The gap between the nominal exchange rate and the estimated equilibrium rate was narrowest in three periods: that up to 1961, then 1967–74 and in the more recent period since 1984. There were two long periods of substantial disequilibrium: 1962–7 (the cedi was first devalued in 1967), and 1975–84. The equilibrium exchange rate has been on a steady path of decline since 1962, except for a brief upturn in 1967–9. Attempts to hold the nominal exchange rate above the equilibrium rate have been fruitless as there have ultimately been devaluations throughout the period. However, the tendency for the nominal rate to lag persistently behind the equilibrium rate implies the constant use of scarce reserves in support of unviable exchange rates. This policy can be expected to have had a major destructive effect on the export sector.

Production and Growth

The analysis suggests that the effort to promote economic growth based on the preparations made in the 1950s was not successful. Per capita real income fell from C501.5 to C396.5, a reduction of 21%, an average annual decline of 1.0% (Table A6.7). In 1977–8 there was a temporary improvement associated with the partial monetary reforms of the short-lived Akuffo regime. The observed recovery in recent years coincides with the economic recovery strategies since 1983. The fact that the upward trends follow quickly from policy reform, would suggest that per capita growth rates have been responsive to the short-term benefits of monetary and economic reforms.

The trends in the pattern of savings and investment provide some explanations for the failure of development. Due to lack of reliable data, domestic savings have been estimated from the national accounts as the Gross Domestic Fixed Capital Formation (GDFCF) minus the import surplus, (Table A6.5, cols 10 and 11). Investment far exceeded savings in the period to 1965. From 1976 to 1983, investment was compressed to the level of savings and the two moved in tandem along a sharp downward path. In this period of decline, Ghana had seen the rate of domestic savings drop from 18% of GNP in 1958 to 0.6% in 1983, and the rate of investment from 20.8% in 1961 to 3.5% in 1982. In this trend, the strong influence of the export sector on savings, and of imports on investment has been unmistakable. This observation again suggests that the cocoa sector, as the prime mover of exports, has had a direct influence on the rate of savings and an indirect effect on the rate of investment through imports. This observation suggested the detailed investigation into the cocoa sector in this study for some of the primary explanations for the decline of the Ghana economy.

Table A6.9 provides a measure of the productivity of investment in the period 1957–85.

Productivity of capital began to fall in 1961. The process of decline in the 1973–6 phase was peculiar in the sense that it coincided with the period of high capital investment, indicating, as in the early 1960s, that the type of investment was highly unproductive.

Money and Inflation

The results of the analysis of fiscal performance show that, though both government revenues and expenditures fell in the long period of decline, the fall in expenditures always lagged behind the fall in revenues, thus retaining an accumulation of demand in the economy. The trends in money supply and inflation (Table A6.10) reflect well the resulting demand-led inflation deriving from the fiscal process. A careful observation of the trends in money supply and in inflation shows four peaks of inflation: a smaller peak in the mid-1960s, and three major peaks in 1977, 1981 and 1983 (the highest). The incidence of very high inflation thus occurred towards the latter half of the period of decline, when productivity was at its lowest.

The severe monetary and economic instability in the latter part of the period under study was both demand and supply induced. Up to 1975, inflation generally lagged behind the money supply. From 1976 it was the money supply that lagged behind inflation. This would suggest increasingly severe supply problems.

Notes

1. Charts are drawn from smoothed data employing 3-year moving averages centred on the middle year.
2. The study was conducted by a team consisting of the Directors of Research of all Central Banks in the region under the direction of this author.
3. A country that loses external credibility usually has to hold larger than normal external reserves before import credits can be negotiated.
4. This term describes import contraction resulting from the loss of capacity to import due to the loss of foreign exchange earning capability. See Besley and Collier (1987) and London (1987).

Table A6.1 Ghana Fiscal Performance, 1955–85 (million cedis)

Year	GDP current prices	Revenue current prices	Expenditure current prices	Revenue ratio (%) of GDP	Expenditure ratio (%) of GDP	Moving average of Col.5	Moving average of Col.6
1	2	3	4	5	6	7	8
1955	680	128	141	18.8	20.7	16.4	18.7
1956	706	99	118	14.0	16.7	16.4	17.6
1957	740	120	114	16.2	15.4	15.8	17.2
1958	780	133	151	17.1	19.4	16.3	18.1
1959	890	140	174	15.7	19.6	16.8	20.8
1960	956	167	224	17.5	23.4	15.8	21.1
1961	1022	144	207	14.1	20.3	15.3	22.3
1962	1094	157	253	14.4	23.1	14.2	21.9
1963	1208	170	269	14.1	22.3	15.7	24.1
1964	1357	254	365	18.7	26.9	17.4	24.8
1965	1466	284	371	19.4	25.3	17.8	23.4
1966	1518	231	273	15.2	18.0	16.8	21.5
1967	1504	236	321	15.7	21.3	16.1	21.0
1968	1700	298	400	17.5	23.5	16.6	21.5
1969	1999	332	395	16.6	19.8	17.8	21.3
1970	2259	437	468	19.3	20.7	18.0	20.5
1971	2501	451	524	18.0	21.0	17.4	20.3
1972	2815	420	543	14.9	19.3	14.6	18.6
1973	3501	382	549	10.9	15.7	12.8	17.1
1974	4660	584	754	12.5	16.2	13.0	17.9
1975	5241	810	1146	15.5	21.9	13.8	20.3
1976	6478	870	1484	13.4	22.9	13.1	21.3
1977	11163	1171	2137	10.5	19.1	10.2	19.0
1978	20986	1393	3165	6.6	15.1	9.0	16.9
1979	26222	2600	4296	9.9	16.4	7.8	14.1
1980	42853	2951	4668	6.9	10.9	7.1	12.6
1981	72526	3279	7719	4.5	10.6	5.7	10.9
1982	86450	4856	9530	5.6	11.0	5.2	9.9
1983	184038	10242	14755	5.6	8.0	6.5	9.6
1984	270561	22642	26694	8.4	9.9	8.5	10.4
1985	344182	40311	45763	11.7	13.3	10.1	11.6

Sources: Table 6.1, and 6.5, International Financial Statistics, IMF, Yearbook 1988

Table A6.2   Ghana Fiscal Performance, 1955–85: Cocoa Export Tax Base Erosion (million cedis)

Year	Cocoa exports	Total imports	GDP current prices	Cocoa export ratio to GDP	Total import ratio to GDP	Moving average of col.2 three yr	Moving average of col.3 three yr	Moving average of col.4 three yr	Smoothed cocoa tax base erosion	Smoothed import tax base erosion
1	2	3	4	5	6	7	8	9	10	11
1955	131	176	680	19.3	25.9	134.1	176.0	620.0	21.6	28.4
1956	102	178	706	14.4	25.2	111.7	182.3	708.7	15.8	25.7
1957	102	193	740	13.8	26.1	109.7	180.0	742.0	14.8	24.3
1958	125	169	780	16.0	21.7	121.7	196.0	803.3	15.1	24.4
1959	138	226	890	15.5	25.4	132.0	230.3	875.3	15.1	26.3
1960	133	296	956	13.9	31.0	136.7	282.7	926.0	14.8	30.5
1961	139	326	932	14.9	35.0	135.3	297.3	961.7	14.1	30.9
1962	134	270	997	13.4	27.1	136.3	295.3	1010.0	13.5	29.2
1963	136	290	1101	12.4	26.3	135.3	281.0	1111.7	12.2	25.3
1964	136	283	1237	11.0	22.9	135.7	321.7	1268.0	10.7	25.4
1965	135	392	1466	9.2	26.7	129.3	324.3	1407.0	9.2	23.1
1966	117	298	1518	7.7	19.6	127.7	335.0	1496.0	8.5	22.4
1967	131	315	1504	8.7	20.9	143.0	327.3	1574.0	9.1	20.8
1968	181	369	1700	10.6	21.7	177.7	370.7	1734.3	10.2	21.4
1969	221	428	1999	11.1	21.4	234.3	445.3	1986.0	11.8	22.4
1970	301	539	2259	13.3	23.9	241.7	552.0	2253.0	10.7	24.5
1971	203	689	2501	8.1	27.5	259.7	552.0	2525.0	10.3	21.9
1972	275	428	2815	9.8	15.2	291.7	572.3	2939.3	9.9	19.5
1973	397	600	3502	11.3	17.1	379.3	694.0	3659.0	10.4	19.0
1974	466	1054	4660	10.0	22.6	473.0	876.0	4481.7	10.6	19.5
1975	556	974	5283	10.5	18.4	512.7	1025.0	5489.7	9.3	18.7
1976	516	1047	6526	7.9	16.0	584.0	1103.3	7657.3	7.6	14.4
1977	680	1289	11163	6.1	11.5	728.0	1456.3	12891.7	5.6	11.3
1978	988	2033	20986	4.7	9.7	1171.3	2038.0	20123.7	5.8	10.1
1979	1846	2792	28222	6.5	9.9	1799.3	2886.7	30687.0	5.9	9.4
1980	2564	3835	42853	6.0	8.9	1842.7	3497.7	47867.0	3.8	7.3
1981	1118	3866	72526	1.5	5.3	1584.7	3426.3	67276.3	2.4	5.1
1982	1072	2578	86450	1.2	3.0	2844.3	7824.0	114338.0	2.5	6.8
1983	6343	17028	184038	3.4	9.3	6736.7	13492.3	180349.7	3.7	7.5
1984	12795	20871	270561	4.7	7.7	12487.0	25908.3	266260.3	4.7	9.7
1985	18323	39826	344182	5.3	11.6	10372.7	20232.3	204914.3	5.1	9.9

Source: IMF Data Fund, IFS Yearbook, 1988

Table A6.3 Ghana External Sector, 1955–85: External Reserves as Percentage of GDP

Year	Gross reserves mill.US$	Net reserves mill.US$	Gross reserves mill. cedi	Net reserves mill. cedi	GDP current mill.cedi	Gross reserves ratio of GDP	Net reserves ratio of GDP
1	2	3	4	5	6	7	8
1955	336	336	240	240	680	35.3	35.3
1956	320	320	229	229	706	32.4	32.4
1957	273	269	194	192	740	26.2	25.9
1958	281	277	201	198	780	25.8	25.4
1959	304	295	217	211	890	24.4	23.7
1960	294	259	210	185	871	24.1	21.2
1961	163	159	117	114	932	12.6	12.2
1962	197	180	141	129	997	14.1	12.9
1963	219	187	156	133	1101	14.2	12.1
1964	136	89	97	68	1237	7.8	5.5
1965	118	−10	84	−7	1466	5.7	−0.5
1966	113	−39	81	−28	1518	5.3	−1.8
1967	95	−51	94	−52	1504	6.3	−3.5
1968	106	−62	109	−44	1700	6.4	−2.6
1969	80	−101	82	−103	1999	4.1	−5.2
1970	74	−23	75	−24	2259	3.3	−1.1
1971	53	−6	96	−11	2501	3.8	−0.4
1972	115	98	147	126	2815	5.2	4.5
1973	194	184	223	212	3502	6.4	6.1
1974	108	2	124	2	4660	2.7	0.0
1975	167	110	192	126	5283	3.6	2.4
1976	109	17	126	19	6526	1.9	0.3
1977	169	−3	195	−3	11163	1.7	0.0
1978	190	9	522	23	20986	2.5	0.1
1979	302	118	831	325	28222	2.9	1.2
1980	232	85	638	234	42853	1.5	0.5
1981	198	−72	544	−198	72526	0.8	−0.3
1982	215	−6	589	−15	86450	0.7	0.0
1983	220	−193	6607	−5790	184038	3.6	−3.1
1984	393	−358	19650	−17890	270561	7.3	−6.6
1985	544	−554	32575	−33230	344182	9.5	−9.7

Source: IFS Yearbook 1988

Table A6.4   Ghana External Sector Performance, 1955–85: Import Compression (million cedis)

Year	Exports fob	Imports cif	GDP current prices	Export ratio to GDP (%)	Imports ratio to GDP (%)	Smoothed col.5 %	Smoothed col.6 %
1	2	3	4	5	6	7	8
1955	191	176	680	28.1	25.9	28.1	25.9
1956	173	178	706	24.5	25.2	25.8	25.7
1957	183	193	740	24.7	26.1	25.3	24.3
1958	209	169	780	26.8	21.7	25.6	24.4
1959	226	226	890	25.4	25.4	26.8	27.0
1960	246	296	871	28.2	34.0	26.6	31.5
1961	244	326	932	26.2	35.0	26.2	32.0
1962	240	270	997	24.1	27.1	23.8	29.5
1963	234	290	1101	21.3	26.3	21.8	25.4
1964	247	283	1237	20.0	22.9	19.4	25.3
1965	251	392	1466	17.1	26.7	17.2	23.1
1966	222	298	1518	14.6	19.6	16.7	22.4
1967	274	315	1504	18.2	20.9	18.7	20.8
1968	396	369	1700	23.3	21.7	21.3	21.4
1969	447	428	1999	22.4	21.4	22.9	22.3
1970	523	539	2259	23.2	23.9	22.3	24.3
1971	537	689	2501	21.5	27.5	21.8	22.2
1972	582	428	2815	20.7	15.2	21.2	20.0
1973	751	600	3502	21.4	17.1	20.2	18.3
1974	868	1054	4660	18.6	22.6	19.8	19.4
1975	1023	974	5283	19.4	18.4	17.9	19.0
1976	1025	1047	6526	15.7	16.0	15.2	15.3
1977	1171	1289	11163	10.5	11.5	11.5	12.4
1978	1754	2033	20986	8.4	9.7	10.1	10.4
1979	3259	2792	28222	11.5	9.9	9.4	9.5
1980	3521	3835	42853	8.2	8.9	8.2	8.1
1981	3454	3866	72526	4.8	5.3	5.4	5.8
1982	2886	2578	86450	3.3	3.0	4.7	5.9
1983	11238	17028	184038	6.1	9.3	5.6	6.6
1984	20161	20871	270561	7.5	7.7	7.7	9.5
1985	33185	39826	344182	9.6	11.6	8.6	9.7

Source: IMF Data Fund, World Bank Data Bank, IFS Yearbook, 1988

Table A6.5 Ghana External Sector, 1955–85: Cocoa Sector Income Share in GNP (million cedi)

Year	Total cocoa sales	Public revenue from cocoa	Cocoa sector after tax income	Effective tax rate	Gross national product	Cocoa sector Income ratio of GNP	PPP Index base 1960	Cocoa Sector net income at 1960 PPP adjusted prices	Moving average of cocoa sector income ratio of GNP
1	2	3	4	5	6	7	8	9	10
1955	155	93	54	60.0	676	8.0	1.0218	52.8	8.7
1956	105	31	65	29.5	702	9.3	1.0188	63.8	9.2
1957	101	14	77	13.9	734	10.5	1.0167	75.7	8.8
1958	126	66	52	52.4	776	6.7	1.0021	51.9	8.0
1959	142	69	61	48.6	884	6.9	1.0030	60.8	6.8
1960	140	61	65	43.6	946	6.9	1.0000	65.0	7.4
1961	143	38	84	26.6	1008	8.3	0.9994	84.1	7.7
1962	138	34	84	24.6	1084	7.7	1.0703	78.5	7.6
1963	138	36	81	26.1	1190	6.8	1.0859	74.6	6.9
1964	154	50	82	32.5	1342	6.1	1.0812	75.8	7.0
1965	142	−10	115	−7.0	1447	7.9	1.7428	66.0	6.3
1966	105	13	75	12.4	1504	5.0	1.6129	46.5	6.2
1967	147	46	83	31.3	1479	5.6	1.4380	57.7	5.7
1968	338	111	107	32.8	1650	6.5	1.4923	71.7	5.6
1969	253	143	94	56.5	1941	4.8	1.5281	61.5	5.6
1970	343	201	123	58.6	2211	5.6	1.4693	83.7	5.2
1971	279	118	127	42.3	2449	5.2	1.5574	81.5	5.3
1972	328	146	140	44.5	2775	5.0	1.6573	84.5	4.9
1973	352	133	156	37.8	3471	4.5	1.7848	87.4	4.3
1974	462	230	157	49.8	4613	3.4	1.8282	85.9	3.9
1975	667	350	193	52.5	5241	3.7	2.0881	92.4	3.6
1976	635	226	243	35.6	6478	3.8	2.9644	82.0	3.2
1977	880	518	248	58.9	11123	2.2	5.2588	47.2	2.6
1978	1143	446	387	39.0	20938	1.8	5.4114	71.5	2.3
1979	2973	1784	763	60.0	28124	2.7	11.6925	65.3	2.5
1980	2946	969	1292	32.9	42671	3.0	15.6925	82.3	2.4
1981	1789	−362	1136	−20.2	72294	1.6	30.3110	37.5	2.7
1982	1240	−3026	2976	−244.0	86225	3.5	33.9527	87.7	2.1
1983	6051	1497	2376	24.7	182398	1.3	71.6073	33.2	2.0
1984	10380	2249	3460	21.7	266918	1.3	94.7615	36.5	1.4
1985	15748	1758	5670	11.2	338414	1.7	98.9180	57.3	1.5

Sources: World Bank Data from Agricultural Pricing Study (Stryker, *et al.*)
IMF, IFS Yearbook, 1988

Table A6.6 Ghana External Sector, 1955–85: Equilibrium Exchange Rates and Measures of Overvaluation (base year 1960)

Year	Domestic inflation	Trading partners' inflation	PPP indicator	Nominal exchange rate US$:1cedi	Equilibrium exchange rate US$:1cedi	Index of valuation	Measure of over or under valuation	Equilb'rm exchange rate in cedis:US$	cf. World Bank Estimates Method(a) base 1960 cedis:US$	Method(b) base 1960 cedis:US$
1	2	3	4	5	6	7	8	9	10	11
1955	84.3	81.1	1.03946	1.4000	1.3469	103.95	3.95	0.74	na	na
1956	90.2	88.3	1.02152	1.4000	1.3705	102.15	2.15	0.73	na	na
1957	97.5	95.9	1.01668	1.4000	1.3770	101.67	1.67	0.73	na	na
1958	97.5	97.3	1.00206	1.4000	1.3971	100.21	0.21	0.72	0.69	0.58
1959	98.7	98.4	1.00305	1.4000	1.3957	100.30	0.30	0.72	0.70	0.63
1960	100.0	100.0	1.00000	1.4000	1.4000	100.00	0.00	0.71	0.71	0.71
1961	106.3	106.4	0.99906	1.4000	1.4013	99.91	-0.09	0.71	0.70	0.77
1962	112.5	108.1	1.04070	1.4000	1.3452	104.07	4.07	0.74	0.74	0.74
1963	118.8	110.6	1.07414	1.4000	1.3034	107.41	7.41	0.77	0.87	0.83
1964	137.5	112.6	1.22114	1.4000	1.1465	122.11	22.11	0.87	0.92	0.88
1965	168.8	116.1	1.45392	1.4000	0.9629	145.39	45.39	1.04	1.00	1.21
1966	193.8	120.9	1.60298	1.4000	0.8734	160.30	60.30	1.14	1.09	1.20
1967	175.0	124.2	1.40902	1.1907	0.9936	119.84	19.84	1.01	1.07	1.05
1968	193.8	129.4	1.49768	0.9800	0.9348	104.84	4.84	1.07	1.13	1.12
1969	206.3	135.4	1.52363	0.9800	0.9189	106.65	6.65	1.09	1.13	1.10
1970	212.5	145.1	1.46451	0.9800	0.9560	102.52	2.52	1.05	1.12	1.14
1971	231.3	149.8	1.54406	0.9693	0.9067	106.90	6.90	1.10	1.08	1.30
1972	256.3	155.2	1.65142	0.6984	0.8478	82.38	-17.62	1.18	1.12	1.07
1973	300.0	169.5	1.76991	0.7202	0.7910	91.05	-8.95	1.26	1.11	1.09
1974	356.3	195.4	1.82344	0.7231	0.7678	94.18	-5.82	1.30	1.12	1.29
1975	462.5	222.3	2.08052	0.7162	0.6729	106.43	6.43	1.49	1.25	1.34
1976	718.8	244.4	2.94108	0.7532	0.4760	158.23	58.23	2.10	1.59	1.95
1977	1556.3	298.6	5.21199	0.7448	0.2686	277.28	177.28	3.72	2.05	3.69
1978	2693.8	316.7	8.50584	0.5273	0.1646	320.37	220.37	6.08	2.90	5.29
1979	4162.5	358.4	11.61412	0.2815	0.1205	233.53	133.53	8.30	4.02	7.37
1980	6250.0	413.5	15.11487	0.2794	0.0926	301.65	201.65	10.80	5.36	10.51
1981	13531.3	449.2	30.12311	0.3084	0.0465	663.57	563.57	21.52	10.46	26.39
1982	16550.0	490.5	33.74108	0.3294	0.0415	793.88	693.88	24.10	12.69	26.65
1983	36881.3	518.2	71.17194	0.2712	0.0197	1378.70	1278.70	50.84	25.33	66.10
1984	51506.3	547.1	94.14421	0.0276	0.0149	185.60	85.60	67.25	46.50	na
1985	56818.8	587.0	96.79523	0.0195	0.0145	134.82	34.82	69.14	62.71	na

Trading partners' inflation is based on seven largest sources of imports plus Côte d'Ivoire and Togo (Frimpong-Ansah *et al.*, 1987). World Bank methods below rely on US and UK prices only.

World Bank Method(a) is the equilibrium exchange rate of .803 in 1958 multiplied by the ratio of the non-agricultural, non-tradable CPI for Ghana to the Manufacturing Unit Value (MUV) index of industrial countries

World Bank Method(b) is the estimation of the equilibrium exchange rate using the Elasticities approach. (Stryker *et al.*, 1988 page 2.18 in Annex 2) Both estimates are converted to Base 1960 equilibrium rate of .71 for comparison with my series

Source: Bank of Ghana, IMF IFS Yearbook, 1988

Table A6.7 Ghana Growth Indicators, 1957–85: Real Per-Capita Growth Rate (constant 1975 prices)

Year	Population million	GDP fixed 1975 prices (million cedis)	Incre-mental GDP (million cedis)	Per capita incre-mental GDP (cedis)	Per-capita growth rate constant prices 1975 %	Per-capita GDP 1975 prices (cedis)
1	2	3	4	5	6	7
1957	6.20	3109	105	16.9	–1.0	501.5
1958	6.39	3095	–14	–2.2	–4.7	484.4
1959	6.58	3557	462	70.2	10.0	540.6
1960	6.78	3825	268	39.5	3.4	564.2
1961	6.85	3961	136	19.9	1.1	578.2
1962	6.93	4153	192	27.7	2.4	599.3
1963	7.01	4297	144	20.5	1.0	613.0
1964	7.40	4389	92	12.4	–0.2	593.1
1965	7.74	4449	60	7.8	–2.4	574.8
1966	7.91	4453	4	0.5	–2.1	563.0
1967	8.08	4533	80	9.9	–0.2	561.0
1968	8.26	4597	64	7.7	1.8	556.5
1969	8.44	4867	270	32.0	1.2	576.7
1970	8.61	5197	330	38.3	4.6	603.6
1971	8.86	5486	289	32.6	2.5	619.2
1972	9.09	5349	–137	–15.1	–5.3	588.4
1973	9.39	5646	297	31.6	2.5	601.3
1974	9.61	6033	387	40.3	3.7	627.8
1975	9.87	5283	–750	–76.0	–15.0	535.3
1976	10.31	5097	–186	–18.0	–6.5	494.4
1977	10.41	5212	115	11.0	1.2	500.7
1978	10.75	5645	433	40.3	4.8	525.1
1979	11.09	5435	–210	–18.9	–6.7	490.1
1980	11.54	5475	40	3.5	–3.3	474.4
1981	11.94	5322	–153	–12.8	–9.0	445.7
1982	12.24	5043	–279	–22.8	–7.6	412.0
1983	12.70	5035	–8	–0.6	–3.9	396.5
1984	13.13	5300	265	20.2	1.8	403.7
1985	13.59	5600	300	22.1	2.2	412.1

Source: IMF Data Fund, International Financial Statistics, Yearbook 1988

Table A6.8 Ghana Growth Indicators, 1956–85: Per-Capita Domestic Saving and Investment (million cedi)

Year	Gross National Product	Gross domestic capital formation	Import surplus	Domestic savings	Population (million)	Per-capita GNP (cedis)	Per-capita domestic saving (cedis)	Per-capita GDFCF (cedis)	Per-capita saving ratio to GNP	Per-capita CDFCF ratio to GNP	Moving average of Col.10	Moving average of Col. 11
1	2	3	4	5	6	7	8	9	10	11	12	13
1956	702	112	15	97	6.02	116.6	16.1	18.6	13.8	16.0	13.1	13.9
1957	734	112	21	91	6.20	118.4	14.7	18.1	12.4	15.3	14.8	15.1
1958	776	110	-30	140	6.39	121.4	21.9	17.2	18.0	14.2	15.5	15.6
1959	884	154	12	142	6.58	134.3	21.6	23.4	16.1	17.4	16.4	17.4
1960	946	194	50	144	6.78	139.5	21.2	28.6	15.2	20.5	14.7	19.6
1961	1008	210	82	128	6.85	147.2	18.7	30.7	12.7	20.8	14.0	19.4
1962	1084	184	30	154	6.93	156.4	22.2	26.6	14.2	17.0	13.5	18.7
1963	1190	218	56	162	6.01	198.0	27.0	36.3	13.6	18.3	14.1	17.5
1964	1345	232	36	196	7.40	181.8	26.5	31.4	14.6	17.2	12.3	18.0
1965	1447	266	141	125	7.74	187.0	16.1	34.4	8.6	18.4	10.4	16.2
1966	1504	197	76	121	7.91	190.1	15.3	24.9	8.0	13.1	8.6	14.4
1967	1479	174	41	133	8.08	183.0	16.5	21.5	9.0	11.8	10.0	12.1
1968	1650	187	-27	214	8.26	199.8	25.9	22.6	13.0	11.3	11.0	11.0
1969	1941	195	-19	214	8.44	230.0	25.4	23.1	11.0	10.0	11.8	11.2
1970	2211	271	16	255	8.62	256.5	29.6	31.4	11.5	12.3	9.7	11.7
1971	2449	311	152	159	8.86	276.4	17.9	35.1	6.5	12.7	10.8	11.2
1972	2775	244	-154	398	9.09	305.3	43.8	26.8	14.3	8.8	11.0	9.7
1973	3471	268	-151	419	9.39	369.6	44.6	28.5	12.1	7.7	11.5	9.5
1974	4613	555	186	369	9.61	480.0	38.4	57.8	8.0	12.0	10.9	10.5
1975	5241	614	-49	663	9.87	531.0	67.2	62.2	12.7	11.7	10.1	11.2
1976	6478	641	22	619	10.31	628.3	60.0	62.2	9.6	9.9	10.2	10.3
1977	11123	1049	118	931	10.41	1068.5	89.4	100.8	8.4	9.4	7.3	8.2
1978	20938	1128	279	849	10.75	1947.7	79.0	104.9	4.1	5.4	6.1	6.3
1979	28064	1184	-467	1651	11.09	2530.6	148.9	106.8	5.9	4.2	5.0	5.1
1980	40802	2368	314	2054	11.54	3535.7	178.0	205.2	5.0	5.8	4.6	4.5
1981	76471	2699	412	2287	11.94	6404.6	191.5	226.0	3.0	3.5	4.0	4.3
1982	86225	3053	-308	3361	12.24	7044.5	274.6	249.4	3.9	3.5	2.5	3.6
1983	182398	6922	5790	1132	12.70	14362.0	89.1	545.0	0.6	3.8	3.7	4.8
1984	266918	18542	710	17814	13.13	20328.9	1356.7	1412.2	6.7	6.9	5.0	6.8
1985	338414	32689	6641	26048	13.59	24901.7	1916.7	2405.4	7.7	9.7	7.2	6.1

Sources: IMF Data Fund, IFS Yearbook, 1988

Table A6.9 Ghana Growth Indicators, 1957–85: Productivity Indicators

Year	Gross Domestic Product fixed 1975 prices	GFDCF fixed 1975 prices	Incre-mental GDP	Indicator of capital productivity Col.6/Col.5	Per capita incre-mental GDP (million cedis)	Per capita gross fixed domestic capital formation (million cedis)
1	2	3	4	5	6	7
1957	3109	471	105	0.22	16.94	75.97
1958	3095	437	−14	−0.03	−2.19	68.39
1959	3557	616	462	0.75	70.21	93.62
1960	3825	776	268	0.35	39.53	114.45
1961	3961	814	136	0.17	19.85	118.83
1962	4153	700	192	0.27	27.71	101.01
1963	4297	775	144	0.19	20.54	110.56
1964	4389	751	92	0.12	12.43	101.49
1965	4449	806	60	0.07	7.75	104.13
1966	4453	578	4	0.01	0.51	73.07
1967	4533	524	80	0.15	9.90	64.85
1968	4597	505	64	0.13	7.75	61.14
1969	4867	474	270	0.57	31.99	56.16
1970	5197	623	330	0.53	38.33	72.36
1971	5486	682	289	0.42	32.62	76.98
1972	5349	464	−137	−0.30	−15.07	51.05
1973	5646	432	297	0.69	31.63	46.01
1974	6033	719	387	0.54	40.27	74.82
1975	5283	614	−750	−1.22	−75.99	62.21
1976	5097	501	−186	−0.37	−18.04	48.59
1977	5212	490	115	0.23	11.05	47.07
1978	5645	303	433	1.43	40.28	28.19
1979	5435	228	−210	−0.92	−18.94	20.56
1980	5475	316	40	0.13	3.47	27.38
1981	5322	187	−153	−0.82	−12.81	15.66
1982	5043	177	−279	−1.58	−22.79	14.46
1983	5035	122	−8	−0.07	−0.63	9.61
1984	5300	460	265	0.58	20.18	35.03
1985	5600	653	300	0.46	22.08	48.05

Sources: IMF Data Fund, IFS Yearbook, 1988

Table A6.10 Ghana Monetary Sector, 1952–85: Money Supply and Price Trends (billion cedis)

Year	Money supply (a)	Money plus quasi money (b)	Money supply change over previous year (%)	Money plus quasi money change over previous year (%)	Consumer price index base 1980 (c)	Rate of inflation (%)
1	2	3	4	5	6	7
1951	0.08	0.08	7.2	7.9	1.4	14.9
1952	0.08	0.09	8.8	9.3	1.4	−1.4
1953	0.09	0.09	1.1	2.9	1.4	−3.9
1954	0.09	0.10	7.3	8.1	1.3	−0.5
1955	0.10	0.11	8.5	9.4	1.3	0.5
1956	0.12	0.14	4.4	5.7	1.4	4.1
1957	0.11	0.13	−10.6	−7.5	1.4	1.0
1958	0.10	0.12	−7.3	−2.6	1.4	0.0
1959	0.12	0.14	13.6	14.9	1.5	2.9
1960	0.13	0.16	11.4	13.3	1.6	0.9
1961	0.15	0.17	15.4	6.3	1.7	6.2
1962	0.17	0.20	13.3	17.6	1.8	5.9
1963	0.17	0.22	0.0	10.0	1.9	5.6
1964	0.24	0.29	41.2	31.8	2.2	15.8
1965	0.24	0.30	0.0	3.4	2.7	22.7
1966	0.25	0.32	4.2	6.7	3.1	14.8
1967	0.24	0.32	−4.0	0.0	2.8	−9.7
1968	0.26	0.35	8.3	9.4	3.1	10.7
1969	0.29	0.39	11.5	11.4	3.3	6.5
1970	0.31	0.43	6.9	10.3	3.4	3.0
1971	0.32	0.47	3.2	9.3	3.7	8.8
1972	0.46	0.67	43.8	42.6	4.1	10.8
1973	0.59	0.79	28.3	17.9	4.8	17.1
1974	0.70	1.01	18.6	27.8	5.7	18.8
1975	1.01	1.39	44.3	37.6	7.4	29.8
1976	1.43	1.90	41.6	36.7	11.5	55.4
1977	2.39	3.04	67.1	60.0	24.9	116.5
1978	4.13	5.13	72.8	68.8	43.1	73.1
1979	4.68	5.94	13.3	15.8	66.6	54.5
1980	6.09	7.95	30.1	33.8	100.0	50.2
1981	9.41	12.03	54.5	51.3	216.5	116.5
1982	11.20	14.84	19.0	23.4	264.8	22.3
1983	16.72	20.80	49.3	40.2	590.1	122.8
1984	26.85	31.96	60.6	53.7	824.1	39.7
1985	38.31	46.72	42.7	46.2	909.1	10.3

Sources: IMF, IFS Supplement on Money, 1983, IFS Yearbook 1980

Notes: (a) Money supply is defined as demand deposits plus currency in circulation

(b) Quasi money is financial savings

(c) Consumer price index is the national index of the cost of living

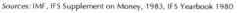

Figure A 6.1 Fiscal Performance: Revenue and Expenditure as % of GDP

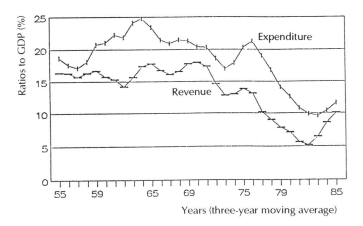

Years (three-year moving average)

Figure A6.2 Fiscal Performance: Cocoa and Import Tax Base Erosion

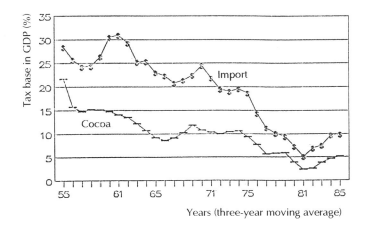

Years (three-year moving average)

Figure A6.3 External Sector: External Reserves Ratio of GDP

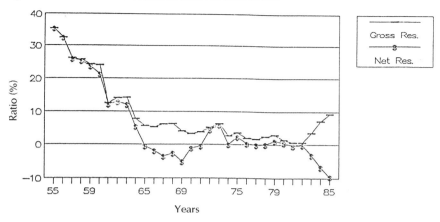

Figure A6.4 External Sector: Import Compression

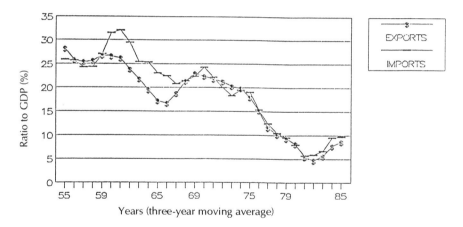

Figure A6.5 External Sector: Cocoa Sector Income Ratio of GNP

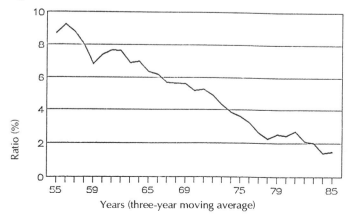

Figure A6.6 External Sector: Official and Equilibrium Exchange Rates

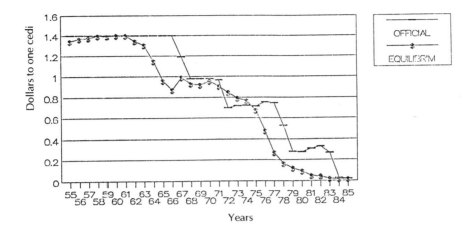

Figure A6.7 Ghana Growth Indications: Per Capita Domestic Savings and Investment

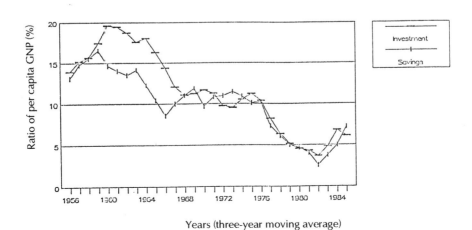

ANNEX II
Cocoa: A Summary of the Econometric Analysis

Supply Function, 1906–86: Modelling Cocoa Production by OLS

I: Equation

Variable	Coefficient	Std Error	HCSE	T-Value	Partial r²
L.Cocoa Prod $_{t-1}$	.70411	.06689	.07455	10.52644	.5964
L.Capacity base	.40480	.09726	.09511	4.16205	.1876
L.Producer price	.06755	.02638	.03118	2.56099	.0804
L.Maize price	−.08108	.04089	.04654	−1.98304	.0498
Constant	−.64022	.30147	.29734	−2.12369	.0567

$R^2 = .999570$ DW = 2.02 Test for Serial Correlation Lagged dependent variable: $Chi^2(1) = .039$
$F[1,74] = .04$
$F[1,74]$ Crit. Value = 3.97

II: Diagnostics

Test of ARCH Errors:
Resid. sum of Sqs = .155551D+03, $\sigma = 1.45956$, $F[1,73] = .68$
Crit.Value = 3.97

Analysis of Scaled Residuals: Sample size 80

Mean	.000000
Std Deviation	.974355
Skewness	−.082160
Excess Kurtosis	.191900
Minimum	−2.472303
Maximum	2.290680

Chi^2 Test for Normality : $Chi^2(2) = .199$

Test for Heteroscedastic Errors:
Test $80*R^2 = 11.3086$ with 9 variables. $F[8,65] = 1.3376$
$F[8,65]$ Crit. Value = 2.09

General Test of Functional Form:
Heteroscedasticity Test $80*R^2 = 19.4593$ with 15 variables.
$F[14,59] = 1.3546$
$F[14,59]$ Crit. Value = 1.86

Wald Test of four static long-run restrictions

Log Prod = 1.368 LBase + .228 LC.Price − .274 LMaize −2.164 Const.
S.E.   (.15386)   (.09550)   (.16303)   (.85013)
F [1,75] 110.806   17.323   6.559   3.932   4.510
Critical Value = 3.969 (maize price is not significant)
WALD Test Chi^2 (4) = 14149.606

173

Supply Function, 1906–55

I: Equation

Variable	Coefficient	Std Error	HCSE	T-Value	Partial r^2
L.Cocoa Prod$_{t-1}$	.45029	.10820	.12422	4.16180	.2779
L.Capacity Base	.71405	.15588	.17297	4.58088	.3180
L.Producer Price	.03336	.02460	.02849	1.35638	.0393
L.Maize Price	.00329	.03904	.04033	.08415	.0002
Constant	−1.05591	.40165	.44034	−2.62894	.1331

$R^2 = .999752$, DW = 2.27, Test for Serial Correlation Lagged
Dependent Variable Chi^2 (1) = 2.214
$F[1,44] = 2.04$
$F[1,44]$ Crit.Value = 4.06

II: Diagnostics

Test of ARCH Errors:
Resid. Sum of Sqs = .113611D+03 $\sigma = 1.70678$ $F[3,39] = .12$
$F[3,39]$ Crit.Value = 2.85

Analysis of Scaled Residuals   Sample Size 50

Mean	.000000
Std Deviation	.958315
Skewness	.368362
Excess Kurtosis	.761897
Minimum	−2.397168
Maximum	2.949833

Chi^2 Test for Normality : Chi^2 =2.106

Test for Heteroscedastic Errors:
Test $50*R^2 = 13.5988$ with 9 variables. $F[8,35] = 1.6344$
$F[8,35]$ Crit. Value = 2.22

Test of Functional Form
Heteroscedasticity Test $50*R^2 = 16.9465$ with 15 variables
$F[14,29] = 1.0620$
$F[14,29]$ Crit. Value = 2.05

Wald Test of 4 static long-run restrictions

Log Prod = 1.299 LBase + .061LC.Price + .006L.Maize −1.921 Const.
S.E.   (.07912)   (.04351)   (.07049)   (.48268)
F[1,45] 17.321 20.984   1.840   .007   6.911

Critical Value = 4.059 (Cocoa Producer price and Maize Price are not
significant. High significance of constant term suggests
other unaccounted factors in the early period of the industry)

WALD Test Chi^2 = 45692.450

Supply Function, 1944–85

I: Equation

Variable	Coefficient	Std Error	HCSE	T-Value	Partial r^2
L.Cocoa prod$_{t-1}$	.56461	.10809	.10775	5.22368	.4245
L.Capacity Base	.59127	.14569	.13617	4.05849	.3080
L.Producer Price	.18312	.04635	.04701	3.95106	.2967
L.Maize Price	−.08816	.10048	.14576	−.87736	.0204
Constant	−1.49801	.81563	.88251	−1.83663	.0836

R^2 = .999564   DW = 2.01   Test for Serial Correlation
Lagged Dependent Variable:
Chi^2 (1) = .054
F-Form [1,36] = .05
F[1,36] Crit. Value = 4.12

II: Diagnostics

Test of ARCH Errors:
Resid. Sum of Sqs = .718626D+2 σ = 1.47569   F[2,33] = 1.86
F[2,33] Crit.Value = 3.29

Analysis of Scaled Residuals   Sample Size 42
Mean   .000000
Std Deviation   .949968
Skewness   −.258480
Excess Kurtosis   .377394
Minimum   −2.531120
Maximum   2.343906
Chi^2 Test for Normality: Chi^2 = .632

Test for Heteroscedastic Errors:
Heteroscedasticity Test $42*R^2$ = 10.4229 with 9 variables
F[8,27] = 1.1140
F[8,27] Crit. Value = 2.31

Heteroscedasticity Coefficients and T-Values:

Vars.	V1	V2	V3	V4	V5
Coeff.	.99551	−1.66406	−.49311	−.62789	4.46907
T-Value	(1.63)	(−1.17)	(−2.32)	(−1.16)	(1.13)

(Test of Functional Form not possible due to limitations on degrees of Freedom)

WALD Test of 4 static long run restrictions:
Log Prod = 1.358 L.Base + .421L.CPrice − .202L.Maize − 3.441Const.

S.E.	(.21588)	(.11539)	(.24874)	(1.79991)
F[1,37]	16.471	15.611	.770	3.373

Critical Value = 4.111   (maize price and constant term are not significant)

WALD Test Chi^2 = 16087.727

Table A7.1 Cocoa Tree Yield Coefficient

Year	Yield coefficient
	(a)
1	0.000
2	0.000
3	0.000
4	0.033
5	0.100
6	0.357
7	0.500
8	0.533
9	0.548
10	0.567
11	0.581
12	0.948
13	0.976
14	0.990
15	1.000
16	1.000
17	1.000
18	1.000
19	1.000
20	1.000
21	0.971
22	0.943
23	0.914
24	0.886
25	0.857
26	0.829
27	0.800
28	0.771
29	0.743
30	0.714
31	0.686
32	0.657
33	0.629
34	0.600
35	0.571
36	0.543
37	0.514
38	0.486
39	0.457
40	0.429
41	0.400
42	0.371
43	0.343
44	0.314
45	0.286
46	0.257
47	0.229
48	0.200
49	0.171
50	0.143
51	0.114
52	0.086
53	0.057
54	0.029
55	0.000

Source: Bateman (197 : Table II-6, Annex II)

Table A7.2 Farmers' Planting Effort Coefficient, 1895–1985

Year	Farmers' effort coefficient	Estimated vintage factor '000 tons	Year	Farmers' effort coefficient	Estimated vintage factor '000 tons
	(b)	(c)		(b)	(c)
1895	0.9048	9.315	1942	0.0000	0.000
1896	0.9048	9.315	1943	0.0000	0.000
1897	0.9048	9.315	1944	0.0000	74.516
1898	0.9048	18.629	1945	0.0000	74.516
1899	0.9048	18.629	1946	0.8776	74.516
1900	0.9048	37.258	1947	0.9048	74.516
1901	0.9048	37.258	1948	0.9048	74.516
1902	0.9048	37.258	1949	0.9048	74.516
1903	0.9048	37.258	1950	0.9048	74.516
1904	0.9048	37.258	1951	0.9048	74.516
1905	0.9048	37.258	1952	0.9048	74.516
1906	0.9048	37.258	1953	0.9048	74.516
1907	0.9048	37.258	1954	0.9048	74.516
1908	0.9048	37.258	1955	0.9048	74.516
1909	0.9048	37.258	1956	0.9048	74.516
1910	0.9048	74.516	1957	0.9048	74.516
1911	0.9048	74.516	1958	0.9048	74.516
1912	0.9048	74.516	1959	0.9048	74.516
1913	0.9048	74.516	1960	0.8799	74.516
1914	0.9048	74.516	1961	0.7845	56.678
1915	0.9048	74.516	1962	0.5268	26.617
1916	0.9048	74.516	1963	0.0000	6.777
1917	0.8745	74.516	1964	0.0000	0.000
1918	0.0000	53.728	1965	0.0000	0.000
1919	0.8436	0.000	1966	0.0000	0.000
1920	0.0000	43.752	1967	0.0000	0.000
1921	0.0000	0.000	1968	0.0000	0.000
1922	0.0000	0.000	1969	0.0000	0.000
1923	0.0000	0.000	1970	0.0000	0.000
1924	0.4029	0.000	1971	0.0000	0.000
1925	0.0000	3.650	1972	0.0000	0.000
1926	0.8779	0.000	1973	0.0000	0.000
1927	0.9048	55.526	1974	0.0000	0.000
1928	0.8326	74.516	1975	0.0000	0.000
1929	0.8602	37.440	1976	0.0000	0.000
1930	0.0000	47.037	1977	0.0000	0.000
1931	0.3292	0.000	1978	0.0000	0.000
1932	0.5041	2.440	1979	0.0000	0.000
1933	0.0000	6.061	1980	0.0000	0.000
1934	0.0000	0.000	1981	0.0000	0.000
1935	0.0000	0.000	1982	0.0000	0.000
1936	0.9048	0.000	1983	0.0000	0.000
1937	0.2096	74.516	1984	0.0000	0.000
1938	0.0000	1.104	1985	0.0000	0.000
1939	0.0000	0.000	1986	0.0000	0.000
1940	0.0000	0.000	1987	0.0000	0.000
1941	0.0000	0.000	1988	0.0000	0.000

Source: Col. (b) Bateman (1971: p. II-5, Annex II)
Col. (c) As estimated by Stryker *et al.* (1988), Annex 4, Table 1 based on Bateman's method (Bateman 1971: Table II-5). Vintage factor relates to total acreage and is sum of regional acreages. Vintage factor is expressed in tonnage equivalent of acreage

Table A7.3 Econometric Analysis Supply Functions

Listing of ProdAct (actual production, '000 tonnes)

1905	7.00000	8.00000	10.0000	15.0000
1909	19.0000	28.0000	34.0000	44.0000
1913	48.0000	61.0000	68.0000	81.0000
1917	77.0000	112.000	123.000	145.000
1921	146.000	170.000	200.000	213.000
1925	224.000	220.000	222.000	224.000
1929	218.000	224.000	223.000	238.000
1933	233.000	251.000	268.000	263.000
1937	279.000	272.000	262.000	252.000
1941	247.000	227.000	222.000	219.000
1945	209.000	192.000	208.000	278.000
1949	248.000	262.000	211.000	247.000
1953	211.000	220.000	229.000	264.000
1957	206.000	256.000	317.000	430.000
1961	409.000	413.000	428.000	538.000
1965	401.000	368.000	315.000	323.000
1969	403.000	413.000	462.000	415.000
1973	349.000	376.000	394.000	319.000
1977	271.000	265.000	296.000	258.000
1981	225.000	179.000	159.000	175.000
1985	219.000			

Listing of ProdNorm (capacity, base '000 tonnes)

1905	13.1000	18.8000	24.8000	30.9000
1909	37.9000	45.1000	54.0000	63.1000
1913	72.5000	82.6000	94.9000	108.500
1917	122.400	136.200	150.100	163.900
1921	180.500	196.400	210.100	219.400
1925	226.600	232.900	239.600	243.700
1929	246.500	244.400	242.600	243.200
1933	245.700	246.200	245.200	241.300
1937	235.400	233.900	233.900	231.200
1941	229.700	227.400	222.900	216.600
1945	209.200	201.900	209.500	209.400
1949	207.600	207.900	208.800	209.900
1953	211.500	213.500	223.000	225.700
1957	250.100	283.900	321.100	353.200
1961	380.100	393.600	408.400	420.800
1965	415.600	399.300	380.600	380.800
1969	392.800	407.600	412.100	406.800
1973	401.500	393.200	366.400	337.500
1977	310.100	307.000	303.100	294.600
1981	305.200	305.900	315.400	310.100
1985	312.800			

Listing of PPrice (cocoa producer price, 1963 prices)

1905	520.000	702.000	550.000	542,000
1909	502.000	516.000	524.000	540.000
1913	560.000	360.000	498.000	408.000
1917	204.000	126.000	188.000	60.0000
1921	102.000	114.000	96.0000	142.000
1925	132.000	206.000	232.000	184.000
1929	196.000	124.000	141.000	148.000
1933	101.000	125.000	137.000	287.000
1937	144.000	124.000	114.000	83.0000
1941	89.0000	74.0000	74.0000	114.000
1945	130.000	231.000	313.000	475.000
1949	280.000	373.000	435.000	383.000
1953	395.000	368.000	407.000	405.000
1957	361.000	345.000	281.000	260.000

Table A7.3 (cont.)

1961	225.000	202.000	158.000	119.000
1965	97.0000	118.000	155.000	154.000
1969	169.000	166.000	155.000	176.000
1973	179.000	168.000	155.000	124.000
1977	104.000	121.000	117.000	78.0000
1981	108.000	89.0000	66.0000	71.0000
1985	122.000			

Listing of MazPrice (maize producer price, 1963 prices)

1905	7.80000	8.50000	8.40000	8.10000
1909	8.50000	8.70000	9.00000	9.00000
1913	9.00000	10.1000	13.0000	16.1000
1917	20.9000	27.1000	23.1000	27.6000
1921	31.5000	30.0000	33.0000	30.5000
1925	32.0000	34.8000	30.8000	27.3000
1929	47.7000	36.9000	38.9000	36.1000
1933	33.9000	34.4000	32.1000	32.3000
1937	32.6000	30.6000	40.5000	46.3000
1941	48.7000	51.4000	49.8000	55.2000
1945	57.9000	62.8000	67.3000	58.6000
1949	63.8000	67.8000	73.0000	70.0000
1953	73.0000	67.8000	64.5000	77.3000
1957	51.1000	69.3000	53.9000	48.8000
1961	69.3000	61.0000	65.0000	72.9000
1965	73.9000	66.5000	40.2000	60.0000
1969	82.8000	63.5000	59.5000	77.8000
1973	70.8000	65.1000	62.3000	91.0000
1977	87.8000	51.8000	47.5000	76.2000
1981	65.9000	55.3000	115.000	52.2000
1985	40.1000			

Listing of LProdAct

1905	1.94591	2.07944	2.30259	2.70805
1909	2.94444	3.33220	3.52636	3.78419
1913	3.87120	4.11087	4.21951	4.39445
1917	4.34381	4.71850	4.81218	4.97673
1921	4.98361	5.13580	5.29832	5.36129
1925	5.41165	5.39363	5.40268	5.41165
1929	5.38450	5.41165	5.40717	5.47227
1933	5.45104	5.52545	5.59099	5.57215
1937	5.63121	5.60580	5.56834	5.52943
1941	5.50939	5.42495	5.40268	5.38907
1945	5.34233	5.25750	5.33754	5.62762
1949	5.51343	5.56834	5.35186	5.50939
1953	5.35186	5.39363	5.43372	5.57595
1957	5.32788	5.54518	5.75890	6.06379
1961	6.01372	6.02345	6.05912	6.28786
1965	5.99396	5.90808	5.75257	5.77765
1969	5.99894	6.02345	6.13556	6.02828
1973	5.85507	5.92959	5.97635	5.76519
1977	5.60212	5.57973	5.69036	5.55296
1981	5.41610	5.18739	5.06890	5.16479
1985	5.38907			

Listing of LProdNorm

1905	2.57261	2.93386	3.21084	3.43076
1909	3.63495	3.80888	3.98898	4.14472
1913	4.28359	4.41401	4.55282	4.68675
1917	4.80729	4.91412	5.01130	5.09926
1921	5.19573	5.28015	5.34758	5.39090
1925	5.42319	5.45061	5.47897	5.49594
1929	5.50736	5.49881	5.49141	5.49388
1933	5.50411	5.50614	5.50207	5.48604

Table A7.3 (cont.)

1937	5.46129	5.45489	5.45489	5.44328
1941	5.43677	5.42671	5.40672	5.37805
1945	5.34329	5.30777	5.34472	5.34425
1949	5.33561	5.33706	5.34138	5.34663
1953	5.35423	5.36364	5.40717	5.41921
1957	5.52186	5.64862	5.77175	5.86703
1961	5.94043	5.97534	6.01225	6.04216
1965	6.02972	5.98971	5.94175	5.94227
1969	5.97330	6.01029	6.02127	6.00832
1973	5.99521	5.97432	5.90373	5.82157
1977	5.73689	5.72685	5.71406	5.68562
1981	5.72097	5.72326	5.75384	5.73689
1985	5.74556			

Listing of LPPrice

1905	6.25383	6.55393	6.30992	6.29527
1909	6.21860	6.24611	6.26149	6.29157
1913	6.32794	5.88610	6.21060	6.01127
1917	5.31812	4.83628	5.23644	4.09434
1921	4.62497	4.73620	4.56435	4.95583
1925	4.88280	5.32788	5.44674	5.21494
1929	5.27811	4.82028	4.94876	4.99721
1933	4.61512	4.82831	4.91998	5.65948
1937	4.96981	4.82028	4.73620	4.41884
1941	4.48864	4.30407	4.30407	4.73620
1945	4.86753	5.44242	5.74620	6.16331
1949	5.63479	5.92158	6.07535	5.94803
1953	5.97889	5.90808	6.00881	6.00389
1957	5.88888	5.84354	5.63835	5.56068
1961	5.41610	5.30827	5.06259	4.77912
1965	4.57471	4.77068	5.04343	5.03695
1969	5.12990	5.11199	5.04343	5.17048
1973	5.18739	5.12396	5.04343	4.82028
1977	4.64439	4.79579	4.76217	4.35671
1981	4.68213	4.48864	4.18965	4.26268
1985	4.80402			

Listing of LMazPrice

1905	2.05412	2.14007	2.12823	2.09186
1909	2.14007	2.16332	2.19722	2.19722
1913	2.19722	2.31254	2.56495	2.77882
1917	3.03975	3.29953	3.13983	3.31782
1921	3.44999	3.40120	3.49651	3.41773
1925	3.46574	3.54962	3.42751	3.30689
1929	3.86493	3.60821	3.66099	3.58629
1933	3.52342	3.53806	3.46886	3.47507
1937	3.48431	3.42100	3.70130	3.83514
1941	3.88568	3.93964	3.90803	4.01096
1945	4.05872	4.13996	4.20916	4.07073
1949	4.15575	4.21656	4.29046	4.24850
1953	4.29046	4.21656	4.16667	4.34769
1957	3.93378	4.23844	3.98713	3.88773
1961	4.23844	4.11087	4.17439	4.28909
1965	4.30271	4.19720	3.69387	4.09434
1969	4.41643	4.15104	4.08598	4.35414
1973	4.25986	4.17592	4.13196	4.51086
1977	4.47506	3.94739	3.86073	4.33336
1981	4.18814	4.01277	4.74493	3.95508
1985	3.69138			

Table A7.4 Forecast Values for 30 Observations, 1956–85. From 1906–85 Supply Function

		Analysis of one-step forecasts			
Date	Actual	Forecast	Y–Yhat	Forecast SE	t-value
1956	5.575949	5.475016	.100933	.088861	1.135857
1957	5.327876	5.607163	−.279287	.086645	−3.223347
1958	5.545177	5.585461	−.040283	.103689	−.388501
1959	5.758902	5.763560	−.004658	.098213	−.047433
1960	6.063785	5.924916	.138869	.094473	1.469927
1961	6.013715	6.110942	−.097227	.088527	−1.098270
1962	6.023448	6.109301	−.085853	.090560	−.948020
1963	6.059123	6.132053	−.072930	.091209	−.799586
1964	6.287858	6.160394	.127464	.091185	1.397854
1965	5.993961	6.247738	−.253777	.085829	−2.956763
1966	5.908083	6.093021	−.184938	.090199	−2.050336
1967	5.752573	6.027548	−.274975	.090846	−3.026842
1968	5.777652	5.958997	−.181345	.097943	−1.851536
1969	5.998937	5.996604	.002333	.102323	.022797
1970	6.023448	6.121187	−.097739	.092130	−1.060878
1971	6.135565	6.137563	−.001998	.091363	−.021867
1972	6.028278	6.183925	−.155647	.088730	−1.754167
1973	5.855072	6.126505	−.271433	.091009	−2.982469
1974	5.929589	6.031204	−.101615	.096142	−1.056920
1975	5.976351	6.011520	−.035170	.088537	−.397231
1976	5.765191	5.967711	−.202519	.087001	−2.327791
1977	5.602119	5.806182	−.204063	.089026	−2.292182
1978	5.579730	5.728896	−.149166	.089093	−1.674265
1979	5.690360	5.708279	−.017919	.088798	−.201801
1980	5.552959	5.725810	−.172850	.088756	−1.947469
1981	5.416101	5.699560	−.283459	.092324	−3.070265
1982	5.187386	5.632538	−.445152	.097108	−4.584114
1983	5.068904	5.543819	−.474915	.125986	−3.769592
1984	5.164786	5.478208	−.313422	.119973	−2.612447
1985	5.389072	5.544767	−.155695	.112430	−1.384812

Tests of parameter constancy over 1956–85
Forecast Chi^2 ((30)/30 = 5.97
Chow test (30, 45) = 3.17
F[30, 45] Crit Val = 1.72

Table A7.5 Estimated Cocoa Base Capacity Under Conditions of Optimum Incentive

Year	Farmers' long-run planting response variable (c)	Estimated normal capacity tonne '000 (d)	Estimated yielding capacity hectares '000 (e)	Estimated tree population million (f)	Year	Farmers' long-run planting response variable	Estimated normal capacity tonne '000 (d)	Estimated yielding capacity hectares '000	Estimated tree population million (f)
1895					1942	925.3	227.4	1516.0	2577.2
1896					1943	907.0	222.9	1486.1	2526.4
1897					1944	881.2	216.6	1443.8	2454.5
1898	0.3	0.1	0.5	0.8	1945	851.3	209.2	1394.8	2371.1
1899	1.2	0.3	2.0	3.5	1946	821.5	201.9	1346.1	2288.3
1900	4.6	1.1	7.5	12.7	1947	792.2	209.5	1396.4	2374.0
1901	9.5	2.3	15.6	26.5	1948	792.0	209.4	1396.1	2373.4
1902	15.4	3.8	25.3	43.0	1949	785.1	207.6	1383.8	2352.5
1903	24.5	6.0	40.1	68.2	1950	786.3	207.9	1385.9	2356.0
1904	36.3	8.9	59.4	101.0	1951	789.8	208.8	1392.2	2366.8
1905	53.3	13.1	87.3	148.5	1952	794.0	209.9	1399.6	2379.3
1906	76.5	18.8	125.4	213.2	1953	800.0	211.5	1410.1	2397.2
1907	100.8	24.8	165.2	280.9	1954	807.4	213.5	1423.2	2419.5
1908	125.7	30.9	205.9	350.1	1955	843.4	223.0	1486.6	2527.2
1909	154.4	37.9	253.0	430.1	1956	882.4	233.3	1555.4	2644.2
1910	183.6	45.1	300.9	511.5	1957	921.4	243.6	1624.2	2761.1
1911	219.8	54.0	360.2	612.3	1958	962.3	254.4	1696.2	2883.5
1912	256.6	63.1	420.5	714.8	1959	1004.1	265.5	1770.0	3008.9
1913	294.9	72.5	483.2	821.5	1960	1047.2	276.9	1845.8	3137.9
1914	335.9	82.6	550.4	935.7	1961	1091.1	288.5	1923.2	3269.5
1915	386.2	94.9	632.8	1075.7	1962	1136.2	300.4	2002.8	3404.8
1916	441.6	108.5	723.5	1229.9	1963	1182.3	312.6	2084.0	3542.9
1917	497.9	122.4	815.8	1386.8	1964	1227.4	324.5	2163.5	3677.9
1918	554.2	136.2	908.1	1543.7	1965	1272.6	336.5	2243.1	3813.3
1919	610.7	150.1	1000.7	1701.2	1966	1317.6	348.4	2322.5	3948.2
1920	666.7	163.9	1092.4	1857.1	1967	1362.8	360.3	2402.2	4083.7
1921	734.6	180.5	1203.7	2046.2	1968	1407.8	372.2	2481.4	4218.5
1922	799.3	196.4	1309.7	2226.4	1969	1452.9	384.2	2561.0	4353.7
1923	854.7	210.1	1400.4	2380.6	1970	1498.0	396.1	2640.4	4488.8
1924	892.7	219.4	1462.6	2486.5	1971	1543.0	408.0	2719.8	4623.7
1925	922.0	226.6	1510.6	2568.1	1972	1588.1	419.9	2799.3	4758.8
1926	974.7	232.9	1552.8	2639.7	1973	1632.5	431.6	2877.5	4891.8
1927	970.7	238.6	1590.5	2703.8	1974	1675.0	442.9	2952.4	5019.1
1928	991.4	243.7	1624.4	2761.5	1975	1715.2	453.5	3023.3	5139.6
1929	1002.8	246.5	1643.1	2793.2	1976	1753.5	463.6	3090.8	5254.3
1930	994.3	244.4	1629.1	2769.5	1977	1789.5	473.1	3154.2	5362.2
1931	987.1	242.6	1617.3	2749.5	1978	1823.3	482.1	3213.9	5463.7
1932	989.5	243.2	1621.2	2756.0	1979	1855.2	490.5	3270.1	5559.2
1933	999.7	245.7	1638.0	2784.6	1980	1884.9	498.4	3322.5	5648.3
1934	1001.9	246.2	1641.6	2790.7	1981	1912.7	505.7	3371.5	5731.6
1935	997.5	245.2	1634.4	2778.5	1982	1939.8	512.9	3419.2	5812.7
1936	981.9	241.3	1608.9	2735.1	1983	1967.0	520.1	3467.2	5894.2
1937	957.8	235.4	1569.4	2667.9	1984	1993.0	526.9	3513.0	5972.1
1938	951.6	233.9	1559.1	2650.5	1985	2018.2	533.6	3557.5	6047.7
1939	951.8	233.9	1559.5	2651.1	1986	2041.5	539.8	3598.4	6117.3
1940	940.6	231.2	1541.1	2619.9	1987	2062.5	545.3	3635.5	6180.3
1941	934.5	229.7	1531.1	2602.9	1988	2081.7	550.4	3669.4	6238.0

Notes: As in Table 7.2

Table A7.6 Long-Run Optimum Cocoa Yield Capacity, 1955–85: Estimated at Producer Prices Equal Border Prices

Year	Estimated optimum traditional capacity hect.'000	Estimated tree population million	Estimated optimum traditional capacity tonne'000	Insecticide yield factor tonne'000	Swollen shoot cutout tonne'000	Hybrid yield tonne'000	Estimated total capacity tonne'000	Actual production tonne'000	Variation from opt. capacity loss (–) tonne'000	Percentage variation loss (–)
1	2	3	4	5	6	7	8	9	10	11
1955	1486.7	2379.3	223.0	9.6	–9.6		223.0	229	6.0	2.7
1956	1555.3	2644.1	233.3	4.2	–11.8		225.7	264	38.3	17.0
1957	1624.0	2760.8	243.6	12.3	–5.8		250.1	206	–44.1	–17.6
1958	1696.0	2883.2	254.4	37.6	–8.1		283.9	256	–27.9	–9.8
1959	1770.0	3009.0	265.5	67.0	–11.4		321.1	317	–4.1	–1.3
1960	1846.0	3138.2	276.9	96.7	–20.4		353.2	430	76.8	21.7
1961	1923.3	3269.7	288.5	116.3	–24.7		380.1	409	28.9	7.6
1962	2002.7	3404.6	300.4	117.9	–24.7		393.6	413	19.4	4.9
1963	2084.0	3542.8	312.6	116.4	–20.6		408.4	428	19.6	4.8
1964	2163.3	3677.7	324.5	121.2	–24.8		420.9	538	117.1	27.8
1965	2243.3	3813.7	336.5	104.8	–24.8		416.5	401	–15.5	–3.7
1966	2322.7	3948.6	348.4	79.3	–24.8		402.9	368	–34.9	–8.7
1967	2402.0	4083.4	360.3	54.4	–24.8		389.9	315	–74.9	–19.2
1968	2481.3	4218.3	372.2	51.3	–24.8		398.7	323	–75.7	–19.0
1969	2561.3	4354.3	384.2	61.4	–24.8		420.8	403	–17.8	–4.2
1970	2640.7	4489.2	396.1	75.0	–24.8		446.3	413	–33.3	–7.5
1971	2720.0	4624.0	408.0	78.6	–24.8	0.1	461.9	462	0.1	0.0
1972	2799.3	4758.9	419.9	74.3	–24.8	0.2	469.6	415	–54.6	–11.6
1973	2877.3	4891.5	431.6	73.2	–24.8	0.5	480.5	349	–131.5	–27.4
1974	2952.7	5019.6	442.9	71.8	–24.8	0.8	490.7	376	–114.7	–23.4
1975	3023.3	5139.7	453.5	53.3	–24.8	1.3	483.3	394	–89.3	–18.5
1976	3090.7	5254.2	463.6	33.1	–24.8	2.0	473.9	319	–154.9	–32.7
1977	3154.0	5361.8	473.1	14.8	–24.8	3.1	466.2	271	–195.2	–41.9
1978	3214.0	5463.8	482.1	20.2	–24.8	5.3	482.8	265	–217.8	–45.1
1979	3270.0	5559.0	490.5	23.7	–24.8	9.2	498.6	296	–202.6	–40.6
1980	3322.7	5648.6	498.4	21.1	–24.8	15.2	509.9	258	–251.9	–49.4

Table A7.6 (cont.)

Year										
1981	3371.4	5731.3	505.7	35.7	-24.8	23.4	540.0	225	-315.0	-58.3
1982	3419.4	5812.9	512.9	42.1	-24.8	29.7	559.9	179	-380.9	-68.0
1983	3467.4	5894.5	520.1	53.9	-24.8	38.9	588.1	159	-429.1	-73.0
1984	3512.7	5971.6	526.9	50.4	-24.8	48.4	600.9	175	-425.9	-70.9
1985	3557.4	6047.5	533.6	55.0	-24.8	57.4	621.2	219	-402.2	-64.7

Notes:

Col.2 Hectarage calculated at 150kg yield per hectare

Col.3 Tree population estimated at an average of 1,700 trees per hectare

Col.4 Optimum Traditional Yield from Table A7.3 (Annex II)

Col.4 Insecticide yield factor from Bateman (1971)

Col.6 Swollen shoot effect is assumed to be stabilized from 1964 (Bateman 1971)

Col.7 Hybrid yield capacity from Stryker et al. (1988), World Bank

Col.8 Optimum Yield capacity is sum of Cols 4–7

Col.10 is Col.9 less Col.8

Col.11 is Col.10 as percentage of Col.8

Table A7.7 Maximum and Minimum Incentive Cocoa Prices and Output

Year	Cocoa fob price cedis per tonne (a)	Price index base 1980 (b)	Optimal incentive prices (c)	Minimum incentive prices (d)	Actual producer prices (e)	Price Gap actual less optimal (f)	Price gap actual less minimum (g)	Output optimal incentive tonnes (h)	Output minimum incentive tonnes (i)	Output fall distortion tonnes (j)
1	2	3	4	5	6	7	8	9	10	11
1954	637	1.40	6.2	3.5	7.0	0.8	3.5	235	241	229
1955	436	1.45	6.4	3.6	7.0	0.6	3.4	272	259	264
1956	391	1.50	6.6	3.7	7.2	0.6	3.5	200	210	206
1957	632	1.53	6.7	3.8	7.2	0.5	3.4	339	281	256
1958	550	1.53	6.7	3.8	7.0	0.3	3.2	367	349	317
1959	439	1.57	6.9	3.9	6.0	-0.9	2.1	462	453	430
1960	342	1.59	7.0	4.0	5.4	-1.6	1.4	392	420	409
1961	318	1.68	7.4	4.2	5.4	-2.0	1.2	444	426	413
1962	337	1.84	8.1	4.6	5.4	-2.7	0.8	489	473	428
1963	357	1.91	8.4	4.7	5.0	-3.4	0.3	703	637	538
1964	278	2.17	9.5	5.4	5.0	-4.5	-0.4	461	460	401
1965	262	2.74	12.1	6.8	4.0	-8.1	-2.8	492	433	368
1966	396	3.10	13.6	7.7	4.0	-9.6	-3.7	403	357	315
1967	562	2.84	12.5	7.1	6.5	-6.0	-0.6	465	377	323
1968	761	3.07	13.5	7.6	7.0	-6.5	-0.6	565	483	403
1969	818	3.29	14.5	8.2	8.0	-6.5	-0.2	494	462	423
1970	643	3.39	14.9	8.4	8.0	-6.9	-0.4	554	489	462
1971	688	3.71	16.3	9.2	8.0	-8.3	-1.2	461	436	415
1972	824	4.09	18.0	10.2	10.0	-8.0	-0.2	493	417	349
1973	1294	4.81	21.2	12.0	12.0	-9.2	0.0	666	480	376
1974	1688	5.68	25.0	14.1	15.0	-10.0	0.9	620	463	394
1975	1526	7.38	32.5	18.3	16.0	-16.5	-2.3	568	443	319
1976	2596	11.52	50.7	28.6	20.0	-30.7	-8.6	712	455	271
1977	3942	24.93	109.7	62.0	35.7	-74.0	-26.3	714	407	265
1978	10396	43.15	189.9	107.3	71.4	-118.5	-35.9	757	443	296
1979	9120	66.63	293.2	165.6	107.1	-186.1	-58.5	624	386	258
1980	6300	100.00	440.0	248.6	107.1	-332.9	-141.5			

Prices are cedis/60lb bag

Table A7.7 (cont.)

Year										
1981	5000	216.49	952.6	538.1	321.4	-631.2	-216.7	510	300	225
1982	30558	264.76	1164.9	658.1	321.4	-843.5	-336.7	406	229	179
1983	60666	587.61	2585.5	1460.6	535.7	-2049.8	-924.9	425	225	159
1984	83323	823.70	3624.3	2047.5	803.6	-2820.7	-1243.9	452	236	175
1985	120983	909.21	4000.5	2260.0	1516.1	-2484.4	-743.9	441	245	219
1986		1127.60	4961.4	2802.9	2316.9	-2644.5	-486.0			
1987		1346.24	5923.5	3346.4	3750.0	-2173.5	403.6			

Notes:

(a) Fob prices supplied by CMB.   (b) Consumer price Index, IFS, IMF 1988

(c) Optimum Incentive Price base on 1954 price in Bateman Incentive Model

(d) Minimum Incentive Price based on 1954 cut-off price for planting

(e) Source CMB.   (f) Col.7 less Col.4   (g) Col.7 less Col.5

(h) Optimal output taken from Very Long-Run Supply Function, Table 7.12

(i) Minimum Incentive Output is equivalent to no new planting ie. Short-Run
   Price Distortion level output

(j) Full Distortion output is equivalent to actual production

Table A7.8 Estimated Transfer of Cocoa Producers Incomes to Treasury Under Optimum Incentive

Year	Optimum production level tonnes'000 (a)	Optimum export unit value cedis/tonne (b)	Total export value mill. cedis (c)	Nominal optimum producer price cedis/tonne (d)	Total farmers' revenues mill. cedis (e)	Total estimated transfer to treasury mill. cedis (f)	Non-agric. price index base 1963 (g)	Real value of transfer to treasury mill. cedis (h)
1	2	3	4	5	6	7	8	9
1955	235	380.5	89.4	234.7	55.1	34.3	74.1	46.2
1956	272	331.5	90.2	242.0	65.8	24.3	75.9	32.1
1957	200	558.6	111.7	245.7	49.1	62.6	79.6	78.6
1958	339	473.2	160.4	245.7	83.3	77.1	79.6	96.9
1959	367	372.0	136.5	253.0	92.9	43.7	79.6	54.9
1960	462	278.5	128.7	256.7	118.6	10.1	81.6	12.4
1961	392	256.5	100.5	271.3	106.4	−5.8	83.3	−7.0
1962	444	282.9	125.6	297.0	131.9	−6.3	87.0	−7.2
1963	489	311.9	152.5	308.0	150.6	1.9	100.0	1.9
1964	703	270.2	190.0	348.3	244.9	−54.9	109.3	−50.3
1965	461	308.7	142.3	443.7	204.5	−62.2	124.1	−50.1
1966	492	535.8	263.6	498.7	245.3	18.3	137.0	13.3
1967	403	466.9	188.2	458.3	184.7	3.5	138.9	2.5
1968	465	686.8	319.4	495.0	230.2	89.2	150.0	59.5
1969	565	760.7	429.8	531.7	300.4	129.4	159.3	81.2
1970	494	565.1	279.2	546.3	269.9	9.3	163.0	5.7
1971	554	590.4	327.1	597.7	331.1	−4.0	170.4	−2.4
1972	461	533.9	246.1	660.0	304.3	−58.1	185.2	−31.4
1973	493	1079.7	532.3	777.3	383.2	149.1	211.1	70.6
1974	666	1445.6	962.8	916.7	610.5	352.3	259.3	135.9
1975	620	1426.2	884.2	1191.7	738.8	145.4	329.6	44.1
1976	568	4035.3	2292.1	1859.0	1055.9	1236.1	446.3	277.0
1977	712	10687.4	7609.4	4022.3	2863.9	4745.5	648.1	732.2
1978	714	36980.2	26403.9	6963.0	4971.6	21432.3	1161.1	1845.9
1979	757	23258.4	17606.6	10750.7	8138.3	9468.4	1757.4	538.8
1980	624	19238.6	12004.9	16133.3	10067.2	1937.7	2564.8	75.5
1981	510	30874.8	15746.1	34928.7	17813.6	−2067.5	5644.4	−36.6
1982	406	11612.8	4714.8	42713.0	17341.5	−12626.7	6448.1	−195.8
1983	425	67702.8	28773.7	94801.7	40290.7	−11517.0	12651.9	−91.0
1984	452	102197.5	46193.3	132891.0	60066.7	−13873.5	22661.1	−61.2
1985	441	87273.8	38487.7	146685.0	64688.1	−26200.3	29287.0	−89.5

3582.7

Notes: (a) Optimum production is taken from Very Long-Run Supply Function, Table 8.12
           (b) Optimum Export Value is from Table 8.9 Col.8, adjusted for equilibrium exchange rate and excludes CMB costs
           (c) Col.2 multiplied by Col.3.
           (d) Source CMB (tonnes).
           (e) Col.2 multiplied by Col.5.   (f) Col.4 less Col.6.
           (g) Source: Stryker *et al.*, Table 3.5(1), Annex Page 3.13

Table A7.9 Estimated Transfer of Cocoa Producer Incomes to Public Revenue (sub-optimal)

Year	Distorted production level tonnes'000 (a)	Optimum export unit value cedis/tonne (b)	Total export value mill.cedis (c)	Nominal actual producer price cedis/tonne (d)	Total farmers' revenues mill.cedis (e)	Total estimated transfer to treasury mill.cedis (f)	Non-agric. price index base 1963 (g)	Real value of transfer to treasury mill.cedis (h)
1	2	3	4	5	6	7	8	9
1955	229	380.5	87.1	256.7	58.8	28.4	74.1	38.3
1956	264	331.5	87.5	264.0	69.7	17.8	75.9	23.5
1957	206	558.6	115.1	264.0	54.4	60.7	79.6	76.2
1958	256	473.2	121.1	256.7	65.7	55.4	79.6	69.6
1959	317	372.0	117.9	220.0	69.7	48.2	79.6	60.5
1960	430	278.5	119.8	198.0	85.1	34.6	81.6	42.4
1961	409	256.5	104.9	198.0	81.0	23.9	83.3	28.7
1962	413	282.9	116.8	198.0	81.8	35.1	87.0	40.3
1963	428	311.9	133.5	183.3	78.5	55.0	100.0	55.0
1964	538	270.2	145.4	183.3	98.6	46.7	109.3	42.8
1965	401	308.7	123.8	146.7	58.8	65.0	124.1	52.4
1966	368	535.8	197.2	146.7	54.0	143.2	137.0	104.5
1967	315	466.9	147.1	238.3	75.1	72.0	138.9	51.8
1968	323	686.8	221.8	256.7	82.9	138.9	150.0	92.6
1969	403	760.7	306.6	293.3	118.2	188.3	159.3	118.2
1970	423	565.1	239.0	293.3	124.1	115.0	163.0	70.5
1971	462	590.4	272.8	293.3	135.5	137.2	170.4	80.5
1972	415	533.9	221.6	366.7	152.2	69.4	185.2	37.5
1973	349	1079.7	376.8	440.0	153.6	223.3	211.1	105.8
1974	376	1445.6	543.5	550.0	206.8	336.7	259.3	129.9
1975	394	1426.2	561.9	586.7	231.1	330.8	329.6	100.4
1976	319	4035.3	1287.3	733.3	233.9	1053.3	446.3	236.0
1977	271	10687.4	2896.3	1309.0	354.7	2541.5	648.1	392.2
1978	265	36980.2	9799.8	2618.0	693.8	9106.0	1161.1	784.3
1979	296	23258.4	6884.5	3927.0	1162.4	5722.1	1757.4	325.6
1980	258	19238.6	4963.6	3927.0	1013.2	3950.4	2564.8	154.0
1981	225	30874.8	6946.8	11784.7	2651.6	4295.3	5644.4	76.1
1982	179	11612.8	2078.7	11784.7	2109.5	−30.8	6448.1	−0.5
1983	159	67702.8	10764.7	19642.3	3123.1	7641.6	12651.9	60.4
1984	175	102197.5	17884.6	29465.3	5156.4	12728.1	22661.1	56.2
1985	219	87273.8	19113.0	55590.3	12174.3	6938.7	29287.0	23.7

3529.4

Notes: (a) Actual production data, representing distorted output

(b) Optimum export value is from Table 8.9 Col.8, adjusted for equilibrium exchange rate and excludes CMB costs

(c) Col.2 multiplied by Col.3.

(d) Source CMB (tonnes).

(e) Col.2 multiplied by Col.5.

(f) Col.4 less Col.6.

(g) Source: Stryker *et al.*, Table 3.5(1), Annex Page 3.13

Figure A7.1 Plot of Estimated Capacity Base Against Actual Production, 1905–85 (tonnes)

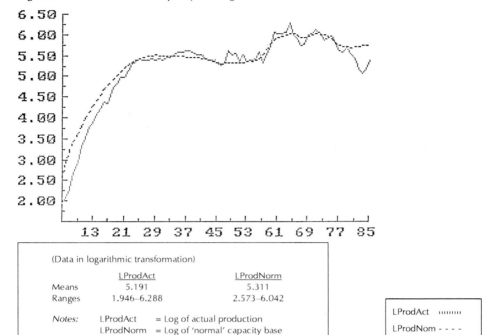

(Data in logarithmic transformation)

	LProdAct	LProdNorm
Means	5.191	5.311
Ranges	1.946–6.288	2.573–6.042

Notes: LProdAct = Log of actual production
LProdNorm = Log of 'normal' capacity base

LProdAct ΙΙΙΙΙΙΙΙ
LProdNom - - - -

Figure A7.2 Plot of Estimated Capacity Base Against Actual Production, 1940–85 (tonnes)

(Data in logarithmic transformation)

	LProdAct	LProdNorm
Means	5.639	5.680
Ranges	5.069–6.288	5.308–6.042

Notes: LProdAct = Log of actual production
LProdNorm = Log of 'normal' capacity base

LProdAct ΙΙΙΙΙΙΙΙ
LProdNom - - - -

Figure A7.3 Plot of Fitted Output Against Actual Production, 1906–85

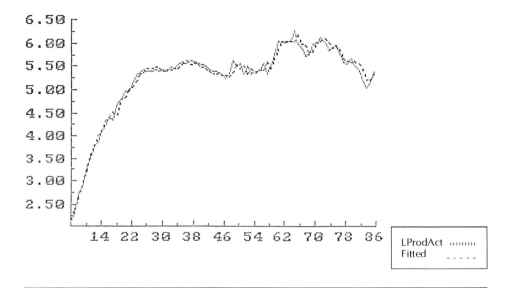

Figure A7.4 Plot of Forecast Values Against Actual Values, 1906–85

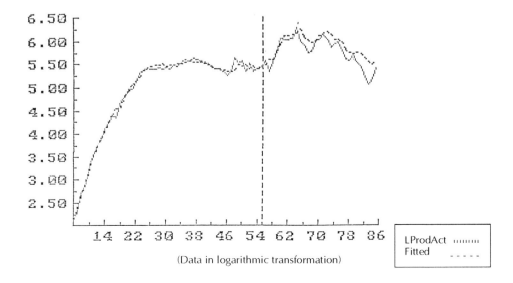

(Data in logarithmic transformation)

Figure A7.5   Cocoa Yield Profile (Yield Coefficients of Tree Life 55 Years)

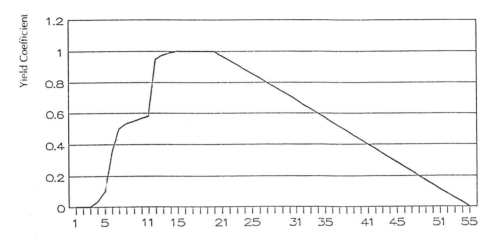

Tree Life (Years)

Bibliography

Abbey, J.S. and Clark, S. (1974): 'A Macroeconomic Model of the Ghana Economy 1956–1969', *Economic Bulletin of Ghana*, Vol. 4, No. 1.

Acquah, P.A. (1972): 'A Macro-Economic Analysis of Export Instability in Economic Growth (The Case of Ghana and the World Market)', Ph.D thesis, University of Pennsylvania.

ADB/ECA (1987): *Economic Report on Africa*, Abidjan and Addis Ababa.

Ady, P. (1968): 'Supply Functions in Tropical Agriculture', *Bulletin of the Oxford Institute of Statistics*, Vol. 30, No. 2.

African Centre for Monetary Studies (ACMS) (1985): *The Structure and Role of Interest Rates in African Countries*, Dakar.

African Centre for Monetary Studies (1987): *The Role of Interest Rates in Economic Development in Africa*, Dakar.

Afrifa, A.A. (1967): *The Ghana Coup*, Frank Cass, London.

Akiyama, T (1985): *Cocoa Supply Projections*, Draft Annex C Commodity Studies and Projections Division, World Bank.

Akiyama, T. and Duncan R.C. (1982): *Analysis of the World Cocoa Market*, World Bank Staff Commodity Working Paper No. 8.

Akiyama, T. and Bowers, A. (1984): *Supply Responses of Cocoa in Major Producing Countries*, World Bank Commodity Studies Division Working Paper No. 1984-3.

Akiyama, T. and Trivedi, P.K. (1987): 'Vintage Production Approach to Perennial Crop Supply: An Application to Tea in Major Producing Countries', *Journal of Econometrics*, 36.

Akoto, A.O. (1985): 'Public Policy and Agricultural Development in Ghana', unpublished Ph.D. thesis, University of Cambridge.

Amamoo, B. (1981): *Ghana 1957–1966: Politics of Institutional Dualism*, Allen and Unwin, London.

Amin, S. (1974): Unequal Development, *Monthly Review Press*, New York.

Andoh, A.S.Y. (1984): 'The Ashanti National Liberation Movement (of the Nineteen Fifties) in Retrospect', Mimeo, University of Science and Technology, Kumasi.

Apter, D. (1972): *Ghana in Transition*, Princeton University Press,

Armah, K. (1974): *Ghana: Nkrumah's Legacy*, Rex Collings, London.

Balassa, B (1977): *Policy Reform in Developing Countries*, Oxford University Press, Oxford.

Bateman, M. J. (1965a): 'Cocoa in the Ghanaian Economy', Ph.D thesis, MIT.

Bateman M. J. (1965b): 'Supply Relations for Perennial Crops in Less Developed Areas' in C. R. Wharton (ed.): *Subsistence Agriculture and Economic Development*, Aldine, Chicago.

Bateman, M. J. (1971): 'Cocoa Prospects, 1971–1985', World Bank Mimeo.

Bateman, M. J. (1974): 'An Economic Analysis of Ghanaian Cocoa Supply', in Kotey, Okali and Rourke (1974).

Bateman M. J., Meeraus, A., Newbery D. M., Okyere, W. A. and O'Mara, G.T. (1989): *An Analytical Review of Ghana's Cocoa Pricing Policy with Recommendations for Future Policy Formation*, Agricultural Policies Division, World Bank, Washington DC.

Bates, R. (1981): *Markets and States in Tropical Africa*, University of California Press, Berkeley.

Bates, R. (1983): *The Political Economy of Rural Agriculture in Africa*, Cambridge University Press.

Bates, R. (ed.) (1988): *Towards a Political Economy of Development*, University of Calfornia Press, Berkeley.

Bauer, Lord (P.T.) (1954): *West African Trade*, Cambridge University Press, Cambridge.

Bauer, Lord (P.T.) (1971): *Dissent on Development*, Weidenfeld and Nicolson, London.

Bauer, Lord (P.T.) (1981): *Equality, The Third World and Economic Delusion*, Methuen, London.

Bauer, Lord (P.T.) (1984): *Reality and Rhetoric: Studies in the Economics of Development*, Harvard University Press, Cambridge, Mass.

Baumol, W.J., Panzar, J.C., Willig, R.D. (1982): *Contestable Markets and the Theory of Industry Structure*, Harcourt Brace, Jovanovich, San Diego.

Beckett, W.H. (1944): *Akokoaso: A Survey of a Gold Coast Village*, Percy Lind, London School of Economics and Political Science.

Beckman, B. (1976): *Organizing the Farmers: Cocoa Politics and National Development in Ghana*, Scandinavian Institute of African Development, Uppsala.

Berhman, J.R. (1968): 'Monopolistic Cocoa Pricing' *Journal of Farm Economics* 50 (3).

Benneh, G. (undated): 'Some Policy Issues in the Quest for Food Self-Sufficiency in Ghana', Public Lecture, University of Ghana.

Besley, T. and Collier, P. (1987): 'Import Compression and Trade Policy', Discussion Paper, Unit for the Study African Economics, Institute of Economics and Statistics, Oxford University, November 1987.

Bhagwati, J.N. (1978), *Anatomy and Consequences of Exchange Control Regimes*, Ballinger, Cambridge, Mass.

Birmingham, W., Neustadt, I. and Omaboe, E.N. (eds) (1965): *A Study of Contemporary Ghana, Vol. I: The Economy of Ghana*, Allen and Unwin, London.

Bissue, I. (1965): 'An Appraisal of Ghana's Seven Year Development Plan'. B. Litt Thesis, University of Oxford.

Boahen, A. (1988): 'The Ghanaian Sphinx: Reflections on the Contemporary History of Ghana, 1972–1987', J. B. Danquah Memorial Lecture, Ghana Academy of Arts and Sciences, Accra.

Brennan, G. and Buchanan, J.M. (1980): *The Power to Tax: Analytical Foundations of a Fiscal Constitution*, Cambridge University Press, Cambridge.

Buchanan, J.M. (1980): *Towards a Theory of the Rents-Seeking Society*, Texas A & M University Press.

Cardinall, A. W. (1931): *The Gold Coast 1931*, Government Printer, Accra.

Caves, Richard E. (1965): 'Vent for Surplus Models of Trade and Growth', in R.E. Baldwin *et al.*, *Trade Growth and the Balance of Payments*, North Holland, Amsterdam.

Central Bureau of Statistics, *Economic Survey*, Various Issues from 1956.

Central Bureau of Statistics, *Quarterly Digest of Statistics*, Various Issues.

Chazan, N. (1983): *An Anatomy of Ghanaian Politics: Managing Political Recession, 1969–1982*, Westview Press, Boulder, Col.

Chazan, N. (1988): 'Ghana: Problems of Governance and the Emergence of Civil Society' in Diamond, L., Linz, J.J. and Lipset, S.M. (eds): *Democracy in Developing Countries, Vol. 2, Africa*, Lynne Rienner Publishers.

Chenery, H.B. and Eckstein, P. (1970): 'Alternative Policies for Latin America', *Journal of Political Economy*, July Pt. 2.

Church, R.J. (1936): 'The Railways of West Africa – A Geographical and Historical Analysis', Ph.D thesis, University of London.

Clauson (1944): Various minutes on Colonial Office files – C0967/13, C0852/503/6, C0852/1003/3, Public Record Office, London.

CPP (1951): *Manifesto, for the 1951 Elections,* Accra.

Crook, R. (1986): 'Decolonization, The Colonial State and Chieftaincy in the Gold Coast', *African Affairs,* Vol. 85, No. 338, January.

Dadson, J. A. (1970): 'Socialized Agriculture in Ghana, 1962–1965', Unpublished Ph.D Thesis, Harvard University.

Dadson, J.A. (1973): 'Farm Size and Modernization of Agriculture in Ghana' in I.M.Ofori (ed.).

Domar, E.D. (1946): 'Capital Expansion, Rate of Growth and Employment', *Econometrica.*

Dunn, J. and Robertson, A.F. (1973): *Dependency and Opportunity,* Cambridge University Press.

Economic Commission for Africa (ECA) (1986): *Agricultural Credit and the Mobilization of Resources in Rural Areas,* Addis Ababa, May.

ECOWAS, (1987): A Single ECOWAS Monetary Zone, Lagos.

Ewusi, K. (1973): 'The Rate of Inflation, Variations in Local Food Prices and Effect of Transport Facilities on Local Food Prices in Ghana in the Sixties', in I. M. Ofori (ed.).

Ewusi, K. (1986): *Economic Trends in Ghana in 1984–1985 and Prospects for 1986,* ISSER, Legon.

Fei, J. and Ranis, G. (1964): *The Development of the Labour Surplus Economy,* Homewood, Illinois: Richard D. Irwin.

Findlay, R. and Wilson, J. (1984): 'The Political Economy of Leviathan', Paper presented at the 3rd Pinhas Sapir Conference on 'Economic Policy in Theory and in Practice', Tel Aviv.

Flint, J. (1983): 'The Failure of Planned Decolonization in British Africa', *African Affairs,* Vol. 82, No. 328.

Frimpong-Ansah, J.H. (1971): 'Stabilization and Development', *Economic Bulletin of Ghana,* 2nd Series, Vol. 1, No. 1.

Frimpong Ansah, J. H. (1987):'Professor Sir W. Arthur Lewis, A Patriarch of Development Economics', Salford Papers in Economics, 87–8, University of Salford.

Frimpong-Ansah, J. H. (1988): 'Policy Perspectives on Trade in Africa', Salford Papers in Economics, 88–2, University of Salford.

Frimpong-Ansah, J. H. (1989a): 'The Challenge to Private Entrepreneurship in Sub-Saharan Africa', *Tanzanian Journal of Economics,* Vol. 1, No. 1, July.

Frimpong-Ansah, J. H. (1989b): 'The Adjustment Process in Ghana in the Historical Context', DERC/ODA Symposium, University of Warwick, April 1989.

Frimpong-Ansah, J. H. and Ingham, B. (forthcoming) (1992): *Saving for Economic Recovery in Africa,* James Currey, London.

Frimpong-Ansah, J. H. and Kanbur, Ravi (1989): 'Exchange Rate Policy and Trade Policy in the Context of Structural Adjustment in Africa: An Overview of Theory and Practice', Paper presented at the Commonwealth Secretariat-Rockefeller Workshop in Nairobi, March.

Frimpong-Ansah, J. H., Kanbur, Ravi and Svedberg, P. (eds) (1991): *Trade and Development in Africa,* Manchester University Press.

Ghana Cocoa Board (1988): 'Memorandum on Cocoa Tree Stock, Producer Prices and Production', July.

Ghana Government (1951): *Development Plan 1951,* Government Printer, Accra.

Ghana Government (1953): *Golden Harvest, The Story of the Gold Coast Cocoa Industry,* Ghana Information Services Department, Accra.

Ghana Government (1955): *Development Progress Report,* Government Printer, Accra.

Ghana Government (1957): *The Report of the Committee on Agricultural Indebtedness (Quaidoo Report).*

Ghana Government (1959): *Gold Coast, The Second Development Plan, 1959–1964* Government Printer, Accra.

Government of Ghana (1984): *Economic Recovery Programme 1984–1986: Review of Progress in 1984 and Goals for 1985 and 1986.* Second Meeting of Consultative Group for Ghana, Paris, Accra, November.

Government of Ghana (1985): *Progress of Economic Recovery Programme 1984–1986 and Policy Framework, 1986–1988,* Third Meeting of the Consultative Group for Ghana, Paris, Accra, October.

Government of Ghana (1987a): *Public Investment Programme 1986–1988,* Vol. I & II, Accra, March.

Government of Ghana (1987b): *National Programme for Economic Development* (Revised), Accra, July.

Guggisberg, Sir Gordon (1924): *Post War Gold Coast,* Government Printer, Accra.

Haavelmo, T. (1965): Comment on W. Leontief's Paper on 'The Rate of Long Run Economic Growth and Capital Transfer from Developed to Underdeveloped Areas', in *Study Week on the Economic Approach to Development Planning.* Pontificaiae Academia Scientiarum Scripta Varia, No. 28, North Holland.

Hammond, P. S. (1962): 'Cocoa (A. Agronomy)', in J. Brian Wills (ed.): *Agriculture and Land Use in Ghana,* Oxford University Press for the Ghana Minstry of Food and Agriculture.

Hancock, W. K. (1942): *Survey of British Commonwealth Affairs, Vol II: Problems of Economic Policy, 1918–1939,* Oxford University Press, Oxford.

Hart, Keith (1982): *The Political Economy of West African Agriculture,* Cambridge University Press, Cambridge.

Harrod, R. F. (1939): 'An Essay in Dynamic Theory', *Economic Journal.*

Helleiner, G. K. (1964): 'The Fiscal Role of Marketing Boards in Nigerian Economic Development, 1947–1961', *Economic Journal,* September.

Hendry, D. (1989): *An Interactive Econometric Modelling System,* Institute of Economics and Statistics, University of Oxford.

Hicks, J. R. (1979): *Causality in Economics,* Blackwell, Oxford.

Hill, Polly (1956): *The Gold Coast Farmer: A Preliminary Survey,* Oxford University Press, Oxford.

Hill, Polly (1963): *The Migrant Cocoa Farmers of Southern Ghana: A Study in Rural Capitalism,* Cambridge University Press, Cambridge.

Hill, Polly (1986): *Development Economics on Trial: An Anthropological Case for Prosecution,* Cambridge University Press, Cambridge.

Hirschman, A. O. (1958): *The Strategy of Economic Development,* Yale University Press, New Haven.

Hirschman, A. O. (1984): 'A Dissenter's Confession: "The Strategy of Economic Development" Revisited', in Meier and Seers.

IMF (1986a): *Ghana Stand-By Arrangement,* Washington DC, October.

IMF (1986b): *Ghana: Recent Economic Developments,* Washington DC, May.

IMF (1988): *International Financial Statistics,* Yearbook, Washington DC.

Ingham, B. M. (1973): 'Ghana Cocoa Farmers – Income Expenditure Relationships', *Journal of Development Studies,* Vol. 9, No. 3.

Ingham, B. M. (1987): 'Colonialism and the Economy of the Gold Coast 1919–1945', in Ingham and Simmons (eds) (1987).

Ingham, B. M. and Simmons, C. (eds) (1987): *Development Studies and Colonial Policy,* Frank Cass, London.

Jefferson, Thomas, *Notes on Virginia.*

Jeffries, R. (1978): *Class, Power and Ideology in Ghana: The Railwaymen of Sekondi,* Cambridge University Press, Cambridge.

Jeffries, R. (1982): 'Ghana: Jerry Rawlings ou un populisme à deux coups', *Politique Africain,* 2, 8.

Kay, G. B. and Hymer, S. (1972): *The Political Economy of Ghana. A Collection of Documents and Statistics,* Cambridge University Press, Cambridge.

Kesse, G. O. (1985): *The Mineral and Rock Resources of Ghana,* A. A. Balkema, Rotterdam.

Keynes, J. M. (1936): *The General Theory of Employment, Interest and Money,* Macmillan, London.

Killick, Tony (1965): 'The Economics of Cocoa' in Birmingham *et al.*

Killick, Tony (1978): *Development Economics in Action, A Study of Economic Policies in Ghana,* St Martins Press, New York.

Kimble, D. (1963): *A Political History of Ghana: The Rise of Gold Coast Nationalism 1850–1928,* Oxford University Press, Oxford.

Kotey, R. A., Okali, C. and Rourke, B. E. (eds) (1974): *Economics of Cocoa Production and Marketing,* ISSER, University of Ghana.

Koutsoyiannis, A. (1977): *Theory of Econometrics,* second edition, Macmillan, London.

Krueger, A. O. (1974): 'The Political Economy of the Rent-Seeking Society', *American Economic Review.*

Krueger, A. O., Schiff, M. and Valdes, A. (1984): *A Comparative Study of the Political Economy of Agricultural Pricing Policies: A Framework for the Country Studies,* World Bank.

Krueger, A. O., Schiff., M. and Valdes, A. (1986): 'Note 7 on Measurement of Quantitative Effects of Regression Residuals', World Bank Memo, No. 27.

Krueger, A. O., Schiff, M. and Valdes, A. (1987): 'Measuring the Impact of Sector-Specific and Economic-Wide Policies on Agricultural Incentives in LDCS'. Paper presented at the American Economic Association Annual Meetings, Chicago, December 28–30, 1987.

Krueger, A. O., Schiff, M. and Valdes, A. (1989): *The Political Economy of Agricultural Pricing Policies: Country Studies,* Johns Hopkins University Press.

Lal, Deepak (1983): The Poverty of 'Development Economics', IEA, Hobart Paperback 16.

Lal, Deepak (1984): 'The Political Economy of the Predatory State', DRD Discussion Paper, World Bank.

Lal, Deepak (1986): 'The Political Economy of Industrialization in Primary Exporting Countries: Some Cautionary Tales', DRD Discussion Paper, World Bank.

Lal, Deepak (1988): *The Hindu Equilibrium, Volume I: Cultural Stability and Economic Stagnation, India c.1500BC–AD1980,* Clarendon Press, Oxford.

Leith, Clark J. (1974): *Foreign Trade Regimes and Economic Development: Ghana,* Columbia University Press, New York.

Lewin, Thomas J. (1978): *Ashante Before the British: The Prempean Years, 1875–1900,* University Press, Kansas.

Lewis,. W. A. (1944a): *Machinery for Economic Development in the Colonies,* Colonial Economic Advisory Committee, London.

Lewis, W. A. (1944b): *Some Aspects of the Flow of Capital into the Colonies,* Colonial Economic Advisory Committee, London.

Lewis, W. A. (1944c): *The Promotion of Secondary Industries in the Colonies,* Colonial Economic Advisory Committee, London.

Lewis, W. A. (1950): 'The Industrialization of the British West Indies', *Caribbean Economic Review,* May.

Lewis, W. A. (1953): Report on Industrialization and the Gold Coast, Government Printer, Accra.

Lewis, W. A. (1954): *Economic Development with Unlimited Supplies of Labour,* Manchester School of Economics and Social Studies, May.

Lewis, W. A. (1955): *The Theory of Economic Growth,* Allen & Unwin, London.

Lewis, W. A. (1959): 'Valedictory Address to Fellows of the Ghana Economic Society: On Assessing a Development Plan', *The Economic Bulletin of Ghana,* Vol. 3, Nos 6–7.

Lewis, W. A. (1968): *Some Aspects of Economic Development,* Aggrey-Fraser-Guggisberg Memorial Lectures, University of Ghana.

Lewis, W. A. (1984): 'Development Economics in the 1950s', in Meier and Seers.

Libby, R. T. (1976): 'External Cooptation of a Less Developed Country's Policy-Making: The Case of Ghana', *World Politics,* XXIX, I.

Lipton, M. (1977): *Why Poor People Stay Poor: Urban Bias in World Development,* Harvard University Press, Cambridge, Mass.

London, A. (1986): 'Import Compression and External Adjustment Policy: Some Evidence for Selected African Countries', unpublished mimeo, ADB, Abidjan.

Loxley, J. (1988): *Ghana: Economic Crisis and the Long Road to Recovery,* North-South Institute, Ottawa.

MacKinnon, J. G. and White, H. (1985): 'Some Heteroscedastic Covariants Matrix Estimators with Improved Finite Sample Properties', *Journal of Econometrics,* 29, pp. 305–25.

Mandelbaum, K. (1945): *The Industrialization of Backward Areas,* Blackwell, Oxford.

Manu,. J.E.A. (1972): 'The Balance of Payments Constraint and Economic Development', *Economic Bulletin of Ghana,* Vol. 2, No. 4.

Marx, Karl (1906): *Capital.*

May, E. (1985): 'Exchange Controls and Parallel Market Economies in Sub-Saharan Africa – Focus on Ghana', World Bank Staff Papers, No. 711.

McPhee, A. (1926): *The Economic Revolution in British West Africa,* Frank Cass (1971 edition), London.

Meeraus, A., Okyere, W. A. and O'Mara, G. T. (1989): 'Analysis of Cocoa Producer Investment Response to Pricing Policy – Ghana', in Bateman *et al.*

Meier, G. M. and Seers, D. (1984): *Pioneers in Development,* Oxford University Press, Oxford.

Meier, G. M. (ed.) (1987): *Pioneers in Development,* Second Series, Oxford University Press, Oxford.

Metcalfe, G. E. (1964): *Great Britain and Ghana: Documents in Ghana History, 1807–1957,* University of Ghana (Thomas Nelson), Legon.

Myint, H. (1958): 'The Classical Theory of International Trade and the Underdeveloped Countries', *Economic Journal,* June.

Myint, H. (1984): 'Comment on Gunnar Myrdal's Paper on "International Inequality and Foreign Aid in Retrospect" ', in Meiers and Seers.

Nerlove, M. (1956): 'Estimates of the Elasticities of Supply of Selected Agricultural Commodities', *Journal of Farm Economics,* Vol. 38.

Nerlove, M. (1958): *Distributed Lags and Demand Analysis,* US Department of Agriculture, Agriculture Handbook No. 141, Washington DC.

Nerlove, M. and Addison, W. (1958): 'Statistical Estimation of Long-Run Elasticities of Supply and Demand', *Journal of Farm Economics,* XL4.

Newbery, D. M. (1989a): 'Optimal Trade Taxes on Agriculture in Developing Countries', Department of Applied Economics, University of Cambridge, paper presented at the RES-AUTE Conference, Bristol, April 1989.

Newbery, D. M. (1989b): 'The Agricultural Sector and ERP – Ghana', DERC/ODA Symposium, University of Warwick, April 1989.

Niculescu, B. (1965): *Colonial Planning: A Comparative Study*, Allen and Unwin, London.

Nkrumah, K. (1957): *Autobiography*, Panaf.

Nkrumah, K. (1963): *Africa Must Unite*, International Publishers, New York.

Nkrumah, K. (1965): *Neo-Colonialism: The Last Stage of Imperialism*, International Publishers, New York.

Nkrumah, K. (1973): *Revolutionary Path*, International Publishers, New York.

Nurkse, R. (1961): *Equilibrium and Growth in the World Economy*, Harvard University Press, Cambridge, Mass.

Nyanteng, V. K. (1980): *The Declining Ghana Cocoa Industry: An Analysis of Some Fundamental Problems*, ISSER, Legon.

Nyanteng, V. K. and Apeldoorn, G. J. (1973): 'Some Development Implications of Farmers' Problems in Marketing Their Food Crops', in I. M. Ofori (ed.).

Ocquaye, M. (1980): *Politics in Ghana, 1972–1979*, Tornado Publications, Accra.

Odling-Smee, J. (1972): *Economic Decision Making in 1971*, unpublished memorandum, Ministry of Finance and Economic Planning,. Accra.

Ofori, I. M. (ed.) (1973): *Factors in Agricultural Growth in West Africa*, ISSER, University of Ghana, Legon.

Oluwasanmi, H.A. (1966): *Agriculture and Nigerian Economic Development*, Oxford University Press, Ibadan.

Oluwasanmi, H. A. (1976): 'African Institutions and Rural Development', *Land Tenure Newsletter*, No. 53, University of Wisconsin, Madison.

Ormsby-Gore, W.G.A. (1926): *Report by the Hon. W.G.A. Ormsby-Gore, MP (Parliamentary Under-Secretary of State for the Colonies), on his visit to West Africa*, Cmd, 1744, HMSO, London.

Oti-Boateng, E. and Kanbur, Ravi (1989): 'The Ghana Living Standard Survey and a Poverty Profile of Ghana', DERC/ODA Symposium, University of Warwick, April 1989.

Pearce, Richard (1989): 'The Agricultural Sector and ERP – Ghana'. DERC/ODA Symposium, University of Warwick, April 1989.

Ranis, G. and Okhawa, K. (1985): *Japan and the Developing Countries*, Blackwell.

Ray, D. (1986): *Ghana: Politics, Economics and Society*, Pinter/Rienner, London.

Ricardo, David (1817): *Principles of Political Economy and Taxation*.

Rimmer, D. (1966): 'The Crisis in the Ghana Economy', *Journal of Modern African Studies*, 4,1.

Roemer, M. (1983): 'Missed Opportunities: Ghana 1950–1980', Development Discussion Paper No. 148, HIID, Harvard University.

Roemer, M. (1983a): *Dutch Disease in Developing Countries: Swallowing the Bitter Medicine*, Development Discussion Paper, HIID, Harvard University.

Rosenstein-Rodan, P. N. (1943): 'Problems of Industrialization of Eastern and South-Eastern Europe', *Economic Journal*, Vol. 53, June–September.

Rothchild, D. (1984): 'Middle Africa: Hegemonial Exchange and Resource Allocation' in Groth, A. and Wade, L. (eds): *Comparative Resource Allocation*, Sage, London.

Rothchild, D. and Gyimah-Boadi, E. (1986): 'Ghana's Economic Decline and Development Strategies' in Ravenhill, J. (ed.): *Africa in Economic Crisis*, Macmillan, London.

Sampson, Magnus, J. (1969): *Gold Coast Men of Affairs (Past and Present)*, Dawson of Pall Mall, London.

Seers, D. and Ross, C. (1952): *Report on the Financial and Physical Problems of Development in the Gold Coast*,. Government Printer, Accra.

Seers, D. (1970): 'The Transmission of Irregularity' in Gardner, R. *et al.* (eds): *Africa and the World*, Oxford University Press.

Seers, D. (1972): 'What Are We Trying to Measure?' *Journal of Development Studies*, Vol. 8, No. 3 (April).

Seers, D. (1977): 'The New Meaning of Development', *International Economic Review*, 19.3.

Seini, W., Howell, J. and Commander, S. (1987): 'Agricultural Policy Adjustment in Ghana', Paper for ODI Conference on the Design and Impact of Adjustment Programmes on Agricultural Institutions, 10–11 September, London.

Simmons, C. (1987): 'Economic Development and Economic History' in Ingham and Simmons.

Slater, R. (1930): *Address to the Legislative Council*, Government Printer, Accra.

Smith, Adam (1776): *The Wealth of Nations*.

Steuart, Sir James (1767): *An Enquiry into the Principles of Political Economy*, Book I.

Stoces, F. (1966): 'Agricultural Production in Ghana, 1955–1965', *Economic Bulletin of Ghana*, Vol. X, No. 3.

Streeten, P. (1984): 'Comment on A. O. Hirschman "A Dissenter's Confession" ' in Meier and Seers.

Stryker, J. D. *et al.* (1988): 'A Comparative Study of the Political Economy of Agricultural Pricing Policies: Ghana' (Associates for International Resources and Development), World Bank unpublished mimeograph, June.

Svedberg, P. (1991): 'Trends in African Exports, 1956–1985', in Frimpong-Ansah, Kanbur and Svedberg.

Szereszewski, R. (1965): *Structural Changes in the Economy of Ghana*, Weidenfeld and Nicolson, London.

Teal, F. (1984): 'Growth, Comparative Advantage and Economic Effects of Government: A Case Study of Ghana', Ph.D thesis, School of Oriental and African Studies, University of London.

Uphoff (1970): 'Ghana's Experience in Using External Aid for Development, 1957–1966', Ph.D. thesis, Berkeley, University of California.

White, H. (1980): 'A Heteroscedasticity-Consistent Covariants Matrix Estimator and a Direct Test for Heteroscedasticity', *Econometrica*, 48, 4, pp. 817–838.

World Bank (1970): *Ghana – Eastern Region Cocoa Project*, Washington DC.

World Bank (1984a): *Ghana: Policies and Programmes of Adjustment, Vols I & II*, Washington DC.

World Bank (1985): *Ghana: Towards Structural Adjustment, Vols I & II*, Washington DC.

World Bank (1987a): *Mining Sector Rehabilitation Project, Republic of Ghana*, Staff Appraisal Report No. 7039-GH, December.

World Bank (1987b): *Ghana: Policies and Issues of Structural Adjustment*, Washington, March.

Index